THE EVOLUTION OF GERALD DURRELL

THE EVOLUTION OF GERALD DURRELL

Biography of an Author and Wildlife Conservationist

Mary Sanders Pollock

BLOOMSBURY ACADEMIC
LONDON • NEW YORK • OXFORD • NEW DELHI • SYDNEY

BLOOMSBURY ACADEMIC
Bloomsbury Publishing Plc
50 Bedford Square, London, WC1B 3DP, UK
1385 Broadway, New York, NY 10018, USA
29 Earlsfort Terrace, Dublin 2, Ireland

BLOOMSBURY, BLOOMSBURY ACADEMIC and the Diana logo are
trademarks of Bloomsbury Publishing Plc

First published in Great Britain 2024

Copyright © Mary Sanders Pollock, 2024

Mary Sanders Pollock has asserted her right under the Copyright, Designs and
Patents Act, 1988, to be identified as Author of this work.

For legal purposes the Acknowledgments on p. xi constitute an
extension of this copyright page.

Cover design: Rebecca Heselton
Cover image © The Estate of Gerald Durrell

All rights reserved. No part of this publication may be reproduced
or transmitted in any form or by any means, electronic or mechanical,
including photocopying, recording, or any information storage or retrieval
system, without prior permission in writing from the publishers.

Bloomsbury Publishing Plc does not have any control over, or responsibility
for, any third-party websites referred to or in this book. All internet addresses
given in this book were correct at the time of going to press. The author and
publisher regret any inconvenience caused if addresses have changed or sites
have ceased to exist, but can accept no responsibility for any such changes.

A catalogue record for this book is available from the British Library.

A catalog record for this book is available from the Library of Congress.

ISBN: HB: 978-1-3503-8545-0
PB: 978-1-3503-8546-7
ePDF: 978-1-3503-8547-4
eBook: 978-1-3503-8548-1

Typeset by RefineCatch Limited, Bungay, Suffolk

To find out more about our authors and books visit www.bloomsbury.com
and sign up for our newsletters.

In memory of Mimi Hall

FIGURE 0.1 Gerald Durrell with chimpanzee. (Gerald Durrell Estate)

CONTENTS

List of Illustrations viii
Foreword by Lee Durrell ix
Acknowledgments xi

Introduction 1

1 Corfu 15

2 The Wide World 41

3 Africa 61

4 South America: The Human Factor 91

5 Islomania 115

6 Madagascar and the Mascarenes 139

7 The Zoo 161

Afterword: How to be Whole 179

Select Bibliography 189
Index 193

ILLUSTRATIONS

0.1	Gerald Durrell with chimpanzee (Gerald Durrell Estate)	vi
2.1	Père David's deer	55
3.1	Agama lizard	64
3.2	Gerald and Jacquie Durrell with Animals in Bournemouth. (Gerald Durrell Estate)	81
4.1	Magellenic penguin	104
5.1	Wilson and MacArthur's Theory of Island Biogeography	119
5.2	Leadbeater's possum	126
6.1	Rodrigues fruit bats	142
7.1	Emperor tamarin	161
A.1	Statue of Gerald Durrell with Lemurs, Jersey Zoo	180
A.2	The Durrell Index, 2020	182

FOREWORD

The story of Gerald Durrell as told by Mary Pollock is written with thought and care, whilst engaging the reader and moving at a lively pace. Mary has neatly pulled together much disparate material and put it into the historical and geographical contexts of the unfolding years.

She skillfully weaves time and place, not necessarily chronologically, which is refreshing, but thematically, layering where and when Gerry's worldwide travels took him in the evolution of his conservation philosophy. He was fine-tuning his view of our species' place in nature and recognising the depths of our own anthropocentricity. The ramifications were not pretty. And he was working out what he could do to mitigate them.

Mary paints the huge canvas of Gerry's life with the spaces and species that affected him most, from Corfu to the continents, from islands big and small, from earwigs to elephants and lizards to lemurs. She saves Gerry's "ark" until the penultimate chapter, although it has been more than sixty years in the making. The "ark" is not just his zoo where threatened species are cared for, but his reach all over the world, from sites of active conservation for species and habitats in danger to the international cohort of graduates of his conservation academy. She concludes that Gerry's "activism is a model of hope and encouragement", so badly needed in this world now. "Environmental grief" is affecting more and more people, causing more and more despair.

The early chapters may attract the notice of some of today's readers, as they cover the period when Gerry began his expeditions to remote areas of the world collecting animals to sell to zoos. This activity was the norm then, but it may grate on contemporary sensitivities. As he recounted his adventures, he described the places, people and animals in the words of the 1950s and 1960s, some of which may not be pleasing to modern ears.

Mary points out that Gerry writes about these early days as "a man of his time'" She makes it crystal clear, however, that Gerry glimpses a calamitous future—literally earth-shattering—already in the making, though precious few were aware of it then. He was single-mindedly determined to do something about it. The rest of the story reveals, honestly and joyfully, just what he did in his own inimitable, unique way. This book will be an essential read in the chronicles of conservation.

Lee Durrell
Corfu, June 2023

ACKNOWLEDGMENTS

This book could not have been written or published without the participation of colleagues, family, and friends. More than they know, I appreciate the support of my department chairs, Tom Farrell, Lori Snook, and Joel Davis, and my dean, Elizabeth Skomp. Over the years, Stetson University Professional Development committees have awarded indispensable financial aid for travel, sabbatical leave, and summer research. The Stetson University library system staff have helped me solve problems and find essential research materials. Maribel Velazquez, Ryan Byers, and Xan Pack-Brown have cheerfully provided additional technical support.

Elsewhere, librarians at the Southern Illinois University at Carbondale, especially Aaron Lisek and Nicholas Guardiano, guided me through the Lawrence Durrell archive in the Special Collections Research Center. Without their assistance, one layer of Gerald's story could not have been told here.

Michelle Bezanson's illustrations for one of my previous books inspired the design of this one, and she generously provided one of the drawings. Additional drawings are from Hallie Martin. Kirsten Work read drafts and helped me revise for accuracy. My brothers Jim Sanders, Tom Sanders, and John Sanders provided material support and indispensable dialogue. Jack Brown at the Santa Fe Teaching Zoo taught me that not all zoos are evil. Without the dedicated help of Kathy Barnard and Katie Burk, this publication might not have been completed. In her special way, Kiri made my work lighter and happier.

Lee Durrell's commitment to this project has been unflagging. When I began, she granted me interviews at her flat at the center of the Durrell Zoo; introductions to the staff; technical support; and what seemed unfettered access to the zoo and the adjoining campus of the Durrell Conservation Academy. She read and corrected drafts, forwarded photographs, and consented to write a Foreword. Her involvement has been so generous that I feel sure I have forgotten some of the details.

Durrell Zoo and Durrell Trust staff members Amy Hall, Joya Ghose, Tim Wright, and Mike Hudson also generously gave me their time and answered my questions.

Finally, I am grateful to the editorial staff at Bloomsbury, especially Lucy Brown and Aanchal Vij, for their faith in this project and their hard work to complete it.

Permissions

The Durrell Trust for the Durrell Index.
The Durrell Estate for photographs:

- Gerald and Jacquie with animals in Bournemouth.
- Gerald with angwantibo.
- Gerald with chimpanzee.

Getty Images for photograph:

- Statue of Gerald at the Durrell Zoo in Jersey.

Lawrence Durrell Archive, Special Collections Research Center, Morris Library, Southern Illinois University Carbondale, for personal letters from Gerald Durrell to Lawrence Durrell.

INTRODUCTION

During his lifetime, Gerald Durrell's charm and magical rapport with animals made him an international celebrity. While he was still a young man, Gerald foresaw the sixth extinction and founded a conservation zoo on the Isle of Jersey to save the animals he could, especially some of the small, rare, and little-known creatures endemic to environmental hotspots around the world. To support his travels and conservation projects, he wrote more than thirty books. The best known, *My Family and Other Animals*, (1956) has been adapted by the BBC in two series about his free-range childhood on the Greek island of Corfu in the 1930s (1987 and 2019). Gerald died in 1995, but his work lives on in the zoo, the international wildlife conservation academy adjacent to the zoo, the conservation projects he supported in the animals' native habitat, the nature programs on television, and the marvelous books. Although Gerald's commitment to wildlife conservation was shared by environmental activists on the international stage, his journey and his legacy were uniquely his own.

This is a story of his evolution within a global system of extraction, imperialism, and care for "the little ones of God," as Yani, an elderly childhood friend on the island of Corfu described Gerald's love for animals.[1] Gerald was a passionate man, a writer of high good humor, grief, and rage. His books and his life give us permission to acknowledge our own emotions when we consider mass extinction, deforestation, dangerous chemicals and plastics everywhere, pandemics, and the disastrous effects of climate change. This permission to feel may be his greatest legacy, but the legacy begins and ends with the animals he studied, collected, and, most of all, protected.

Umwelt. It is the world as I perceive it, or as my dog does, or, in the famous elaboration of this concept by Jacob von Euxküll, as a tick experiences it. Sometimes my dog barks at objects and events I don't perceive. She knows things I don't know—things important to her. Chumley the chimpanzee, who returned with Gerald from an early collecting adventure in Cameroon, was an influential personage in his life. Escaping from the zoo to ride a city bus, he endangered his own life, but, within his own self-centered world, being an escape artist, and striking out to explore his London surroundings, must have given him a sense of territory and resources for survival, just as the adventure would have done in the woodlands of his home. We humans are limited by our sensorium, history, and culture, and thus we fail, time after time, to understand the reactions of the dog and the chimpanzee, or the tick, to the world we all share.[2]

More than most of us, Gerald Durrell was born preternaturally equipped to open windows into the *Umwelten* of nonhuman animals, and his representations of animal being have much in common with what scholars now understand as "critical anthropomorphism," an approach Richard Louv describes as "steeped in scientific knowledge and then in imaginative identification."[3] His life and work provide a supreme example of what E. O. Wilson calls "biophilia," the instinct of life *for* life.[4]

To all appearances, Gerald was born with this gift of biophilia, but his family and friends allowed him to keep the windows open and gave him a wider experience of the world than most people ever know. "I have been a very lucky man and throughout my life the world has given me the most enormous pleasure," he wrote in 1972. "I feel indebted to it," he continues, "and I would like to try and do something to repay the debt. People look at you in a rather embarrassed sort of way when you talk like this, as though you had said something obscene, but I only wish that more people felt that they owed they world a debt and were prepared to do something about it"[5]

He was indeed lucky and indebted. Gerald grew up as a cosmopolitan in the most literal sense of the word. From his birth in 1925, he was a citizen of the world. From his earliest childhood he recalled his *ayah* and the animals he met in Bihar province of India, where his father Lawrence Samuel Durrell served as a civil engineer under the auspices of the Raj. For several generations, both sides of Gerald's family had served in India, and their outlook on the world was shaped by their family history. Gerald lost his father when he was only three years old, and the Durrells moved back to England, never to return to India except for brief visits. In 1935, after alighting first in London and then spending time near relatives in Bournemouth, Gerald's mother Louisa and his brother, the novelist

2   THE EVOLUTION OF GERALD DURRELL

Lawrence Durrell (thirteen years older than Gerald), made a dramatic decision to settle on the Greek island of Corfu.[6] (Throughout this book, I will refer to the Durrells by their first names because all members of this family are part of the story. They sometimes instructed people that the surname rhymes with "squirrel.")

After feeling displaced for seven years, the Durrells quickly came to feel at home there. With his dog Roger and his donkey Sally, Gerald trekked constantly through orchards, fields, and forests and explored coastal fauna in the family boats. When he wished to travel to the ends of the island, he caught rides in the taxi of Spiro Chalikiopoulos. He was home-schooled by Lawrence, the brilliant Greek polymath Dr. Theodore Stephanides, and a succession of additional worldly and eccentric tutors. He counted local farmers, fishermen, and aristocrats among his friends and learned Greek more quickly than anyone else in the family, partly because he was the youngest and partly because he became intimately acquainted with the Corfiots as he explored their landscape. (Years later, in 1956, the Greek returned quickly for both Gerald and Lawrence after Lawrence's diplomatic posting to Cyprus.)[7] These boyhood experiences, casual though they might appear, laid the groundwork for his profound and original understanding of what later came to be understood as "island biogeography." (In the twenty-first century, this field is integrated into "conservation biology.")

Besides Louisa, Lawrence, and Gerald, the Durrell household included a middle brother Leslie, a sister Margo, Lugaretzia the Greek maid, dogs, and almost countless wild creatures—mammals and birds, reptiles and amphibians, all manner of sea creatures, and insects. The animals were more than pets. Gerald studied them, and literally dozens of them became characters with agency and subjectivity in Gerald's memoirs about the years in Corfu. Along with the neighbors, Lawrence's colorful friends from all over Europe and India circulated in and out of the Durrells' various houses, eating and drinking and entertaining each other with heady, clever conversation.

And so they all lived for almost five years. In late 1939, at almost the last minute, after Italy invaded Corfu and the German war machine could no longer be ignored, Louisa returned to England, along with Gerald and Leslie. Margo married an aircraft engineer and followed him to Africa. Lawrence and his wife Nancy remained in the Mediterranean. All of them left the island with a store of memories, and Gerald was blessed with the best education a young naturalist could receive. Back in England,

INTRODUCTION 3

he continued his education by working as a pet shop assistant, a farm hand, and an "odd beast boy" in the Whipsnade Zoo.

From the early days, Gerald knew people—writers and artists, politicians, actors, scientists, editors and television producers, politicians and royalty, the powerful and those with no power at all. He inherited the privilege, not of great wealth or social standing, but of feeling entitled and unafraid to move about the world as he wished and just enough financial support to live as he wished, in the company of animals. Although the British Empire was unraveling even before Gerald began his travels as a young man, colonial officials, commercial networks, and influence remained. He was born into this system and knew how to navigate within it.

A modest financial inheritance funded Gerald's first animal collecting adventures, in 1947, to the west African colony of British Cameroon, undertaken when he was only twenty-two years old. For his adventurous way of life to continue, he had to sell the animals he collected to British zoos when he returned. It was difficult to part with the monkeys, especially the troublesome but entertaining drills, as well as the little Red River hogs, pangolins, bats, birds, rodents, and snakes, brought back with great care and difficulty, but he quickly organized a second journey to Cameroon and, in 1949, another to British Guiana (now Guyana), on the northern coast of South America. There, he collected anteaters large and small—douroucouli night monkeys, birds, frogs, and more. Again, he had to sell the animals to zoos to cover the costs of the adventure. In 1953, he returned to South America, this time to Argentina and Paraguay. Once more, he sold all his animals—birds, anteaters, armadillos, foxes, deer, and snakes.

At the insistence of his first wife, Jacquie, and with Lawrence's encouragement, Gerald started writing about his travels to fund future expeditions and the zoo that he had always wanted. In 1957 and 1958, Gerald scraped together the resources (including the loan of Margo's back garden back in Bournemouth) to keep the animals he collected during more journeys to Africa, South America, and elsewhere—Madagascar, the Mascarenes, and even (briefly and unsuccessfully) Cyprus, where he visited with Lawrence during his brother's diplomatic posting there in 1953–54. He already considered zoos defensible only if they helped to save animals rather than simply keeping them for display. After two years of trying to find a permanent English home for this backyard menagerie, he had a stroke of luck. His publisher introduced him to Hugh Fraser, who had just decided that his manor on the Isle of Jersey required too much attention. Fraser was willing to lease and later to sell the property—a large farm with useful outbuildings and a beautiful manor house of pink granite.

Within a few months of establishing the zoo there in 1959, Gerald decided to concentrate his efforts on animals whose numbers were already diminishing in the wild. This would be a conservation zoo. In North America, the demise of the passenger pigeon and near extinction of the bison could scarcely be overlooked, and no expansionist power tried to hide the deliberate mass culling of wildlife considered dangerous or inconvenient. However, Gerald was one of the earliest adventure travelers of the twentieth century to notice first-hand and write about the impact of European and neo-European expansion on lesser-known wildlife populations; he and Jacquie observed a drastic decline in South American animal populations, even within a short period during the 1950s and early 1960s. As Gerald became continually more aware of the problems, he was deeply troubled by them. During the 1960s, 1970s, and 1980s, he made more voyages to Africa and South America—and to New Zealand, Australia, Maylasia, Mexico, the Mascarene Islands, Madagascar, the Indian subcontinent, Russia, and North America, for collecting, filming, and fund-raising for conservation projects.

Most of Gerald's expeditions followed the paths laid down by British colonialism and commercial interests, and he consulted government functionaries employed in colonial or post-colonial bureaucracies whenever he could. When he first began to collect animals for zoos, Gerald seems to have taken for granted these advantages. With time, he became more conscious of his own privilege, more vexed by the tensions of his situation as a supplier in the animal trade, more aware of the ways in which colonialism and its aftermath damaged the land and all who depended on it. Ironically, the very system which enabled him to see wild nature first-hand caused terrible environmental degradation because it was—and still is—fundamentally extractive. As Gerald matured, his sympathies widened to include dispossessed human beings as well as their animal neighbors, all of whom were brought into conflict by the same extractive practices.

The success of any conservation effort depends, in part, on a clear and appealing message, and Gerald's work has remained some of the best wildlife advocacy literature ever written. What is more, according to one definition, at its core, travel writing is "the hunt for a strange animal in a remote land."[8] Every animal Gerald encountered, every human he met, and every corner of the earth he visited made for some of the best travel and adventure writing in the English language.

He first began to write about his travels in an almost impossibly crowded garret in Margo's house, bringing the world into a tiny space in order to write about it. The situation eventually improved. After moving to Jersey and establishing himself in the manor house at the center of the zoo, he worked at the kitchen table, an enormous board. The table accommodated his piles of books, maps, and papers. The room is filled with light. The windows overlook the zoo with its beloved inhabitants, whose calls punctuate the morning and evening air. According to his widow, Lee Durrell, Gerald wrote at top speed, without revising. But no doubt he dreamed of words and animals when he was asleep and meditated on phrasing while he went through the routine chores. Lee also recalls that he bitterly objected to editors' requests or demands.

Still, he had high standards, sometimes calling other travel writers to task. Most recent books about Africa, for instance, he described as "yawn-provoking," "ill-writ tomes produced by big-game hunters or frustrated governors' wives"[9] He felt there were notable exceptions, of course. These included books written by early explorers and others by Lawrence, whose persona in *Prospero's Cell: Guide to the Landscape and Manners of the Island of Corfu* and *Bitter Lemons*Gerald parodies in his own comic novel, *The Mockery Bird*. (Lawrence had it coming: he extracted as much humor as possible from Gerald's collecting misadventures in Cyprus.) Gerald's letters to Lawrence reveal not just a pragmatic investment in his writing, but an aesthetic investment as well. After finishing his first piece of published fiction, an elephant story entitled *Rosie Is My Relative*, he asked Lawrence's advice. Gerald knew the Rosie story would sell because animal lovers everywhere were becoming addicted to his books, but "is it any good is what I asks meself."[10] Who better to ask than another writer whom he greatly admired, who had always encouraged him?

Gerald's early literary environment deserves part of the credit, but the animals and the adventures of catching and caring for them account for even more of the energy in these stories. For Gerald, all animals were charismatic, and however much he adored the big cats and great apes, he objected to the common preoccupation with charismatic megafauna to the exclusion of small, lesser-known creatures. Always, the animals are personages, not objects. Predictably, every primate has a different (and usually entertaining) personality. But so do all the other animals. Seals were unpredictably sexy. Cuthbert, the curassow captured in Guyana, made the team's lives difficult because he insisted on sitting on their feet whenever he could. Gerald was bitten by cute baby kusimandas while they played in his bed, by a brilliantly colored agama lizard in Cameroon, and in Jujuy by a fierce Geoffrey's cat (a mere kitten, smaller than the tabby kitten who became its companion). When he relentlessly pursued a fer de lance in Argentina—before ascertaining its species—it turned to attack him and narrowly missed his leg.

So, sometimes Gerald's luck saved his life. Without thinking things through, he took risks—putting his hand into a shallow, dark cave without knowing what kind of critter resided there, suggesting that his helpers hold on to his feet so he could dangle over a cliff to catch a lizard, or bagging deadly gaboon vipers while suspended over their pit by a rope around the ankle. Gerald almost sat on crocodiles in Malaysia and elephant seals on the Valdes Peninsula in Argentina, almost died during a bone-breaking ride in a ramshackle kit car after a venomous snakebite in Cameroon. In Jujuy, he tried to tempt vampire bats to bite him so he could catch a close-up look at them. (The bats preferred the horses.) He endured broken bones, sleeping on stony ground in the rain, ramshackle hotels (including one in which the doors locked outside but not inside the rooms), transportation delays and vehicle breakdowns, a revolution in Paraguay, tropical diseases, and strenuous all-night drinking bouts with local officials. More than once, he had to be swung by a crane when moving from sea to land and back again.

Even Gerald's hands-on approach at the Jersey Zoo subjected him to dangerous or inconvenient encounters. Once, he and the zoo's head reptile keeper John Hartley were nearly strangled together in the coils of a reticulated python named Pythagoras, to be saved at the last minute when another keeper heard their desperate cries. On another occasion, he was severely bitten by a palm civet named Potsil while trying to charm zoo visitors. Potential donors had to be headed off at the pass when red-headed Simon Hicks, secretary of the Trust, got too near the orangutan enclosure. Since Gambar, a dominant male, was convinced that Simon was a competitor for his mate Gina, he always exerted his rights and authority in the most extreme and unseemly ways possible whenever he caught sight of Simon. Claudius the peccary escaped one rainy night and destroyed a nearby farmer's back garden and field of anemones before he could be caught (by four grown men). Delilah the African great crested porcupine escaped and was gingerly recaptured, but not before she destroyed a great deal of woodwork and injured her captors with the spines she released when backing into their legs.

The animals' diseases were often puzzling, and deaths were heartbreaking. In *Menagerie Manor*, a series of animal biographies from the first five years of the Jersey Zoo, Gerald tells the stories of a lethargic boa constrictor who had to be force-fed with chunks of dead rat stuffed down his throat; Louie the sweet tempered black gibbon, who died of jaundice contracted before she came to the zoo; and Lulu the chimpanzee, whose cranial tumor Gerald lanced on the living room couch, releasing copious amounts of pus and the foulest odor imaginable. Most inexplicable were the injuries inflicted by zoo visitors, who gave razorblades and lighted cigarettes to chimpanzees, lipsticks to monkeys, and aspirins to a chinchilla, who died after eating them. Sometimes badly behaved humans pelted sleeping animals with sticks and stones.

Considering his own experience of trial and error in meeting the needs of the zoo residents, Gerald and his Jersey collaborators organized international zoo conferences and launched *The Dodo*, a professional journal devoted to zookeeping practices, including zoo veterinary medicine and captive breeding. During a publishing career that lasted almost forty years, Gerald's calls for conservation became ever angrier and more insistent. As Ursula Heise points out, "Only occasionally has conservationist writing mobilized the resources of comedy, a genre that offers an alternative mode for thinking about biodiversity. Comedy emphasizes contingency and improbable modes of survival over predictability and extinction and thereby opens up different cognitive and emotional attachments to the lives of other humans as well as nonhuman species."[11] After a series of comic accounts in the 1950s and 1960s, Gerald's anger surfaced. He became aware, little by little, of the looming tragedy of extinction.

He raged against the destruction of lemur habitat in Madagascar. He sneered at red tape in the United States, which in his view contributed to the extinction to Florida's dusky seaside sparrow. He took note of bureaucratic egos in Mexico, which he felt retarded potential progress in saving the volcano rabbit. The outrageous human behaviors Gerald witnessed and wrote about are too many to list. The passages in his books about policy and behavior sometimes veer close to "green imperialism"— in the words of Ramachandra Guha and Juan Martinez-Alier, "an updated version of the White Man's Burden" to save endangered habitats and species, and to blame the indigenous people living those habitats for declining animal populations.[12]

With time, Gerald's views of human nature—especially of indigenous people—became more nuanced. However, neither his projects nor his emotions were ever simple. Throughout his career, the language in which Gerald wrote about the animals he loved and the humans who helped or hindered was often raw and untethered. (He admitted to setting filters in place only because he was aware that children enjoyed his books.) Everyone and anyone became at one time or another a target of his rage or a butt of his jokes—Malagasy housewives purchasing lemurs to cook in casserole, his African helpers, the Fon of Bafut in Cameroon, Dutch traders of rare animals, queer politicians, European colonizers, drunken Englishmen, lecherous Englishmen, women, his fellow laborers in conservation organizations, his family and friends. The dialogue in his stories relentlessly mimics accents and pillories affectations.

Readers, writers, and teachers who devote their energies and direct their students to Gerald's work must sometimes participate in a balancing act. Gerald seems to have understood only later in his career that, if mocking the red-faced Englishman as a purveyor of colonial and post-colonial extractive policy amounted to a useful and necessary critique, mocking subject peoples sometimes recirculated damaging racist tropes. *The Mockery Bird* is a case in point. In this unhinged parody of colonial greed, he managed to stereotype almost everyone. He wrote the novel in 1979 and 1980, at the apex of his outrage, and it shows. The novel is sometimes side-splitting, often uncomfortable reading. At the same time, *The Mockery Bird* should be considered a neglected classic of popular science—a brilliant and original explanation of evolution, extinction, and island biogeography.

Gerald's bawdy Shakespearean humor was a family vice. Caricature, among other verbal extravagances, was also a family vice which Gerald eventually learned was not universally understood or appreciated. In his memoir of Lawrence, published in 1987 in a special issue of *Twentieth Century Literature*, Gerald remembers that one of Lawrence's fans treated the "humorous lampoon" of his brother as a "vicious attack." According to Gerald, when asked if he intended to "answer" the attack, Lawrence "solemnly assured the person that he had challenged me to a duel in Hyde Park, but, as my choice of weapons had been cobras, to which he had always had a strange aversion, he had been forced to call the whole thing off."[13] Throughout his life, a literary style which veers from lyricism to raw humor, and from pathos to polemic, remained Gerald Durrell's idiom.

Nevertheless, even the early books reveal sympathy for those who saw the world as he did, especially those who labored in the shadows for the same ends. In *The Whispering Land* (1961), Gerald describes the reverence for Indian artifacts expressed by a Patagonian landowner whose indigenous ancestors were exterminated by European settlers or absorbed into the general population. In the same volume, Gerald's sympathy for an impassioned and impoverished rural sugar factory worker in Jujuy is as touching as anything he ever wrote. "Coco," as Gerald calls him in the story, painted beautiful, accurate portraits of the local birds, fearing that they might never be known. With remarkable tact, Gerald realized that the offer of money would be insulting, so he sent books.

> And now, when I get discontented with my lot, when I get irritated because I can't afford some new animal, or a new book, I remember Coco in his tiny study, working hard and enthusiastically with inadequate tools and money, and it has a salutary effect on me.[14]

Almost twenty years later, in 1979, as he was writing *The Mockery Bird*, Gerald was in the early stages of founding a wildlife conservation training school for people like Coco.

Although filming or contributing to nature documentaries often accompanied and partially funded Gerald's collecting adventures, most of Gerald's journeys were directly concerned with collecting animals or supporting *in situ* conservation efforts. Although he does not elaborate and makes only the briefest possible mention of Gerald in *Nature's Saviors: Celebrity Conservationists in the Television Age*, Graham Huggan suggests that conservationist celebrities and field-working naturalists may be qualitatively different.[15] Quite early in his career, Gerald was devoted to conservation, seeming to regard television as a necessary tool, though not the most important one. Gerald's affect in these early television appearances was, by comparison to the persona in the books, restrained, perhaps because the early attempts at filming wildlife were trying and frequently unsuccessful.

There are some exceptions in the pattern. Forays into New Zealand, Australia, and Maylasia became a book, *Two in the Bush* (1966), as well as a television special. In 1984, Gerald and Lee Durrell, with attendant film crews, spent almost a year traveling behind the Iron Curtain, through the cities and countryside, tundra, desert, and steppes of the Soviet Union— to visit the seals of Lake Baikal, butterflies in Samarkand, birds near the Caspian Sea and others closer to the Baltic, and musk oxen north of the

Arctic Circle. One stop was the bioreserve Askania Nova, now in the steppes of occupied Kherson. Gerald and Lee Durrell recorded this journey in *Durrell in Russia* (1986), a book version of the television series with the same title. A primatologist, Lee recorded for the book "all the stern scientific stuff," and Gerald wrote about "the sights, sounds, colours and scents."[16] He was touched by the hospitality and generosity of the Russian people and moved by the depth of the wildlife specialists' commitment to the animals in their care. Much later, Lee has remarked that his experience was a turning point in Gerald's understanding of his place in the world.[17]

It appeared to the Durrells that the commitment of Soviet society to wildlife conservation was deep and sincere. "What I wanted to show," Gerald wrote in the last chapter, about Moscow, "was the Soviet people's love of animal life," in the nature reserves and even in the pet market of Moscow, one of his last stops before leaving the country. For the first time, he was not allowed to film because the venue "did not look very nice."[18] He was furious. He must have remembered the hastily constructed cages of his own zoo a quarter century earlier—assemblages of packing crates, battered baskets, and ordinary fencing. Still, despite its closely guarded image, the Durrells left Russia admiring the commitment and standards the Soviet Union had set for wildlife conservation.

The Russia experience cemented Gerald's increasingly deep understanding of how destructive the world's political boundaries can be. In an interview with Jane Bayer for Channel Television, shortly before his travels there, Gerald said,

> If I could have two wishes, the first is, of course that I'd like to shut [the zoo in Jersey] down. . . . You realize why I'm saying this. I would hope it would no longer be necessary to have to keep and breed animals in captivity, so this place would be useless. There would be no endangered animals.
>
> Second. Animals don't consider all these ridiculous barriers that we put up in the world. We draw a chalk line and say, "That's Russia, Poland, Yugoslavia. . . ." Animals don't consider these barriers at all. They are entirely artificial, man-made barriers. And they create more problems than practically anything else we do in the world. I would like for all these barriers to be swept away so that China merges into Russia, Russian into Poland, Poland into Germany. . . . What I'm talking about I suppose is a sort of world government, really. . . .[19]

In an ideal world, the disappearance of boundaries would mean no national privilege, secrecy, class prejudice, or obstacles to protecting the most vulnerable species among us.

The effectiveness of any international conservation program depends in part on the organizers' awareness of the dangers of environmental imperialism. Complicated as it was, Durrell's life trajectory from collector to protector was straightforward in comparison to the struggle against his own internal green imperialist instincts. Fortunately, his heart was open mostly to small, overlooked species dependent on small land areas: the first *in situ* projects, were developed on small islands, with small endangered species populations—St. Lucia, Mauritius, and tiny Round Island. A few years later, *in situ* breeding programs were developed for tortoises in Madagascar. Unlike some large national parks throughout the world, these projects never displaced local human residents. During the years of traveling through the Indian Ocean, Gerald's cosmopolitan understanding became deeper.

Although he would have objected to Immanuel Kant's anthropocentric exclusion of non-human beings from consideration, he would doubtless have agreed with the philosopher's assessment, in "Idea for a Universal History with a Cosmopolitan Purpose," that "We are cultivated to a high degree by art and science. We are civilized to the point of excess in all kinds of social courtesies and proprieties. But we are still a long way from the point where we would consider ourselves morally mature."[20] Kant required inclusion of all earthly human concerns and societies in his projections for moral advancement. Gerald insists that human moral advancement requires attention and respect for all other living beings, throughout the whole world, not just for the family of the human. Indeed, twenty-first-century environmentalist critiques are beginning to develop Gerald's cosmopolitan understanding of the bond with species other than our own—and all human beings.

Adventure travel, zookeeping, conservation, captive breeding experiments, writing, education, and all his social relationships were of a piece. Gerald did not separate or fragment them. His work endures. His books have influenced not just British schoolchildren and animal lovers. Scientists such as Thomas Lovejoy, whose groundbreaking studies of Amazonia have helped determine wildlife conservation policy since the 1980s, read his books as a boy.[21] Carl Jones, whose spectacular success saving birds in the Mascarenes makes him one of the world's leading conservationists, read all Gerald's books when he was a child.[22] According to E. O. Wilson, perhaps the most powerful contemporary voice in ecology and conservation biology, Gerald's books are the best guide for what a naturalist should be and do.[23] The geographer Paul F. Starrs begins his review of Wilson's memoir *Naturalist* by claiming Gerald as his own "greatest hero," not because of the "hysterically funny" Corfu trilogy, which Starrs discovered as a teenager, but because of the early adventure stories, which were read to him when he was seven: "these were story collages bound by an unsurpassed love of the exotic and Durrell's rare skill at making foreign places and people come alive."[24]

The zoo has developed into a lovely, expansive garden a scant half mile from the northern coast of Jersey. The zoo campus now includes homes for the animals, an organic farm to supply much of their food, a recycling plant which processes almost all of the waste generated in the zoo, a field of yurts for tourists, enclosures and laboratories for captive breeding programs; next door is the wildlife academy, which has trained thousands of conservationists, who return to their homes, mostly in environmental hotspots, in order to protect their own wildlife. The international conservation foundation that bears Gerald Durrell's name continues to develop and fund small, carefully designed projects for saving animal habitat and for the conservation, captive breeding, and reintroduction of endangered species.

This book tells the story of Gerald's adventurous life and his perpetual struggle to balance fear, rage, patience, and love.

Notes

1 Gerald Durrell, *My Family and Other Animals* (London: Penguin, 1956), 70.

2 Jacob von Euxküll, *A Foray into the Worlds of Animals and Humans with A Theory of Meaning*. Trans. Joseph D. O'Neil (Minneapolis: University of Minnesota Press, 2010).

3 Richard Louv, *Our Wild Calling* (Algonquin Books, 2019), 50. Louv's explanation owes much to conversations with the biopsychologist Gordon Burkhardt and evolutionary biologist Harry Greene. "Critical anthropomorphism," however is a core concept in contemporary animal studies, frequently defined and deployed in this field.

4 E. O. Wilson, *The Biophilia Hypothesis* (Washington, DC: Island Press, 1995).

5 G. Durrell, *Catch Me a Colobus* (London: Penguin, 1972), 211.

6 Except where noted, the facts of Gerald Durrell's life recorded here are documented in his own books and in biographies. Most helpful is Douglas

Botting's *Gerald Durrell: An Authorized Biography* (New York: Carroll & Graf, 1999).

7 Lawrence's experience in Cyprus (which includes several comical references to "my brother,") are recorded in *Bitter Lemons* (Mt. Jackson, VA: Axios Press, 1957).

8 Bruce Chatwin, *In Patagonia* (Penguin 2003), xiv.

9 G. Durrell, "Introduction," in June Kay, *Okavango*, (London: The Adventurers Club, 1963), 13.

10 G. Durrell, Gerald to Lawrence Durrell, December 3, 1966. (Unpublished letter on zoo letterhead.)

11 Ursula Heise, *Imagining Extinction: The Cultural Meanings of Endangered Species* (Chicago, IL: University of Chicago Press, 2016), 15.

12 Ramachandra Guha and Juan Martinez-Alier, *Varieties of Environmentalism* (London: Earthscan, 1997), 104.

13 G. Durrell, "My Brother Larry," *Twentieth Century Literature*, 33, no. 3 (1987). 262–65, 262.

14 G. Durrell, *The Whispering Land* (London: Penguin, 1961), 196.

15 Graham Huggan, *Nature's Saviors: Celebrity Conservationists in the Television Age* (New York: Routledge, 2013).

16 G. Durrell and L. Durrell, *Durrell in Russia* (New York: Simon and Schuster, 1986), 5.

17 Interview with Lee Durrell, October 24, 2012.

18 Durrell and Durrell, *Durrell in Russia*, 184-86.

19 G. Durrell and Jane Bayer, "A Chance to Meet Gerald Durrell," Interview, Channel TV, March 16, 1983. https://www.youtube.com/watch?v=AiqupY-_7VM).

20 Immanuel Kant, "Idea for a Universal History with a Cosmopolitan Purpose," in *The Cosmopolitan Reader*, ed. Garrett Wallace Brown and David Held (Cambridge, MA: Polity Press, 2013), 17–26.

21 Botting, *Gerald Durrell: An Authorized Biography*, 388.

22 James Fair, "Did You Hear the One about the Kestrel, the Pigeon, the Fody, the Skink, the Bat and the Boa?" *Discover Wildlife*. From the team at *BBC Wildlife Magazine*. https://www.discoverwildlife.com/uncategorized/did-you-hear-the-one-about-the-kestrel-the-pigeon-the-fody-the-skink-the-bat-and-the-boa/

23 E. O. Wilson, Interview about *Genesis*, *New York Times*, February 28, 2018, 7.

24 Paul F. Starrs, "Review of *Naturalist* by E. O. Wilson," *Annals of the Association of American Geographers*, 86, no. 2 (1996), 358–60.

1 CORFU

On the way from Pérama to Benitses, the road curves westward, circling Lake Halkiopoulou, a shallow salt lagoon separated from the sea by a weir, along which foot traffic goes back and forth between mainland Corfu and Kanoni, the peninsula south of Corfu town. The famously photographed island church of Vlacherna is connected to Kanoni by a narrower walkway, and the even better known lush, green island Pontikonissi, with its monastery, is a five-minute boat ride away. Pontikonissi shelters birds and fish in abundance, and it is rumored that critically endangered Mediterranean monk seals still find a haven there. When Edward Lear painted this scene in the middle of the nineteenth century, the hills were less cluttered, the airport, of course, absent, and the wildlife doubtless more abundant; the scene was much the same until after the middle of the twentieth century.

South of Corfu town, the main road turns south and upward along the bluffs. With a closer look, the botanical tangle on both sides resolves into a patchwork of tiny groves, loosely demarcated by agave, yucca, opuntia, palms, an occasional fig tree, and falls of vining succulents. Flights of tall, slender cypress trees follow the flow of rain through creases in the hillsides. Below the road, the hills descend precipitously, ending in shingle beaches and short strips of sand. Houses cling to the slopes, each surrounded by its own grapevines, tiny garden, and trees bearing olives, oranges, lemons, and tangerines.

In *Prospero's Cell* (1945), Lawrence describes Corfu, or "Corcyra," or "Kerkyra," as "a peninsula nipped off while red hot to cool in an Antarctica of lava."[1] Corfu is a sickle shape in the Adriatic sea, about a hundred miles southeast of the heel of Italy's boot. It is a continental island, forty miles north to south, the largest in the Ionian Archipelago, with the Albanian mountains visible in the north and Epirus, the rugged northwest corner of the Greek mainland, not much more than a stone's throw from the island's east coast. The climate here is balmier than in mainland Greece.

March is brisk but mostly sunny in Corfu. Until plants blossom later in the spring, brilliant citrus fruit still hangs from the trees. In late March of 1935, the Durrell family—Gerald, his mother Louisa, Roger, a curly-haired black dog, Gerald's brother Leslie, and his sister Margo—made their way along what was then a dusty track to their first home on Corfu. In *My Family and Other Animals*, Gerald remembered the house as "the Strawberry pink villa." The oldest brother, Lawrence, with his wife Nancy Myers, had preceded the rest of the family by a week and settled temporarily in Corfu town.

The family had left Bournemouth, a Victorian spa town in Dorset, on Britain's south coast, traveling by rail and sea before they disembarked at Corfu's port. The welter of sensations, as Gerald left town in the taxi driven by Spiro Chalikiopoulos (known to the family as Spiro "Americanus"), must have been overwhelming, as was Spiro himself. Larger-than-life, vociferous, experienced in the ways of the world (especially the United States), Spiro became the family's friend and chief problem solver. Gerald remembers the occasion this way:

> [W]hen we arrived, the island lay breathless and sun-drugged in a smouldering, peacock-blue sea under a sky that had been faded to a pale powder-blue by the fierce rays of the sun.... I found myself prey to the most curious sensation of unreality. It was rather like being born for the first time. In that brilliant, brittle light I could appreciate the true huntsman's red of a lady-bird's wing case, the magnificent chocolate and amber of an earwig, and the deep shining agate of the ants. Then I could feast my eyes on a bewildering number of creatures unfamiliar to me.... Each brilliant day brought some new puzzles of behavior to underline my ignorance. [2]

All islands, of course, are distinct and eccentric, but the differences between Corfu and the rest of the Mediterranean (not to mention its distinctness from "Pudding Island," as Lawrence called England) stamped themselves on the whole family. If geographical islands are analogous to other isolated individuals or groups, the history of any island, biological or cultural, consists of lengthy or brief periods of isolation interspersed with cultural, social, and material inputs. When islands and their eccentric inhabitants meet influences from elsewhere—one could think of this elsewhere as mainstream, normal, central—everything changes.

Corfu marked a respite from the sense of exile and displacement felt by every member of the family, whose security was in tatters after the sudden death of father and husband Lawrence Samuel in 1928. Both the Durrells and the Dixies—Louisa's family—had for generations occupied mid-level colonial positions in the Raj and thought of themselves as Anglo-Indian to the core. Their conversation was as laden with elephants hauling camping gear and cobras under the dining table as their dining tables with chutneys and fiery curries. In *The Garden of the Gods*, Gerald remembered his mother's confiding about family history, "When most people talked of home and meant England, when we said home we meant India."[3] Whenever the Durrells traveled to "Pudding Island" for visits with extended family, medical consultations, or schooling (in the case of Lawrence and Leslie), they were in a foreign land. Leslie felt alienated both at his day school in Dulwich and, a bit later, at Caldicott, a Methodist boarding school. Lawrence attended three schools in England. St. Edmunds, the last, gave him a solid grounding in the general knowledge he would need as a novelist, but did not inspire him to attempt Oxford or Cambridge. Until their father died, both boys wanted to return from school to India, and no doubt they would have done so at the earliest opportunity if they could have.

However, despite mixed feelings about England, when Louisa received a generous settlement from her husband's business partners (over half a million pounds in today's currency), she and her English relatives agreed that moving back to the metropolis would provide the stability her family needed. There was really nowhere else to go—and the decision was not simply personal. By 1928, the Raj was under pressure from negative public opinion throughout India, strong regional movements for independence, and violent localized anti-British protests. By 1935, the Government of India Act passed by the British Parliament weakened the Raj further by granting provincial governing powers throughout the subcontinent.

After a false start in London, the Durrells joined family and friends in Bournemouth. Once back in the United Kingdom, Lawrence pursued his literary career while Nancy painted. The family encountered predictable financial difficulties as they alternated between London and Bournemouth. Leslie soon refused to attend another day at school. After one term, Margo, too, refused to return to school. Gerald was frequently overcome by stomach pains on school mornings and "stumbled through his lessons until, one day, falsely accused of a misdemeanour by the school sneak," he was beaten. Louisa removed him.[4] That ended his formal schooling and initiated his friendship with Roger, bought from a pet shop to console him. Roger was the dog of his heart, apparently Gerald's life-long favorite dog, his collaborator and companion throughout the years in Corfu.

Bournemouth itself was part of the problem. A century earlier, the Godwins and Shelleys had spent time in the town, and Robert Louis Stevenson took up residence for his health before emigrating to the South Seas. Bournemouth boasted an orchestra, theater, and bookstores, but it also boasted a pine-tree-lined avenue to the beach called "Invalid's Walk" and a fair share of respectability. Later, Gerald would make disparaging, off-hand remarks about the town and its links with English officialdom: Argentinian armadillos resemble "small, rotund colonels on a Bournemouth seafront".[5] More directly, he notes in "Ludwig," a sketch in the story collection *Marrying Off Mother*, "in my day, all you saw in the streets were portly brigadiers and elderly ladies."[6]

The Durrells did not fit in, even with their respectable Dixie relatives. Without realizing it, in addition to their private grief, they were experiencing the inevitable tension between the periphery of empire and the center, between Victorian imperial expansion and twentieth-century retrenchment. They were a vanguard in a White diaspora which would develop fully only after mid-century. They were travelers and exiles; expatriates and cosmopolitans; wanderers and sojourners. Like most emigrants, they tried to take flight away from disorder and towards belonging. Later Gerald recalled that "Our reasons for packing up and leaving the gloomy shores of England were somewhat nebulous but based loosely on the fact that we were tired of the drab suburbanness of life in England and its accompanying bleak and unpleasant climate."[7]

The decision was also financial. Reeling from the shock of her husband's death and the loss of an infant daughter a few years earlier, Louisa at first tried to live in England as she had done in India, with servants and a large house. In fact, although she moved into smaller quarters several times in London before moving closer to friends and relatives in Bournemouth, she was financially inexperienced and spent too much money, even as she tried to save it. (Indeed, by the late 1940s, what had been at first a small fortune had all but disappeared.) In 1935, Lawrence, then twenty-three years old and conscientious about his role as the eldest son, convinced his mother that her financial solvency depended on a drastic change in her way of life.

Their destination was partly an accident. In 1934, Lawrence's friend and fellow aspiring novelist George Wilkinson wrote enthusiastically to

Lawrence that, among other appealing features, Corfu was inexpensive. But there was more to recommend it. There is hardly a spot along the island's spine and eastern coast without a view of the snow-capped mountains of the mainland. As much as any place in Europe, Corfu is marked and scarred by history, perhaps because the Ionian Islands are the greenest and, agriculturally, the richest part of Greece. During the Hellenistic period, Corfu was controlled periodically by several mainland Greek city states. The Roman Empire eventually incorporated the island, as did the Byzantine. A little later, the Normans established a Mediterranean outpost there. Corfu was then controlled for several centuries by the Venetians, whose architectural style still dominates much of Corfu town and domestic architecture throughout the island. Ottoman control followed, ending during the Napoleonic Wars, and after the European allies drove the French from the island in 1815, the British remained in control until 1864, when Corfu became part of a unified Greece.

The Durrell family would feel more at home in Corfu than anywhere in England, if only because being foreign means being free of the social expectations that attach to belonging. But if they had a national identity at all, that identity was English. After Britain played a part in administering the island, the colonial occupation left behind administrative buildings, additions to the great Venetian fortress in Corfu town, and the large Doric-styled Church of St. George along the south side of the fortress. The British introduced cricket, ginger beer, and a wave of tourism. The buildings remain, as does cricket. Ginger beer is easy to find. The island still hosts an English expatriate community.

Lord Byron and Oscar Wilde visited the island, as did the Victorian painter William Linton and statesman and novelist Benjamin Disraeli, whose grand tour stop there is described in novellas about Corfu. Lear stayed on Corfu intermittently for several years. Illustrations based on his paintings and humorous Corfu letters are appended to *Prospero's Cell*, Lawrence's travel book about the island. Corfu itself is thus a classroom of history—and for Gerald, it became a classroom of natural history as well.

Left to their own devices, untrammeled children will explore a natural environment with great energy and little fear. Until recently, it was not uncommon for rural and suburban children to walk many miles a day through fields or forests, turning over stones to find insects or small reptiles; building dams in streams to trap turtles, minnows, and crayfish; scrambling through a nightscape to catch fireflies; climbing trees; peering into birds' nests; and, like Tarzan and Jane Porter, swinging from vines. Gerald had more freedom even than most children a generation or two ago: while the family lived in Bournemouth before their Corfu adventure, he had already established his reputation for aggressively riding a bicycle over embankments in the garden, lurking high in the treetops, and bringing indoors captured or adopted fauna (including snakes.)[8]

Edith Cobb, a pioneer in research on children's play, suggests in *The Ecology of Imagination in Childhood* that the middle years of childhood are an especially open period of development, when "awakening to the existence of some potential" involves "an acute sensory response to the natural world."[9] Gerald arrived at his natural island paradise just when the physical, mental, and emotional development of a natural predisposition toward other animals could shape him into the committed environmentalist and naturalist he became. In a little less than five years, Gerald explored the landscape and inhabitants of almost all 226 square miles of the island. A tireless walker, Margo often went along with Gerald, and Roger always kept him company.

Gerald related the adventures of this period in the Corfu trilogy, the best-known volume of which is *My Family and Other Animals* (1956). Gerald admits in "The Speech for the Defense" which opens this first Corfu book that "I have been forced to telescope, prune, and graft, so that there is little left of the original continuity of events."[10] In all three volumes, animals are sometimes anthropomorphized to a greater extent than in his other books; family, friends, neighbors, and chance acquaintances are subjected to caricature; and some names are altered. Enormously popular, *My Family and Other Animals* was followed by *Birds, Beasts, and Relatives* (1969) and *The Garden of the Gods* (1980). Like the two later volumes, *My Family and Other Animals* provides a rich source of biographical details, although the chronology is unreliable.

It is surely not accidental that the second volume of this trilogy is less genial than the first, and the third volume includes more pessimistic interpretations of the Corfu experience, along with characters and episodes more difficult to integrate into the idyllic picture of the "tiger-golden" days of childhood.[11] Published at intervals of about a decade, these books not only reflect Gerald's evolving perspective on his life in Corfu, they also suggest an escalating worry as he saw first-hand, in environmental hot spots across the planet, the beginnings of the sixth extinction. In all Gerald's published work of the 1970s and 1980s, including the latter two volumes of the trilogy, the anger is almost palpable, the style unhinged, and the characterization of those he deemed responsible for species extinction merciless.

Nevertheless, Theodore Stephanides, the genial family friend Gerald called "the most important person in my life," read the manuscript of *My Family and Other Animals* and pronounced it factually accurate. (*Birds, Beasts, and Relatives* is dedicated to him "in gratitude for laughter and learning.") The Corfu trilogy suggests a timeline that can be partially reconstructed from the organization of these first two volumes according to houses the family occupied—the Strawberry Pink Villa in Pérama (March through October 1935), the Daffodil Yellow Villa just north of Corfu town near Kondokali (October 1935–October 1937), and the Snow-White Villa, inland from Pérama (October 1937 until the family's departure in June, 1939). Lawrence and Nancy moved about the island, too. Sometimes they took rooms in Corfu town, sometimes they lodged with the rest of the family, and once, for over a year, they rented the "White House" in Kalami, on the northeast coast of the island, a few feet from the water and dampened by the waves on all but the calmest days.

With each house, including the White House, Gerald's world expanded. Much of Corfu's coastline is so corrugated that the roads along the coast consist of one hairpin curve after another. Boat travel is the fastest way to get from one place to another, so Lawrence's sailboat, the *Van Norden* (named for a character in one of Henry Miller's novels) helped the whole family move about the island quickly and explore the waters around it. Each house was situated in a slightly different landscape and offered a different home base for exploration. Although Gerald learned to swim within days after the family's arrival on the island, he wanted to explore more thoroughly the marine life just out of reach. For his eleventh birthday, while the family lived in Kondokali, he persuaded Leslie to a build him a boat, the naming of which became a family affair. The mobility provided by the "Bootle-Bumtrinket" gave Gerald freedom to explore land and sea on his own terms. The donkey Sally, Gerald's birthday gift when he was thirteen, when the family lived in the white villa, enabled him to ramble more widely through the interior.

A timeline parallel to the sequence of houses reflects the more (and yet not entirely) traditional education provided by Gerald's reading and a succession of tutors and mentors. Gerald was still young enough upon arrival in Corfu that structure for him seemed necessary, at least to his mother. According to Gerald's comic account of the problem, in Leslie's view, shooting and sailing were essential. (Leslie also went in for photography—a pursuit which may explain his absence from family photographs.) Margo insisted on dancing instruction. Nancy sometimes instructed her young brother-in-law in drawing, a skill which he put to use right away in his nature diaries.

Lawrence, of course, insisted on literature and recommended (not entirely in jest, one feels) that it begin with Rabelais—"it's important that he gets sex in its right perspective now."[12] Certainly, Gerald's descriptions of the Durrell entertainments on Corfu are Rabelaisian to the extent of unruly human behavior and vast quantities of food and drink. Rabelais would have appreciated the pack of sexually incontinent dogs at one of these feasts, along with water snakes in the lavatory and drunken Magenpies, who danced in the butter and wrecked a dining table, beautifully decorated by Margo, right before the guests arrived.

Gerald also read stories: Conan Doyle, Sheridan La Fanu, D. H. Lawrence, and T. E. Lawrence. In *My Family and Other Animals*, he reports a delightfully confusing conversation, during one of the Rabelaisian entertainments, between Margo and an aspiring writer—"a short, fat somnambulistic little man who looked like a well-boiled prawn"—in which the author of *Lady Chatterley's Lover* is understood to have written *The Seven Pillars of Wisdom*.[13]

Gerald also no doubt also sampled Miller's work, which Lawrence greatly admired: certainly Lawrence's letters to Miller express pleasure in Gerald's earliest literary productions, which were included in the experimental journal *Booster*, a collaborative effort edited by Miller, William Saroyan, Alfred Perlès, and Lawrence. Gerald contributed a precocious, lugubrious poem about death. Indeed, Gerald's later writing sometimes resonates with Miller's fluid, energetic prose style, and the influence of Lawrence's literary scholarship is evident on every page of Gerald's published work.

A self-educated polymath, Lawrence also found books relevant to Gerald's particular interests.[14] Genres of science and nature writing, especially narratives of scientific and geographical discovery, expanded rapidly in the nineteenth century, with wide appeal. Travel writing had become enormously popular in the nineteenth century, and it remained so. Gerald would benefit doubly from narratives which linked science to travel and adventure.[15] Most of his books, of course, were supplied by Lawrence.

Gerald remembered a childhood reading list that included works by Charles Darwin and Gilbert White; W. H. Hudson, best known for *Green*

Mansions: A Romance of the Tropical Forest (1904); Henry Walter Bates' *The Naturalist on the River Amazons* (1863); G. Evelyn Hutchinson's *The Clear Mirror: A Pattern of Life in Goa and Indian Tibet* (1936). *A Bird Book for the Pocket* by Edmund Sanders was always at hand. The list compiled in Bottings' biography is much longer and includes many British comedy classics. Traces of P. G. Wodehouse are detectable almost everywhere in Gerald's writing, especially in the early books, and Jerome K. Jerome's *Three Men in a Boat, to Say Nothing of the Dog* may be reflected in some of Gerald's own titles—*Three Singles to Adventure* and *Two in the Bush*.[16] During the Corfu years, Leslie and Gerald regularly received *The Boy's Own Paper*, replete with a special brand of nature writing in children's adventure stories, and *The Wide World Magazine*, in which Gerald first read about a collection voyage to Cameroon. Like his brothers, Leslie seems to have been a born storyteller, and when he returned from school in England, he regaled his little brother with tales from Charles Hamilton's series about the fictional Billy Bunter of Greyfriars School. Likely the appeal of Billy—for both boys—was his outrageously anti-social behavior. He is greedy, fat, self-absorbed, deceitful, and not nearly as clever as he thinks (hence, the hilarity). He "emit[s], from time to time, a characteristic cry of 'Yarooooh!'"[17]

Science and nature writing for children was a growth industry which employed women and men shut out of formal scientific training.[18] Stories by the entomologist J. Henri Fabre, a schoolmaster almost entirely self-educated as a scientist, whose observations were made mostly in his own back yard in the south of France, were on Gerald's bookshelf and likely an even greater influence than the adventure tales. Like other popular science stories for children of the time, Fabre's work is strongly narrative, romantic, personal, accurate, and disciplined:

> You rip up the animal and I study it alive; you turn it into an object of horror and pity, whereas I cause it to be loved; you labor in a torture-chamber and dissecting-room, I make my observations under the blue sky to the song of the Cicadas. . . . Well, if I write for men of learning, for philosophers. . . I write above all things for the young. . . .[19]

Fabre's personal story reveals courage—he allowed girls in his science classes and was fired for doing so. John Stuart Mill once rescued him from penury. Eventually, after decades of meticulous publications on insect ecology and behavior, Fabre came to the attention of the literary world: Edmund Rostand, Romain Roland, and Maurice Maeterlinck (later infamous for plagiarizing *The Soul of the White Ant* by Eugène Marais) took note of his work.[20]

No wonder Lawrence knew of Fabre's works and presented his youngest brother with them soon after they arrived in Corfu, and no wonder Fabre provided models for both Gerald's investigations and his writing: "They opened up a magical world," wrote Gerald in the preface to *A Practical Guide for the Amateur Naturalist* (1989):

> Here was a man who could tell me why dung beetles so busily made little balls from horse or cow manure and buried them and how the glow-worm overpowers and consumes snails; who could tell me what a praying mantis did on her wedding night and who could describe exciting experiments to prove his theories—he once borrowed a cannon and fired it off in front of his house (breaking all the windows) to see if cicadas could hear.[21]

Fabre not only gave Gerald the facts he so greedily consumed, he also demonstrated—on every page—an ecological approach to the animals he studied, reinforced the validity of emphasizing ethology before that science was named, and revealed a critical anthropomorphism which allowed the naturalist to consider animals' behavior and cognition, in addition to biology and taxonomy. Fabre's vision resonates with Gerald's no less than Lawrence's literary style echoes on Gerald's pages. Gerald's childhood observation of a mantis as she participates in a complicated predatory event (she and a gecko go after the same prey and then each other) on his ceiling is no less accurate because he characterizes her as a wily villain who gets what's coming to her when she in her turn is snapped up for dinner.[22]

Reading was not enough for Louisa and Lawrence when they considered Gerald's education. They insisted on tutors. George Wilkinson, whose enthusiastic letters inspired Lawrence to bring the family to Corfu, was Gerald's first tutor there. George and his wife Pam had left the house they shared in London with Lawrence and Nancy to complete a bicycle trip of 1,800 km through Europe, pausing in Corfu to assemble the materials for their travel book. George was an expert fencer and secretary to biographer and bibliographer A. J. A. Symons; Pam was an accomplished photographer.[23] Despite the inconveniences of Corfu, they suggested that Larry and Nancy come for an extended stay. George consented to undertake Gerald's education soon after the family's arrival. As a travel writer, he encouraged Gerald in similar pursuits.

Gerald detested conventional classroom routine. He began learning demotic Greek almost immediately from the "plump peasant girls" described and caricatured in *My Family and Other Animals:* they were

> shrill and colourful as parrots. . . . What had at first had been a confused babble became a series of recognizable separate sounds. Then, suddenly, these took on meaning, and . . . then I took my newly acquired words and strung them into ungrammatical and stumbling sentences. Our neighbors were delighted . . . and should Roger and I chance to pass that way entire [families], vociferous and pleased would tumble out to greet us. . . .[24]

Along with the language came folklore and information about the indigenous plants and animals that only local people know. If the biota were "vocabulary," the landscape became a kind of "grammar," and Gerald's need to understand the natural history of Corfu was insatiable. Hardly anything else interested him long enough to hold his attention.

As an educator, George faced terrific obstacles, which he overcame by adapting his teaching methods to his pupil. Gerald learned geography from maps and old encyclopedias, French from a dictionary, literature and reading from "books that ranged from Wilde to Gibbon and mathematics from [George's] memory." Fortunately, George was clever enough to cast story problems in the form of animal narratives ("If it took two caterpillars a week to eat eight leaves, how long would four caterpillars take to eat the same number?")[25]. Tutor and pupil made large maps, generously illustrated with animals. Once, in a tiny bay near the house, they made a map of the world along the edge of the sea out of stones and flotsam, while Roger attempted, always unsuccessfully, to catch fish. Here, too, Gerald captured a spider crab, who, time after time, reconstructed its protective camouflage from various materials lying about.

History lessons were enlivened by such fictional footnotes as names of the elephants who crossed the Alps with Hannibal, Columbus's sighting of a jaguar as he first set foot in the New World, and the birds' egg collection Lord Nelson bequeathed to Hardy. George also knew something of natural history, to which the pair devoted one morning a week, and Gerald quickly discovered the value of George's advice to keep an illustrated notebook recording his outdoor investigations—advice he himself passes on in *The Amateur Naturalist*. George's writing assignments—he suggested that Gerald compose fictional adventures like his older brother's—improved Gerald's writing fluency. Although the nature journals have been lost, some of the fiction from this period remains. Gerald's elementary understanding of the European adventurer's place in the colonies resonates in instructive ways with the early collecting narratives he started publishing in the 1950s. In a headnote to his biography, Douglas Botting quotes a passage from "The Man of Animals," written by Gerald when he was ten years old: "Right in the Hart of the Africn Jungel a small wite man lives. Now there is one xtrordenry fackt him that is that he is the frind of *all* animals." One sees here the challenge Gerald presented to his tutors.

George stayed behind, when, in October 1935, the family moved on from the Strawberry Pink villa to the Daffodil Yellow Villa, closer to the White House at Kalami and just outside Corfu town. Not surprisingly, Louisa observed that Gerald "was running wild again" and arranged French lessons. So, for a time, Gerald rode every morning in Spiro's taxi to the Jewish quarter, where he studied with the Belgian consul. Some of the streets here are so narrow that even a donkey would have trouble negotiating them. "It was a rich and colourful part of the town," he wrote in *My Family and Other Animals*, "full of noise and bustle, the screech of bargaining women, the cluck of hens, the barking of dogs, and the wailing cry of men carrying great trays of fresh hot loaves on their heads." Most colorful of all, perhaps, was the consul himself, a "sweet little man" with a three-pointed beard who constructed the lessons by having Gerald read from the *Larousse* dictionary.[26] These lessons were continually interrupted by the consul's air-rifle volleys to destroy the hundreds of starving stray cats in the area. Since the consul himself lived with three large Persian cats, Gerald understood and agreed that this euthanasia project was a kindness.

Although he did not learn French from these encounters, so very unlike the conditions under which he picked up Greek, he did begin to learn about the impact of human behavior on animal populations—a lesson reinforced by other experiences on the island and, especially, his conversations with Theodore Stephanides, to whom George had introduced him a few months earlier.

Another family friend, Pat Evans (denominated "Peter" in *My Family and Other Animals*), was engaged as a tutor soon after the Durrells settled

26   THE EVOLUTION OF GERALD DURRELL

into the Daffodil Yellow Villa. A recent product of Oxford, Evans at first tried conventional methods, which were "painful to an extreme," but eventually followed George's lead by suggesting that Gerald write an epic, and devoting as much time to natural history as his unruly pupil wished.[27] During Evans' tenure, Gerald found himself in a new landscape, a little farther from the sea (which was still in view) and higher up in the hills, where he watched tortoises in their "courtship" and hatching grounds and collected scorpions from the garden wall (to the alarm of Lawrence, especially, when once he opened the scorpions' new matchbox home by mistake). There were more animals to discover, and larger fauna to shelter—a Scops owl, lizards, more snakes, and the beginning of a marine life collection. One of the most memorable episodes in the Corfu trilogy is Gerald's account of an evening swim with porpoises:

> They rose all around me, sighing luxuriously, their black backs shining as they humped in the moonlight.... Heaving and sighing heavily, they played across the bay, and I swam with them, watching fascinated as they rose to the surface, crumpling the water, breathed deeply, and then dived beneath the surface again.... Presently, as if obeying a signal, they turned and headed out of the bay towards...Albania, and I trod water and watched them go, swimming up the white chain of moonlight, backs agleam as they rose and plunged with heavy ecstasy.... Behind them they left a trail of great bubbles that rocked and shone briefly like miniature moons before vanishing under the ripples.[28]

During these evening swims, the family were sometimes joined by fireflies, and on moonless nights the phosphorescence of air and sea was breathtakingly beautiful.

Evans joined the family on many such occasions. But his tenure as Gerald's tutor lasted only about a year: Louisa ended it because of Margo's infatuation with him (which was apparently mutual), and Margo's depression resulted in physical symptoms which required a visit to England with her mother and Gerald. He could scarcely wait to return to the island.

By the end of the summer of 1936, Gerald was adjusting to still another tutor. He was both unlucky and lucky with his final official tutor, Krajewsky (called Kralefsky in the Corfu Trilogy)—a Polish exile whose Polish-English-French ancestry, like that of so many foreign Corfu residents, reflected the map of Europe. According to Gerald's account in *My Family and Other Animals*, the new tutor's lessons were as tedious as his extra-curricular interests were fascinating. Kralefsky's eccentricities stood out, even among an entire community of eccentrics. He was physically stunted and beautifully groomed. His birdlike mother, whose fantasies about talking flowers apparently resulted from senile dementia, shared her son's living quarters in "a mildewed mansion ... on the outskirts of town," along with an impressive collection of finches and other caged birds. When Gerald was introduced to the birds, "It was as though Kralefsky had opened the gates of Paradise in a grubby corridor."[29] Thus, the tutor passed muster with his resistant pupil, who was sometimes recruited to help with the birds' care. Better yet, Kralefsky's conversation, wherever he happened to be, in the classroom or at a dinner party, was punctuated by tall tales, always involving his heroic rescue of "a lady" from angry wild animals, human evil-doers, or natural disasters.

Beyond his passion for pet birds, Kralefsky seems to have had little interest in the natural world, but his cosmopolitan background and attitudes surely remained a model for kindness, hospitality, and open-mindedness years later, when Gerald became almost overwhelmed by the devastation of the natural world as he tried to conserve animal habitat and save critically endangered animals from extinction.

If other tutors came and went at the average pace of one every year, Lawrence and Theo remained the two stable, committed, convincing teachers and mentors during all of Gerald's years in Corfu. Theo was an eccentric—like Spiro, George, Kralefsky, and a host of other characters Gerald describes in the Corfu trilogy—the peasant girls, the speechless Rose-Beetle Man, Yani the elderly shepherd and his silent wife Aphrodite, Taki the fisherman, Kosti the friendly murderer, obscene old Captain Creech, the ancient Countess Mavrodaki and her opinionated Turkish manservant, unpredictable priests, Larry's numerous bohemian friends from around the globe, and the Durrells themselves. Theo danced, hummed, sang nonsense rhymes, and produced execrable puns. He was also, in the words of Henry Miller, "the most learned man I have ever met, and a saint to boot."[30] "He knew all about plants, flowers, trees, rocks, minerals, microbes, diseases, stars, planets, comets and so on." Gerald himself says, "Theodore looked like a Greek god, and certainly he seemed as omniscient as one."[31]

When George introduced Gerald to Theo in 1935, Theo and Lawrence were already acquainted through their literary conversations. Like

Kralefsky and so many other Corfu residents, Theo belonged to the international community both enriched and displaced by international forces at work during early twentieth century. He was born in India (Mumbai) about twenty years before Lawrence, to Anglophone Greek parents who retired to Corfu, where Theo learned Greek, which he always spoke with a slight accent. After serving in the Greek army during the First World War and then studying in Paris, he returned to the island in 1933. During a long and productive life, Theo composed poetry in English and Greek and translated poetry from Greek to English; he wrote *Climax in Crete*, an autobiographical account of the First World War invasion of Crete; *Island Trails*, a popular work about the Ionian Islands; and a play. Thus, his appeal for Henry Miller, George Wilkinson, and Lawrence. Theo was also a medical doctor and scientist. He set up the first X-ray unit on Corfu; later, during his tenure on the staff of St. Thomas Hospital in London after the Second World War, he wrote a manual about the use of the microscope. Theo's interests coincided most with Gerald's, however, as he researched the insect and aquatic life of Corfu for a survey of the island's freshwater biota, including an anti-mosquito fish in one of the lakes, and published scientific papers on his findings.[32]

If Lawrence's influence on Gerald's literary style remained indelible, Theo's influence on Gerald's understanding of the natural world and even, in the long term, his commitment to an environmentalist vocation was equally powerful. The dedication of *A Practical Guide for the Amateur Naturalist* reads, "This book is for Theo (Dr. Theodore Stephanides), my mentor and friend, without whose guidance I would have achieved nothing." Theo was sociable, genial, and kind—interested equally in the human and nonhuman worlds, and in the ways these worlds intersected.

When Gerald met Theo, he was impressed that Theo spoke to him with respect, not condescendingly, as one might to a child. The burning question of the day was about trapdoor spiders, which Gerald had just discovered; the answer came in a detailed natural history lesson and a short field trip. But even Theo did not know how the female spider discriminated between her mate, whom she did not consider edible, and other prey who were edible. A day or two after the pair met, Gerald was surprised to receive a package with a field magnifying class—a spectacular gift from the man who would remain his mentor for decades to come.

Thursdays became Theo's days. Theo's lessons included experimental science as well as field science. Once, he told Gerald the story of a caddis larva, which constructs a shell from suitable objects in its environment.

When Theo dismantled the shell and replaced the natural materials with beads, bits of glass, and brick fragments, the larva quickly built another shell from the new materials: "They are certainly very clever architects," he concluded.[33] Since the chronology of the Corfu trilogy is impossible to reconstruct completely, one can only guess that Theo's story inspired Gerald's own experiments removing the spider crab's constructed shell and providing materials for a new one. Although Theo's fund of factual knowledge seemed almost inexhaustible, perhaps the most important of Theo's lessons for Gerald was a sense of how life forms, even in a micro-habitat, were connected:

> Every water-filled ditch was, to us, a teeming and water-filled jungle, with the minute cyclops and water-fleas, green and coral pink, suspended like birds among the underwater branches, while on the muddy bottoms the tigers of the pool would prowl: the leeches and the dragon-fly larvae.[34]

Like Theo, Gerald soon understood that "nature" is a fabric of life forms connected in chains of dependence, webs of conflict, and cooperation situated and evolving in particular locations.

Although animals were his passion, he noted plants, as well. One chapter title, "The Cyclamen Woods," begins with a description of a hilltop forest near the "Snow-White Villa," dotted with vivid cyclamens (a sub Caucasus and eastern Mediterranean clumping flower now threatened in its native range because of over-harvesting for sale as house plants). It was a perfect resting place, with a perfect view of fields and sea; on one occasion, Gerald stole two baby magpies from a nest there. Since Spiro insisted on calling them the "Magenpies," that became their official collective name. Predictably, they became some of Gerald's most memorable animals, and they caused a world of trouble.

On one occasion, Theo accompanied the Durrells on a short excursion to Lake Antiniotissa, a shallow salt lake on the northern coast of the island, bordered by a narrow strip of flat, sandy beach with an obvious appeal for the more sybaritic members of the family. While Leslie hunted for game on one side of the lake, Gerald and Theo "pottered among the pools and streamlets, like a pair of eager herons."[35] And while Theo searched for insect and microscopic life, Gerald was on the lookout for larger animals for his ever-growing collection.

Despite the disparity in age, these two were not simply mentor and protégé, but true collaborators. They supported one another by confiding their questions and theories. Theo's obvious interest validated Gerald's devotion to animal collecting and study, despite the understandable objections of family members who had to share a house with captured insects, geckos and toads, jackdaws and various songbirds, snakes, owls, a seagull, tortoises, fish, and far too many dogs. Theo congratulated him on his rare observation of mating snails and explained the complex breeding and migration of eels. Theo was no doubt interested in the willingness of a hoopoe with a broken wing to feed baby jays. (Gerald's intelligence in devising this strategy, probably to keep the chicks from imprinting on him, was remarkable.) Theo would have delighted in the hedgehogs in the garden, drunk on fallen grapes, and was no doubt a rapt audience for Gerald's stories of capture and release of injured birds from his wildlife hospital.

Once, after capturing a pregnant dormouse, Gerald released her offspring, who survived, inspiring a passion for captive breeding which never left him:

> In the evenings, when the sun was setting and the sky was getting green as a leaf, striped with sunset clouds, I used to go down to watch the little masked dormice flitting through the branches with a ballerina-like grace and speaking to each other as they pursued moths, or fireflies or other delicacies through the shadowy branches.[36]

Although Louisa tolerated her son's excesses, and Lawrence fostered his young brother's literary bent, only Theo would have understood the dormice and their new home in both literary and scientific terms.

Some of Gerald's most significant experiences, especially those recorded in the second and third books of the Corfu Trilogy, did not bring delight. He was enraged when Margo accidentally killed a litter of baby hedgehogs by overfeeding them. Even Gerald's observations of wildlife seem less benign in the second and third volumes of the memoir. He was appalled to observe a tarantula as it stalked by smell, with apparent foresight, the nestlings of a lark pair, killing them one by one until the whole clutch was consumed.[37] Wandering herds of goats and flocks of sheep, sometimes with a human herder and sometimes not, sometimes accompanied by a dog and sometimes left to their own devices, still, to this day, follow their belled leaders about on Corfu. Perhaps it was from Theo that Gerald first understood the drastic environmental devastation often caused by these domesticated animals:

"They should not, er … be left unattended," said Theodore, prodding the goat gently with his stick. "Goats do more damage to the countryside than practically anything else." The leader uttered a short sardonic "bah" and then moved away, with his destructive troop following him.[38]

The most horrifying episodes (and the most shocking to contemporary sensibilities) appear in *The Garden of the Gods*, the final book of the trilogy. Captain Creech's vulgar limericks—many quoted in full—Lawrence's mumps, and practical jokes at the expense of Lawrence's visiting homosexual friends—all in this final volume—pale by comparison to Gerald's outrage at what he perceived as the typical Greek attitude toward animals. Leslie's relentless shooting of the local wildlife was apparently, in Gerald's view, far more sporting and less dangerous than the thoughtless and vicious behavior of mainland Greeks and "townee sportsmen" during hunting season, which is also nesting season:

> whereas the peasants would stick to the so-called game bird … the hunters from town would blast everything that flew … their game bags [were] full of a sticky, bloody, feathery conglomeration of anything from robins to redstarts … my room and that portion of the veranda set aside for the purpose always had at least half a dozen cages and boxes containing gape-mouthed baby birds or birds I had managed to rescue from the sportsmen.[39]

Gerald's peasants are no noble savages, however. To the consternation of the rest of the family, Gerald on one occasion brought home a mother dog and eleven puppies, in a tearful rage after he discovered that Agathi, a friend of his, had buried them alive because she could not afford to feed them. Leslie's suggestion that drowning would be preferable, heartily seconded by Lawrence, reflects a view that would have been shared by many people of that era—and was challenged by Luisa's defense of the puppies, which anticipated later twentieth-century views about humane treatment of domesticated animals.

Louisa's love and her views about what it means to be human remained a constant for Gerald until she died; Lawrence's encouragement supported Gerald as a writer; Theo remained a constant source of friendship, inspiration, and information. For Gerald the child, Roger may have been equally important as a collaborator and support, not simply a companion. As this pair rambled across the island and along the shorelines, Gerald habitually watched Roger's reactions to his surroundings. Since Roger's senses were alert to stimuli Gerald could not perceive, the dog's reactions to the landscape and to other fauna provided a valuable perspective and information.

Recent research by Bryan Hare and Vanessa Wood, among others, supports "common sense" assumptions that humans and dogs, especially after long association, also understand one anothers' meaning very well.[40] Attributing a range of emotions and cognitive abilities to other-than-human animals was doubtless one key to Gerald's genius at catching and nurturing them. Understanding their perspective—in large part Roger's gift to Gerald in those years of untrammeled childhood exploration—was one source of Gerald's sympathy for species other than his own, and for his feeling of kinship with them.

Roger proved, as well, to be a valuable confederate, an interface at times between Gerald and other humans. An instance of Roger's assistance in getting a free lunch is especially revealing. In *My Family and Other Animals*, Gerald recorded an encounter with an elderly neighbor. In the middle of hiking on a hot day, considering neighborhood lunch possibilities, Gerald finally decided his neighbor Yani was the best bet, even though he might have been napping: "if I made enough noise he would wake up." When they approached Yani's "minute, sparkling white cottage," Gerald encouraged Roger to bark by interrupting Roger's favorite game of fetch; then, on his own initiative, Roger lunged for the cat under Yani's chair. The cat escaped, hissing loudly as Roger barked "threats and insults." As usual with his neighbors, Gerald was forgiven, and Yani's wife Aphrodite, "her wrinkled face as red as a pomegranate seed, bearing a tray on which was a bottle of wine, a jug of water, and a plate with bread, olives, and figs," emerged from the cottage.

This time, Gerald also garnered a bunch of grapes to take away and some new information. "Here, you are interested in the little ones of God," Yani exclaimed. "[L]ook at this one I caught . . . crouching under a rock like the devil." He held out a tiny, corked bottle of golden oil containing "a small chocolate-brown scorpion, his tail curved like a scimitar over his back." When Gerald asks why the scorpion is in oil, Yani is "greatly amused": "You do not know, little lord, though you spend all your time on your stomach catching these things? . . . Let him simmer, let him die in it, let the sweet oil soak up the poison. Then, should you ever be stung by one of his brothers (and Saint Spiridion protect you from that), you must rub the place with that oil. That will cure the sting for you. . .".[41]

Aside from suggesting Roger's role in Gerald's explorations, this episode reveals much about the position Gerald and his family occupied in Corfu. Childhood comes with privileges: good humored adults offer snacks in such circumstances and laugh when children take fruit from an orchard or flowers from a garden. Gerald made full use of these privileges, even to the extent of milking Agathi's goat one morning, without her knowledge. Other aspects of his position among his Greek neighbors are less innocent. Although Gerald himself expresses neither belief nor disbelief in this "curious information" about scorpions, he evidently passed it along to Lawrence, who included the information in a list of superstitious folk cures in an appendix to *Prospero's Cell*, his travel book about Corfu, which is still regarded as one of the most informative accounts of the island. Transmitted in this way, in what Mary Louise Pratt calls a "timeless 'ethnographic' present," Yani's generosity becomes a mere curiosity and Yani himself more marginalized from the Durrells' metropolitan, worldly identity.[42] Even Yani's generosity conforms to the imperialist trope of "the rough and humble peasant gladly sharing his subsistence with the enlightened man [or boy] of the metropolis whose essential superiority is accepted."[43]

The appearance of privilege—possessed without effort by white northern European visitors to the island—was as good as the real thing. Yani's address to Gerald as "little lord" (probably Yani's phrase would be more accurately translated as "little sir") was perhaps laden with comic irony. Nevertheless, the form of address typifies local attitudes toward the Durrells, who were usually regarded by the local people as aristocratic, rich, and always good for their debts, although Louisa's finances were persistently shaky. Indeed, their ability to live in Corfu in the first place was possible because of the financial capital accumulated by generations of family labor for the Raj and the invisible privileges of northern European whiteness.

Race and skin color were certainly on the minds of the Durrells. Even in the 1930s, racist language was recognized for what it was, and accepting and/or deconstructing racist language remained a theme in Gerald's writing. In "Fred—or A Touch of the Warm South"(1991), the first-person narrator puzzles over racism in the American South, which distinguishes between special Black individuals as "family" and the vast perpetually marginalized Black underclass as other.[44] However, Gerald's narration from a childhood perspective is more ambiguous.

A scene in *The Garden of the Gods* involves Larry's friend the charming Prince Jeejeebuoy (Prince being his given name, much to Louisa's confusion), an aspiring translator, literary critic, and practitioner of "fakyo," Jeejee's blend of yoga and fakir philosophy.[45] Like many other wandering friends, Jeejee stops by from time to time to visit. Although his pursuits leave Jeejee open to relentless jokes, which he blandly accepts (calling to mind the insights of postcolonial theory of the subaltern), Louisa draws the line at racist language. A few months after his first visit, Jeejee returns to celebrate his birthday with the family. The Durrells seemingly invite everyone they know, savory and unsavory, to the party. According to Gerald's account, the feast is Gargantuan, the dancing frenetic, and the conversation untethered from tact or good taste. In the midst of it, Louisa scolds Jeejee for describing a fainting fit as black as "a nigger's bottom," a description applauded by Lawrence and the retired colonial official, obscene Captain Ribbendale.[46]

If Louisa emerged from her colonial experience as truly cosmopolitan—welcoming cultural differences, egalitarian to the core, and consistently kind—her sons had to school themselves to acquire these attitudes. Jeejee's accent; the first name Prince, selected by his socially ambitious mother; the pratfalls resulting from Jeejee's "Fakyo" practice; his scholarly ineptitude; his color; and even his good nature—are part of the stereotypical matrix from which Gerald's human characters are developed. Retired military men like Ribbendale and Creech are obscene; homosexuals are overly emotional; the conversation of elderly women (even countesses) is never rational; "foreigners" never speak English correctly; local Greeks are colorfully caught in a timeless present. Even Theo is a comic god. Few of Gerald's acquaintances escape the sort of Linnean classification in which he arranges his human zoo.

Gerald's Lear-like nonsense and relentless stereotyping might have served as strategies by which a youngest child could negotiate the adult world. Lawrence's sensibilities, like Louisa's, developed into a Kantian cosmopolitanism, as *Bitter Lemons*, his memoir of Cyprus in the 1950's, suggests: while he was the press advisor for the British colonial government on that island, Lawrence formed deep friendships with the Cypriots and deeply lamented the heavy-handed exercise of power by the British—an approach which led to bloodshed and rebellion. Gerald's description of Lawrence's behavior in the Corfu trilogy was based on a childhood memory a quarter of a century in the past and a relentless desire to lampoon even the people he respected. (His descriptions of Lawrence are not unfair: Lawrence did the same to him in *Bitter Lemons*, in which Gerald's collecting endeavors in Crete and his enthusiastic drinking and dancing at a wedding serve as topics for fun in an otherwise serious narrative.)

But Gerald's own Dickensian urge to caricature colored almost everything he wrote. He never quite represented others, human or animal, as his mother would have done. His focus on the eccentric—including the appearances and languages of others—emerged from island life and became part of his trajectory as a student of islands and island biogeography, and island animals. On islands, everything is eccentric.

Ultimately, Gerald's passion for the little ones of God would eventually help him see other human beings with the clarity and compassion necessary for cooperation on a project which should involve us all: the preservation of animal species, brought to the brink of extinction by human carelessness. He would spend almost a lifetime grappling with the tension that resulted from his position in the world of human geopolitics and animal being as he found it. In "A Word in Advance" in *The Garden of the Gods* (1980,) he refers to his family's "curious ways"—and recognizes the immense privilege they enjoyed:

> may I point out that we were in those days, and certainly by Greek standards, comparatively wealthy; none of us worked in the accepted sense of the word and therefore most of our time was spent having fun. If you have five years of doing this, you accumulate quite a lot of experiences.[47]

To the end of his life, Gerald remained uncertain about how to frame the internal conflicts of the White colonial diaspora, of which he was a part; how to confront the political and economic wreckage left behind after the formal dissolution of empires in environmental hot spots around the globe; and how to save both species endangered by the extractive practices of former colonizers and the dire needs of local human populations also damaged by these practices.

However, the years in Corfu would be central to his experience—culturally, emotionally, intellectually. Lawrence's memory of vintage time, celebrated at the villa of their friend Stavrodakis, and Gerald's account reveal their difference in age, yet these two accounts position the older brother and the younger brother within the same milieu, each absorbing the impressions of the moment in his own way. Both were swept away by the rich wines and hearty food, the bustle of preparation, singing and dancing, the crushing of the grapes, and the human bonds which are also celebrated at such a celebration.

Much of Lawrence's story about the occasion, in *Prospero's Cell*, records the conversation of the aristocratic host, who claims that Corfu, not Bermuda, was Shakespeare's model for the island setting in *The Tempest* (hence the title of Lawrence's book). In contrast, Gerald remembers the host as a "wizened" little man who looked like a "half-starved tortoise."[48] To the twelve-year-old boy, the adult conversation among family and friends—Theo, Kralevsky, Spiro, Sven, Max, and Donald—was background noise for an abundant lunch of roast kid and fish, with as much wine as he could drink. Eating was followed by a nap: "I curled up like a dormouse in the protective roots of a great olive and drifted off to sleep...."[49]

At the end of the day, the men sang as the boat heads out to sea from the beach beneath Mount Pantokrator, and then home, first lit by the sunset, then the starry sky.[50] The elegiac tone is partially sustained through the two later books of the Corfu trilogy—this passage ending *Birds, Beasts, and Relatives:*

> Far out in the channel ... the darkness was freckled and picked out with the lights of the fishing boats. It was as though a small section of the Milky Way had fallen into the sea. Slowly the moon edged up over the carapace of the Albanian mountains, at first red like the sun, then fading to copper, to yellow, and at last to white. The tiny wind-shimmers on the sea glimmered like a thousand fish scales. ... It would always be like this, I thought. The brilliant, friendly island, full of secrets, my family and my animals round me and, for good measure, our friends.[51]

And henceforward, both brothers wrote about islands with the nostalgia Lawrence called "islomania."[52]

As Nancy observed, and Lawrence noted in *Prospero's Cell*, the Durrell family cultivated "the tragic sense," an understanding of island societies and ecologies and their own lives as precarious.[53] The Durrells' peripatetic and insular lives contributed to Lawrence's theory about human beings and human culture as expressions of the landscape.

Gerald's understanding of islands was ecological, and his nostalgia would evolve into anger and grief. He became increasingly driven by the need to advocate for animals—a development apparent in his numerous animal collecting and conservationist narratives, which emphasized the increasing danger of mass extinction, especially of the little-known species indigenous to islands and other isolated areas.

Gerald learned all too soon that the safety and stability the family experienced during those Corfu years was in part an illusion—that islands are, in fact, the most vulnerable places on earth.

His writing would always reflect antipathy to parochialism, a passion for islands, and tension between felt exile and a sense of place. Every landscape, every nonhuman animal, and every human in his books would be eccentric, unique, even in caricature and stereotype. Even the self would be understood as "other," incomplete and irreconcilable with prevailing values and conventions. Gerald's universe is granular, chaotic, and morally inflamed. The challenge of understanding his life and work is to reconcile this granular, Linnean worldview with the ecological view first presented to him in Theo's lessons. Gerald's legacy suggests that he succeeded in finding balance. His struggle reflects the disenfranchised grief of many today as we consider climate change, the sixth extinction, and searing inequality among humans, and global pandemics.

Notes

1 Lawrence Durrell, *Prospero's Cell: A Guide to the Landscape and Manners of Corfu* (P: Open Road. Kindle Edition, loc. 176).

2 Gerald Durrell, *Birds, Beasts, and Relatives*, 12–13.

3 G. Durrell, *The Garden of the Gods* (Glasgow: William Collins, 1978), 112.

4 Botting, *Gerald Durrell*, 20.

5 G. Durrell, *The Whispering Land* (Baltimore, MD: Penguin, 1961), 93.

6 G. Durrell, *Marrying Off Mother and Other Stories* (New York: Arcade, 1991), 96.

7 Botting, *Gerald Durrell*, 26.

8 Botting, *Gerald Durrell*.

9 Qtd. Richard Louv, *Last Child in the Woods: Saving Our Children from Nature-Deficit Disorder* (Chapel Hill, NC: Algonquin, 2008), 93.

10 G. Durrell, *My Family and Other Animals*, 9.

11 G. Durrell, *Birds, Beasts, and Relatives*, 27.

12 G. Durrell, *My Family and Other Animals*, 55.

13 Ibid., 119.

14 Botting, *Gerald Durrell*, 57.

15 Mary Terrall, "Heroic Narratives of Quest and Discovery," *The Postcolonial Science and Technology. Studies Reader* (Durham, NC: Duke University Press, 2011), 87.

16 Botting, *Gerald Durrell*, 83–84.

17 Ibid., 198. And "Billy Bunter," *Britannia Academic.* Eb.com/levels/collegiate/article/Billybunter/484148 [accessed July 6, 2018].

18 See Barbara T. Gates, *Kindred Nature: Victorian and Edwardian Women Embrace the Living World* (Chicago: University of Chicago Press, 1999) for a history of how science became segregated at the very moment of becoming more systematic—and how women, in particular, gained and conveyed scientific knowledge.

19 Jean-Henri Fabre, *The Wonders of Insects* (New York: The Century Co., 1981), 5–6.

20 Colin Favret, "Henri Fabre: His Life Experience and Predisposition against Darwinism," *American Entomologist*, 45, no. 1 (Spring 1999), 38–48.

21 G. Durrell, *The Amateur Naturalist*, 14.

22 G. Durrell, The *Garden of the Gods*, 145–48.

23 Ian McNiven, *Lawrence Durrell: A Biography* (London: Faber & Faber, 1998), 100.

24 G. Durrell, *My Family and Other Animals*, 39–40.

25 Ibid., 58.

26 Ibid., 132.

27 Ibid., 142.

28 Ibid.,150.

29 Ibid., 214–16.

30 Ian S. MacNiven, "Afterward," Henry Miller, *The Colossus of Maroussi* (New York: New Directions, 2010. Kindle edition, loc. 3302).

31 G. Durrell, *Birds, Beasts, and Relatives*, 19.

32 Information about Theo is available from his own multifarious publications, Gerald's works, and other publications related to the Durrell family.

33 G. Durrell, *My Family and Other Animals*, 139.

34 Ibid., 138.

35 Ibid., 256.

36 G. Durrell, *The Garden of the Gods*, 20.

37 G. Durrell, *Birds, Beasts, and Relatives*, 50.

38 Ibid., 82.

39 G. Durrell, The *Garden of the Gods*, 98.

40 Bryan Hare and Vanessa Woods, *The Genius of Dogs* (New York: Penguin 2013). In *Adam's Task: Calling Animals by Name* (Akadine Press, 2000), Vicki Hearn, a philosopher, poet, and animal trainer, describes working with her dog Belle in much the same terms that Gerald worked (or played) with Roger.

41 G. Durrell, *My Family and Other Animals*, 68–71.

42 Mary Louise Pratt, *Imperial Eyes: Travel Writing and Transculturation*, 2nd Edition (New York: Routledge, 2007), 63.

43 Ibid., 53.

44 See also "Fred—or A Touch of the Warm South," an account of casual racism in the American South, in *Marrying off Mother and Other Stories* (New York: Arcade Publishing, North Carolina,1991). Botting quotes Gerald as claiming that "all these stories are true, or, on second thought, 'some are true, some have a kernel of truth," *Gerald Durrell*, 568.

45 Lawrence studied Indian philosophy intensively and practiced yoga: see C. Ravindran Nambiar's *Indian Metaphysics in Lawrence Durrell's Novels* (Newcastle: Cambridge Scholars Publishing, 2014). Jeejee is probably a composite character based on some of Lawrence's friends.

46 G. Durrell, *The Garden of the Gods*, 186.

47 Ibid., 9.

48 G. Durrell, *Birds, Beasts, and Relatives*, 231.

49 Ibid., 241.

50 Ibid., 243–44.

51 G. Durrell, *Birds, Beasts, and Relatives* (New York: Viking, 1969), 243–44.

52 L. Durrell, "Of Paradise Terrestre," *The Lawrence Durrell Travel Reader*, ed. Clint Willis (New York: Open Road/International Media, 2021), 99.

53 L. Durrell, *Prospero's Cell* (Open Road. Kindle Edition, loc. 176).

2 THE WIDE WORLD

If arriving in Corfu in 1935 had been abrupt and energizing, departing was painfully slow. "This has become our unregretted home. A world," Lawrence wrote in *Prospero's Cell*.[1] But they tore themselves away in journeys that were by turns epic, heartbreaking, and hilarious. Decades later, Gerald and Margo revisited the island, "Looking for and finding the deserted olive groves and sea caves where we were all so happy," and in many ways, the family never recovered from leaving.[2]

Mussolini's plans for resurrecting the Roman Empire throughout the Mediterranean and beyond were generally understood, and Albania and Greece were in the direct line of fire. Clearly, it wasn't all talk. In 1935, Italy attacked Ethiopia, one of the few independent African states left after the European scramble for Africa around the turn of the previous century. The following year, Mussolini poured enough treasure into Franco's faction in the Spanish Civil War to help the future dictator seize complete control of the country by the end of the decade. After signing agreements with Germany in 1938, Italy confronted France with demands for control of Corsica and the territory east of Nice and the River Var, in addition to shared control of the Suez Canal and French Tunisia. In 1939, Mussolini announced to his Grand Council an expansionist blueprint which included Cyprus, Gibraltar, and Malta. In April of that year, Italy invaded Albania, just across the strait from the northern end of Corfu, within sight of Kalami, where Lawrence and Nancy lived for much of their Corfu sojourn.

Everyone assumed Greece would be invaded soon, but isolated as the Durrells were in their rural domiciles, surrounded by friends and friendly neighbors, they were inclined to hang on. They had progressed from feeling exiled to feeling at home and had no desire to change their state into that of refugees. But the circle was broken and scattered by the end of that sad year. In the months and years that followed, a number of family acquaintances and friends, including Theo's parents, were killed. Paddy fields were destroyed, open stretches paved over, part of the city demolished, and the Jewish Corfiot population decimated.

Theo was the first of the Durrell circle to leave the island, in January, to research malaria on a grant from the Rockefeller Foundation. In June, Louisa's bankers warned her that when war did break out, access to her funds would be cut off, so the future was clear. Margo soon left to stay with relatives In England. In September, Gerald, Leslie, and their mother packed up the family's belongings, caged what residents of Gerald's zoo they could manage, including the Magenpies, put new collars on the dogs, took their "last tearful goodbyes," labored nervously through customs, with Louisa "looking as guilty as a diamond smuggler," and boarded the tender. "As the ship drew across the sea," Gerald recalled fifteen years later,

> and Corfu sank shimmering into the pearly heat haze on the horizon a black depression settled on us, which lasted all the way back to England. The grimy train scuttled its way up from Brindisi towards Switzerland, and we sat in silence, not wishing to talk. Above our heads, on the rack, the finches sang in their cages, the Magenpies chucked and hammered with their beaks, And Alecko gave a mournful yarp at intervals. Around our feet the dogs lay snoring.

At the Swiss border, Louisa "stiffened" at the description an unsmiling official had written on the entry card: "One traveling circus and staff."[3]

By this time, Margo had returned to Corfu, married Jack Breeze, a pilot, and accompanied him to Egypt. Lawrence and Nancy evacuated to the Greek mainland in December, taking with them Henry Miller, who had landed in Corfu in August for a badly timed visit. During their helter-skelter road trip around the countryside in an automobile constantly on the verge of collapse, the couple fought bitterly and delivered Miller to his ship within minutes of its scheduled departure and the expiration of Miller's visa.[4]

Lawrence stayed behind on the mainland, but in the spring of 1941 joined the information branch of the war department. For the duration of the war, he remained in the eastern Mediterranean, controlled by Allied forces. Despite the birth of their daughter, the marriage with Nancy did not survive the pressures of travel and separation. After the war, even though he was promoted to the position of Director of

Information Services on Cyprus and later to Director of Public Relations, as a British subject with non-patrial status, Lawrence became a kind of stateless person, unable to accept the politics of the metropole, a wanderer in spirit. "Fuck the English," he wrote to Henry Miller, more than once.[5]

The lives of the Durrells had changed drastically, several times. They were exiles and settlers, provincial and metropolitan, expatriates and refugees. For this continual uprooting, all three brothers would pay a great price for the rest of their lives. A few years later, Gerald's description of England's pretentious imperial past echoes Lawrence's attitude: it was "fascinating," he wrote, to hear from an elderly English friend about

> a bygone age, an age when the British so arrogantly bestrode the earth and when the world maps were predominantly pink to show it. A world unshakeable in its solidarity and its elegance, with an endless supply of good things for those with the wealth. . .[6]

But the cosmopolite experience also permitted distinct freedoms abroad: not belonging within a culture, sometimes not even knowing the customs by which its members must abide, and certainly not feeling bound by those customs, grants cosmopolites both *de facto* social choices and expanded perspectives, no matter one's economic condition.

Gerald brought that freedom back to England. His unconventional mindset and perspective on the natural world were formed during his childhood years in Corfu and imported to England with considerably less struggle than those confronted by his older brothers. At the age of fifteen, he was freed by his mother's relaxed parenting, and perhaps a certain degree of naivete, to violate class boundaries by working at a pet shop instead of attending a public school. Reluctant though he was to leave Paradise, London's novelty and cultural riches contributed significantly to his education as a future zookeeper, environmentalist, and writer of books and television scripts. Since his mother was preoccupied with housing, Gerald was left to his own devices, just as he had been free to range over field, grove, and seashore in Corfu.

His memoirs of this time reveal a continuity between the untrammeled freedom of his childhood rambles in Corfu and delightfully unsupervised teenage forays into the cityscape. "Although I have never been a lover of big cities," he wrote in the autofictional piece "A Transport of Terrapins,"

I found London, at that time, fascinating. After all, the biggest town I was used to was the town of Corfu, which was about the size of a small English market town, and so the great sprawling mass of London had hundreds of exciting secrets for me to discover."[7]

With access to so many bookstores, he continued to read voraciously. He enjoyed the cinema right around the corner from the family's flat on Kensington High Street. Inevitably, he frequented the nearby Natural History Museum, a Victorian Gothic cathedral to science, with stone monkeys climbing the columns of the nave and a larger-than-life statue of Darwin, visible from the front entrance and commanding the grand staircase at the far end of the nave from the front entrance.

The city of London in Gerald's brain was a city of animals. Most important for this future animal catcher, zookeeper, and conservationist were his forays across the city to the London Zoo in Regent's Park. Like Darwin before him, he befriended the keepers as he studied the animals they cared for. Instead of his own zoo of small, local fauna in Corfu, he observed, for the first time, exotic charismatic megafauna, kept in a large, complicated campus that reflected the reach of the British Empire, and beyond. Not surprisingly, his own practice as a collector and zookeeper would come to include attention to these large members of the animal kingdom, as well as "the little ones of God."

England declared war on Germany in September of 1939, the same month Gerald arrived in London. At that time, the staff of the London Zoo were ordered to prepare for the conflict and conserve resources.[8] They built traveling cages to ship the most valuable animals to the rural branch in Whipsnade and destroyed the most dangerous animals, including the venomous reptiles—a common occurrence for zoos in wartime. (During the 1870 siege of Paris, in fact, many of the zoo animals were eaten.)[9] The aquarium was closed, the most valuable individuals removed to other buildings, and some fish released into nearby waters. Wartime innovations included experimenting with alternative diets in the face of shortages, allowing members of the public to "adopt" individual animals, and extending outreach and education so the public would know the zoo was still open and operational.

Although the zoo was closed for two weeks at the beginning of the September, it would have been open by the time Gerald started to explore the city. Gerald would doubtless have known about these precautions and preparations from his conversations with the keepers in London and later at Whipsnade. Experiments with diets, hearing about or watching the construction of traveling cages, and witnessing a zoo under stress would have provided valuable perspectives for working in the animal trade and managing the Jersey zoo in later years.

As London was Gerald's first city, the zoo in Regent's Park provided his first acquaintance (aside from the shabby neighborhood zoo he visited in infancy with his ayah) with built environments to house and display the zoo animals. In those days, the campus in Regent's Park still included many Georgian-era "stamp collection" cages. The small, barred, rectangular structures were designed for easy optics: they served as frames, without thought for the animals' safety, health, or quality of life. To be fair, zoo veterinary science did not exist: those charged with medical care for the animals did their best.[10]

At this point in history, zoos were, ideologically, expressions of human control, as well as a locus of entertainment. Specimens were considered infinitely replaceable—if one died, another would be caught from the wild and displayed in its place. By the time Gerald frequented the zoo in early 1940, it had also been responsive to the Hagenbeck revolution: for most zoo designers, the early twentieth-century animal collector and dealer Carl Hagenbeck set the standard for zoo architecture in his Hamburg Tierpark, established in 1907 as an extension of his highly successful and lucrative participation in the exotic animal trade. The fundamental philosophy underlying the Tierpark was to provide visitors with high entertainment value and education by redesigning cages so that the animals appeared to mix peacefully, without confinement, without stress, in naturalistic stage settings—mountains, rocky caves, and the moats which actually separated carnivores from ungulates, or any animals which might not co-exist harmoniously in this mock-up of a peaceable kingdom. For Hagenbeck, *seeming* natural was the important value.[11] Although this approach to zoo architecture differs from the postage stamp model, "seeming" natural does not necessarily contradict the zoo as an expression of empire, and may even enhance traditional zoo ideology by presenting images (accurate or not) of the animals' homelands.

Even after the rebuilding phase following the Second World War, the zoo still included many of the old buildings, restored and repurposed, along with new enclosures more suited to the residents and keepers. But in the early 1960s, London Zoo officials also kept up with new trends in zoo architecture: in addition to the new walk-through Snowden aviary (architecturally suggestive of avian physiology) and the Casson elephant

THE WIDE WORLD   **45**

enclosure (which suggests elephant physiology and native habitat), new lion terraces and an insect house were created.[12] So a walk through the London Zoo is now also a walk through the history of zoo architecture. During the 1950s and 1960s, Gerald's dialogues with London Zoo officials were not always easy, but they never stopped, and throughout his career, he organized and participated in cooperative ventures which kept him abreast of developments in zoo design which the relatively well funded London Zoo could initiate.

From his first acquaintance with the London Zoo, it would exert an enormous influence on his endeavors in conservation and zoo practices for both its positive and negative attributes and practices. But the zoo in Regent's Park was far from the only important learning experience in the city. Nearer the family flat, Gerald discovered Potts Lane, a miniscule alley of "shops" which, owing to a very old lease agreement which perpetuated the original rents for commercial properties, sold nothing at all of their stock; the "shops" simply provided cover for a few conveniently located domiciles for a few elderly residents. One of these niches was a bird shop, and Gerald naturally made friends with the owner Mr. Bellow, whose collection had expanded into an entire room of his three-room flat—very like Gerald's tutor Kralefskey's ménage back in Corfu Town. When the Durrell family moved on to Bournemouth, Mr. Bellow presented him with the cardinal, "the bird that I most coveted in his collection."[13]

As for career training, no experience was perhaps more important than working in "The Aquarium," the name of an actual neighborhood pet ship where he was hired as an assistant after inflating his age from fourteen to seventeen. In addition to water creatures, Mr. Romilly the owner stocked a variety of "lovely reptiles," which Gerald could only dream of taking home to his so-far tolerant family.

From this departure point, he became acquainted with the international pet trade, still thriving even in the early days of the war. Then, as now, the Dutch had a significant share of the market.[14] After a few months' dedicated labor, Mr. Romilly trusted Gerald enough to send him on the bus to the East End, notably to Van der Goths, "a big wholesaler who specialized in importing North American reptiles and amphibians."

These we got from wholesalers, whereas the farm (which really ran the shop) sent us all the freshwater stuff that we needed. I enjoyed these jaunts to gloomy, cavernous stores in back streets, where I would find great crates of lizards, basketfuls of tortoises, and dripping tanks, green with algae, full of newts and frogs and salamanders.[15]

Van den Goth himself, "a heavily built man who looked like an orangutan carved out of tallow," must have taken to Gerald, for he allowed him to wander at will through the warehouse. Gerald found there, among other creatures, "beautiful snakes" and "a crate full of iguanas, bright green, and frilled, and dewlapped like a fairy-tale dragon."[16]

The pet shop also alerted him to the fact that people who buy and sell animals sometimes regard them simply as commodities, without the least bit of understanding or curiosity. Romilly, for example, "though a kindly man," proved to be wholly unimaginative in displaying the animals he sold. Gerald became the interface in this activity, first "decorating" the cases, aquaria, and cages to make them more appealing—a skill he perhaps picked up from Margo, whose contributions to the Gargantuan Durrell parties back on Corfu had veered toward outlandish costumes and lavish decorations. Unabashedly flattering his employer to get permission, he attacked the giant tank in the window "with all the dedication of a marine Capability Brown," constructing miniature sand dunes, granite cliffs, and forests of marine plants for the black mollies. Gradually, as he found his efforts were appreciated, he began to make more substantive changes in the animals' housing. Since the leopard toads came from North Africa, Mr. Romilly's imagination could stretch only as far as trying to replicate the white sandy Sahara. When Gerald provided the leopard toads with moss for their habitat of unrelieved white sand, and "surreptitiously" massaged olive oil into their skin, the flakiness disappeared. Treating their "milky" eyes with an ointment developed for dogs had "miraculous results." They "loved" the warm spray he sometimes gave them as a treat. One would expect a pet vendor to know they *were* amphibians, creatures of water as well as earth; one senses in Mr. Romilly the "little England" mind, willing to extract resources from the far reaches of Empire without caring for the details. So the pet shop taught Gerald not only about selling animals (figuratively as well as literally), but about people who bought and traded them.

The most important aspect of animal husbandry—taking care of the dog on the sofa or the beautiful fringed iguana—is feeding. Romilly fed the animals in his care in order to keep them alive long enough to sell them. Gerald wanted to "brighten up their lives." He tried daphnia to give the fish a thrill. Most of the animals were served tubifex, thin red worms which conveniently formed round clumps which could be kept alive under a dripping faucet until needed. Most of Romilly's animals survived reasonably well with this diet, along with meal-worms. But when Gerald thought the toads and lizards might be "bored," he devoted a lunch break to gathering wood lice in the parks, then proceeded to breed the wood lice in the basement of the shop for dietary variety. The toads and lizards croaked in appreciation, he claimed.[17]

If Gerald's interest in decoration reflected the artistic gifts of Margo, Leslie (a gifted painter), and Nancy (who taught him to draw), surely Louisa's obsessions with cooking and gardening contributed to his interest in food—for humans and all other animals. Descriptions of Louisa's feasts in the Corfu trilogy are epic. Gerald could have been a food writer in the tradition of M. F. K. Fisher or Anthony Bourdain, understanding food as a deep current in human culture. Indeed, Adam Gopnik's division of food writing into the epic and the meditative appears too categorical in reference to Gerald's commentaries, which are both meditative and comically epic.[18]

Doubtless, Gerald brought Louisa's willingness to work and experiment to his zookeeping practices. During the earliest days of collecting, Gerald found that many of the animals had specialized diets that could not be easily reproduced for them in captivity—anteaters had to be weaned from ants to milk and mince, for example. Once the animals arrived in Europe, the problems were even more pressing. As he explains in *Menagerie Manor* (1964), the early days of the zoo were a time of ceaseless experimentation. No one knew what a Guinea dragon ate until after numerous trails and failures: finally, after George accepted a handful of garden snails, Gerald and reptile keeper John Hartley examined his mouth, to discover that George had massive square back teeth, perfectly adapted for crushing snails. If the behavior of zoo visitors sometimes brought the Durrell team to the brink of despair, the Jersey neighbors' thoughtfulness was gratifying. Local farmers contributed slaughtered male calves too expensive to keep and too small for marketing; local greengrocers contributed surpluses of produce; another neighbor regularly delivered on her bicycle loads of acorns for the wild pigs. Others caught crickets and other insects to delight the small primates and carnivores. Many of these caring and imaginative neighbors' offerings could not have been purchased for any amount of money.

Moreover, Gerald understood the web of connections among food, animal being, and human culture in a profoundly synthetic way that both prepared him to care for exotic animals and reflected a cosmopolitan way of being in the world. If Louisa brought to Corfu the gustatory traditions and knowledge developed across generations of Anglo-Indian cookery (and consultations with her shelves of cookbooks), as a child, Gerald himself was immersed in the terroir of the food he consumed. He grew up eating tangerines casually plucked from the citrus groves he traversed in his rambles and fish he caught from the sea, sometimes minutes before they were cooked. He and Roger snacked under the olive trees on grapes, which Roger ate whole, while Gerald took advantage of the pips for spitting target practice. Because his writing is always specific, even a simple list not only suggests his family's gustatory sophistication, but also resonates with the land and culture of their adopted home. The Corfu trilogy includes generous lists: seafood of all kinds, citrus of all kinds, figs, olives, breads, meats and vegetables of all kinds, desserts, local wines of various qualities.

Some of Gerald's food descriptions amount to gastroporn. In *My Family and Other Animals*, he recounts an invitation to lunch with an elderly, eccentric countess who has heard of his interest in animals. Ostensibly, she wants to give him a much-coveted owl with a broken wing. In addition, he is treated to a multi-course banquet, much to Lawrence's seething jealousy (for Countess Mavrodaki also possessed a spectacular library). The feast begins with cocktails of brandy and champagne and includes soup, baby fish, snipe with appropriate vegetable accompaniments, platters and pitchers of condiments, wild boar with mushrooms and more vegetables, wines for every course, and meringues filled with cream. The countess (withal a tiny women) and Gerald (still very much a child) eat peanuts between the courses, to which are devoted eight pages of description.

Food is a steady baseline in his other short pieces—twenty or so memoirs, fictions, and fictionalized life writing (besides introductions and occasional pieces for other writers). In several stories about a flighty girlfriend Ursula (a real woman, whose name was Diane), rendezvous always take place in restaurants and bars. When he was on the road, Gerald liked to write in bars and restaurants, and when he met interesting locals, he wrote about them as extensions of his own experiences in these places. In "The Michelin Man," a hedonistic consumption athlete, masquerading as the food reviewer for the Michelin Guides, meets his match and his maker when he eats himself to death, to be converted afterwards into a *pâté* which indeed earns the coveted four stars for the establishment.[19] In "Esmeralda," a Frenchman attempts to murder a rival, not because of the wife the rival has seduced, but because of the gifted truffle pig stolen along with the wife.[20]

Most of Gerald's writing is humorous, even when the genre is horror. Of his several attempts in this genre, "The Entrance," the least funny, is still replete with descriptions of food. The main character, a rare book collector named Gideon, eats human souls, but he is also a gourmet, whose knowledge of and devotion to food and wine, and tales of his larder and cellar, persuade a book dealer to visit his isolated chateau to evaluate his library. Not surprisingly, Gideon's dog, cat, and parrot figure in the plot, and the narrator devotes time and attention to preparing their meals—"For the dog I stewed ... some mutton, and a little chicken for the cat, combined with some boiled rice and potatoes, they were delighted with this menu."[21]

The Corfu memoirs are of course replete with references to animal feeding—chops stolen from Louisa's kitchen for hungry puppies; banquets wrecked by the Magenpies, who escape from their cage, smash a bottle of beer, and rampage drunkenly through the butter; and more technical details about the meals Gerald served up to his charges. Predation and feeding serve to initiate him into the realities of nature. In this traditional countryside, there is no way to avoid initiation into the slaughter of animals for human food, or sport. But Gerald also observes—an inspiration perhaps for "The Michelin Man"—female mantises stalk and devour their prey (including males after mating), ant lion larvae building traps for unwary ants, and the tarantula who predates a lark's chicks.

The London adventure came to an end when Louisa found lodgings to her liking in Bournemouth, but Gerald had by this time become addicted to reading. He haunted bookshops, continued to care for his animals at home, tried to avoid school, and waited until he was called up for service in 1942. Apparently because of his heavy drinking the previous night, he was declared unfit. Unlike Leslie, who was forced to take a job in a munitions factory, Gerald was able to substitute agricultural labor also considered a defense necessity, since so many men his age were consigned to military service. Luckily, he found a job at a riding school, which, because the owner kept a few cows, was considered a farm.

In 1945, following his release from wartime service at the riding concession, Gerald persistently applied for positions as a zookeeper. Like most neophyte job hunters, he encountered the usual demand for experience with the usual reality that experience comes only after occupying a position for a period of time. However, the director of the London Zoo recognized passion when he saw it and procured Gerald work as an "odd beast boy" at Whipsnade, a rural branch of the London Zoo in Regent's Park. The adventure is recorded in *Beasts in My Belfry*, an entertaining memoir which is also a critique of zookeeping practices at the time. With the complex knowledge of food he had acquired as a child, with his experiences in the London pet shop, and with his own abiding interest in gastronomic experiences, Gerald still needed information about caring for large animals. This time, he had to learn about feeding multiple specimens of large and often dangerous animals—not merely making decisions about what they would eat, but handling the logistics of delivering provisions by the bucketful, barrowful, and truckload. And of course, he inevitably devotes descriptive passages to human consumption as well—noting class differences among the foodways of the keepers, whose predictable food preferences can occasionally be brightened by cooking mushrooms gathered from the ungulate paddocks; his landlady Mrs. Bailey, whose generous home cooking nourishes his stomach and his heart; and Captain Beale, the ex-colonial zoo director, whose searing curries are recreational recreations of his service "on the coast":

> What with the temperature in the tropics and the curry, you got a real good sweat on . . . sweat horse-troughs. Sit there in the evening . . . nice pink gin . . . Sit there, mother naked, with a curry and a towel and have a good sweat,

he reminisces. Clearly, the raw language of Henry Miller and even Lawrence Durrell were not the only inspirations for Gerald's vigorous prose style. The curry itself, Gerald recalls (in some typically stereotypical terms),

> seized hold of your throat with a hard, cunning, oriental grasp and built up in thick layers in your lung cavities. We all coughed furtively, but I thanked heaven that I came from a household which specialized in hot dishes . . .

The rest of the family gasp for breath, while the Captain insists that "this is a namby-pamby curry compared to what I *could* have made."[22] Trained in the Colonial Service, Beale was a competent organizer, who kept his distance from human employees, mostly from local farmer stock, and the animals under their care. Beale doubtless considered Gerald's appreciation of Anglo-Indian cookery a signal of hearty masculinity, acceptable class standing, and a cosmopolitan mindset.

Gerald's bundle of books and a habit of using his day off for observation and note-taking earned him the nickname "Bloody Sherlock Holmes" from his co-workers. The vast learning he had absorbed from Theo, along with his own sympathetic genius, taught him observation skills that helped him unpack the *Umwelten* of the animals in his care. Of course, the first thing he needed to learn as he moved from section to section were the routines of feeding. Apparently, during the early days, he was thrown literally to the lions. After learning how to care for the big cats, he worked with the polar bears, then the deer, buffalo, camels, and yaks. Along the way, he came to know the giraffes, whose beauty and character charmed him, and various canids: wolves, whose calls enchanted him, a fox with a broken leg, and huskies (inexplicably considered zoo animals).

Even though Gerald was experienced in feeding animals, there was much to learn, including the logistics of scale. Just as he had done in the pet shop, he thought of new foods and new ways of feeding. Gerald understood the difference between what the philosopher Giorgio Agamben terms *zoë* (bare life) and *bios* (being the subject of a life)[23] If most zoo animals were considered by the public and even some of the keepers as simple, if often dangerous, organic objects, Gerald had always seen members of other species as individual subjects of a life. This fundamentally philosophical perspective on his charges translated first into thinking about their diet.

The nervous arctic foxes emerged from hiding to seize, and sometime cache, their meat, but they clearly had the capacity for joy, and they lost their shyness when Gerald one day presented them with eggs from a fallen bird's nest. After that, he sometimes pilfered hens' eggs from a neighboring farm to give them pleasure and variety, and the foxes acknowledged him as part of that wider life they had lost in confinement. Gerald understood that food functions for many other species precisely as it does for our own—as an aesthetic, psychological, and sometimes cultural enrichment of life. In that same spirit, he shared blackberries with a bear, who responded by singing. He played games with the juvenile yaks, who enjoyed chasing wads of hay as Gerald swung them back and forth over the fence of the yaks' enclosure. He bribed an unruly zebra stallion with handfuls of extra oats. The raccoon dogs were so obsessed with food that they could be even more easily bribed with food, despite

52 THE EVOLUTION OF GERALD DURRELL

their shyness. (Since Gerald's Whipsnade days, these strange creatures, which resemble raccoons but constitute the single member of the canid genus Nyctereutes, have all but disappeared from an originally wide range in Asia.)

Feeding revealed preferences and particular behaviors, sometimes in species and sometimes in individuals. The tigers fought over meat, and Gerald noted how quickly a slab of meat could disappear when one of them licked it with a rasp-like tongue. Wolves ate in hierarchical order. The tapirs squealed with delight when their piles of vegetables arrived. The polar bears would dive into their pool to retrieve bits of bread and cheese.

So what he learned about feeding provided Gerald with a link to other fundamental aspects of sound zookeeping. Diet was connected to what is now called in zoo circles "enrichment"—crickets for the amphibians in the pet shop, blackberries for the bear, eggs for the arctic foxes, and encouraging the baby yaks to play with their food. Zoo residents needed to enjoy their food, not only for its nutritional and aesthetic value, but in the ways it was delivered. A handful of oats can engender a bond between the human keeper and the Chapman zebra; a whole bucketful of oats hanging from a hook cannot.

Feeding also determines important aspects of housing and architecture—ungulates would trample their hay into the ground without proper containers for it. Giraffes need to be able to reach up for their food because they are anatomically unable to reach down. Other infants presented feeding problems. When it became apparent that the mother had no milk, Gerald nearly lost life or limb when he was required to enter the water buffalo corral to retrieve an infant for bottle feeding. He learned that zoo design had to be executed with the keepers in mind, as well as the animals' welfare.

The fine line between zoo habitat that seems natural, zoo enclosures which in fact are more or less "natural," and enclosures designed in the best interests of individual animals who live in them—and the keepers who work there—is not easy to pick out, not least because zoo design and architecture influence human visitors' attitudes about the animals they have come to see. Maintaining appropriate "furniture," feeding stations, and plants within an enclosure can enrich not only the animal's life, but the zoo visitor's experience. For example, because wolves are such attentive and protective parents that their thriving young can be seen only weeks after birth, when their parents allow them to leave the den, this aspect of wolf culture means that the enclosure has to be constructed to allow for denning.

The wealth and resources which had fueled the Hagenbeck revolution thinned out after the war. Animals were becoming scarcer. Finances were tighter. With happy irony, lack of funding for trained staff and other resources seems to have had an unintended value at Whipsnade: because the stage settings were less elaborate, they were in fact more natural. The paddocks were, for the most part, roomy fenced areas of the English countryside which made use of the natural vegetation and other features, with whatever manipulation became necessary to provide the animals with cover or shelter. Most of the animals at Whipsnade adapted with ease to these relatively simple arrangements. The park was not perfect, as Gerald discovered, but it was not bad, and the experience of using the natural landscape for enclosure was useful a few years later when he laid out his own zoo in Jersey around the natural features of the land.

It also became clear to Gerald that size of the enclosures did not necessarily mean freedom for the animals, nor did size equate with quality. A thirty-five acre paddock for a small herd of provisioned ungulates might simply mean that keepers encountered greater difficulty in feeding, especially in a hierarchical herd in which weaker animals might be bullied into starvation. Keepers routinely must move animals and manage their health: chasing an ailing ungulate around a large enclosure only worsens its condition. Weeds and brush sometimes looked more "natural," but such botanical clutter could also result in a habitat distinctly unsuitable for the inhabitants, as well as blocking them completely from the visitors' view and the keepers' access. Lack of safety features nearly resulted in a disaster when Gerald had to rescue the baby water buffalo from its mother for bottle feeding. Lack of a structure for confinement exposed Gerald and another keeper to the razor-sharp tusks and hooves of the Chinese water deer when they rescued him from entanglement in a tall wire fence, over which he had tried to escape. A similar situation in the bear habitat, combined with the carelessness of a co-worker, endangered Gerald when he had to separate a mother from her cubs and walk in between upon releasing them. Routine cleaning and occasional clearing of brush exposed him to these hazards on an almost daily basis.

The only rationale for zoos, Gerald would later insist, was conservation. During his year at Whipsnade, he foresaw the need for a compilation of information about threatened and endangered species and began his own amateur version of the IUCN *Red Data Book*, which was formally

54 THE EVOLUTION OF GERALD DURRELL

established almost twenty years later by the International Union for the Conservation of Nature and Natural Resources. This IUCN publication has been continuously updated since 1964 and has come to be regarded as essential information for zoos, conservation groups, and governments. In fact, it embodies the primary goal of the organization itself—influencing governments by providing reliable information.

The threat of extinction adds urgency to feeding and housing decisions. Gerald's first encounter with a species that had been miraculously saved from extinction took place at Whipsnade. All the young Père David deer had to be bottle fed because they needed nourishment during the night as well as during the day—and because of their rarity, the zoo staff could not risk a missed feeding. "I was overwhelmed," Gerald recalled, when chosen to care for them in a great barn at Woburn Park, the estate where the Duke of Bedford had been able to rescue these rare cervids from extinction during the previous century.[24]

Against all odds, during the late nineteenth century, the Duke managed to build a small herd of these Chinese deer, which had been extinct in the

FIGURE 2.1 Père David's deer.

THE WIDE WORLD   55

wild for several centuries, surviving only within the emperor's palace garden. Since this original herd had been killed in a flood, the herd at Woburn, all the more precious, was split at the beginning of the Second World War, with part of the population now housed at Whipsnade for safety. Territorial animals, breeding seasonally, Père David deer experience stress when confined to densely populated paddocks. The need for frequent feeding, coupled with rarity and these distinctive behavioral traits, is perhaps why the fawns Gerald nursed were transferred back to the Duke's estate at Woburn until they could rejoin the small herd at Whipsnade. In a happy addendum to a fortunate history of saving these deer from extinction, the World Wildlife Fund drew from the Woburn and Whipsnade populations to reintroduce almost sixty individuals to China in the 1980s. By the early years of this century, the Chinese population numbered around a thousand, and new herds have been established there. By the time Gerald was twenty, he knew the stakes, he understood the slender threads by which some species survived in this world, and he was well on the way to improving the odds. Like the deer, most endangered species benefit not only from increases in population, but the separating of populations (when large enough) to ensure species survival in a stochastic event such as the flood which decimated the emperor's herd.

Part of Gerald's genius was finding the right people to help, a lesson he clearly learned at Whipsnade, where the keepers were rural workers who had been kept on after they were hired to put up the original fencing of the park. In addition to risking their own (and Gerald's) safety, most of the staff considered their positions at Whipsnade just gainful employment and acted accordingly. A harmless but telling example was Bert's provision of warm water to a giraffe who had developed a chill six years before and been prescribed warm water to soothe its throat. Until Gerald inquired, Bert had not considered the reason for the warm water or the obvious fact that switching the giraffe back to normally cool water could improve its quality of life and decrease the workload for the staff. Like most of the staff, who took pride in their animals, Bert still lacked the interest to observe closely. And since "wild animals are past masters at concealing the fact that they are ill," close observation is required to see the signs of illness and address them. At this point in his career, Gerald already understood that effective zookeeping required knowledge and training, deep interest, and status not usually associated with "a hard and dirty job."[25] Despite the professionalization of zookeeping, staffing remains a challenge, even in this century, because the work itself—handling raw meat, disposing of dead bodies, necropsies, cleaning up dung and vomit, and picking up human waste thrown into animal cages—is dirty work usually relegated to those who have no choice.[26] When asked by a visitor to the Whipsnade Zoo what kind of meat he was serving the lions, Gerald answered, "Keepers, ma'am. It's an economy measure. When the keepers get too old to work, we feed them to the wolves."[27] At many points during his long career, he must have felt that he was being served up for dinner himself.

Ironically, for Gerald in his teens, England was the wide world, where the focus of his young life widened to include more than family and family friends and the personalities of his pets. Inevitably, tensions emerged within his world and work. Gerald's days at Whipsnade were marked by delight in the individual animals, as well as the danger and drudgery of tending to them. Not everyone involved with animals cared for them as he did. The romance of zookeeping on a large scale could sometimes be eclipsed by the dirty, difficult realities. He knew he would persist in this work, despite the fact that most keepers were uneducated, poorly paid, and so incurious that sometimes they failed to care adequately for their animals. His cosmopolitan sophistication enabled Gerald to devise creative solutions for many of the problems zoo animals and keepers faced, but this same sophistication would sometimes make him impatient with those less worldly and less culturally privileged. On the other hand, this same worldliness propelled him out into the wider world of the British Empire, to seek some of the exotic animals he met or read about.

Some of the tensions Gerald felt in the world of zoos and conservation emerged later. Catching animals in their native habitats deepened the knowledge he already had about the need to consider the lifeways of the whole animal. This understanding of the animal in context later made possible some of his captive breeding and reintroduction projects. When Gerald left Whipsnade, he was poised to discover a cascade of extinctions and near extinctions, as economic imperialism entirely replaced the old political structures, and, if new roads and communication networks meant easier access in his own collecting work, they also contributed to the escalating depletion of wild populations. Throughout recorded human history, zoos represented empire, political power, human control: these forces and institutions now resulted in a shrinking world, with so little room left for animals that zoos were necessary as arks, to save the animals from ourselves.

Furthermore, Gerald's commitment to wildlife conservation meant that, particularly in the zoo he established in Jersey, affection for an individual animal could be secondary to his care for an entire species. When he met Cholmondely the Chimpanzee on his first journey to Cameroon, he did not know this.

Notes

1 L. Durrell, *Prospero's Cell: A Guide to the Landscape and Manners of Corfu.* (Open Road. Kindle Edition, loc. 176).

2 G. Durrell, "Preface," in Margo Durrell, *Whatever Happened to Margo?* (London: Time Warner Books, 1996), n.p.

3 G. Durrell, *My Family and Other Animals*, 298–99, 300, 302.

4 I. MacNiven, "Afterword," Henry Miller, *The Colossus of Maroussi* (New York: New Directions, 2010) offers a sad, hair-raising account of these stressful weeks.

5 *Lawrence Durrell and Henry Miller: A Private Correspondence*, ed. George Wickes (New York: E. P. Dutton, 1963).

6 G. Durrell, "Miss Booth-Wycherly's Clothes," in *Marrying Off Mother* (New York: Arcade, 1991), 150.

7 G. Durrell, *Fillets of Plaice* (New York: Viking, 1971), 52.

8 M. Palmer, "London Zoo during World War Two," September 1, 2013. https://www.zsl.org/about-us/architecture-at-zsl-london-zoo-regents-park [accessed August 5, 2016].

9 Kaspar Hansen and Lars Eriksen, "When They Ate the Zoo, Nobody Wanted to Touch the Hippo." February 11, 2014. Vice Media LLC. https://www.vice.com/en/article/kwpbaw/when-they-ate-the-zoo-nobody-wanted-to-touch-the-hippo [accessed August 11, 2016].

10 Isobel Charman, *The Zoo: The Wild and Wonderful Tale of the Founding of the London Zoo* (New York: Pegasus, 2017), 186–85.

11 Nigel Rothfels, *Savages and Beasts: The Birth of the Modern Zoo* (Baltimore, MD: Johns Hopkins University Press, 2008).

12 "Architecture at ZSL, London Zoo, Regent's Park." https://www.zsl.org/what-we-do/education-learning/zsl-library/zsl-archives [accessed July 16, 2016].

13 G. Durrell, *Fillets of Plaice*, 86.

14 J. Pieters, "Researcher: Netherlands a Key Link in Poaching, Illegal Wildlife Trade." February 9, 2016. https://nltimes.nl/2016/02/09/researcher-netherlands-key-link-poaching-illegal-wildlife-trade [accessed July 18, 2023].

15 G. Durrell, *Fillets of Plaice*, 75.

16 Ibid., 75.

17 Ibid., 50–60.

18 Adam Gopnik, "The Food Critic at Table," *New Yorker*, April 4, 2005, http://www.newyorker.com/magazine/2005/04dining-out-3 [accessed July 18, 2023].

19 G. Durrell, "Michelin Man," in *The Picnic and Suchlike Pandemonium* (Glasgow: Fontana Collins, 1981).

20 Ibid.

21 "The Entrance," in G. Durrell, *The Picnic and Suchlike Pandemonium*, 173.

22 G. Durrell, *Beasts in My Belfry* [UK title], 83–84. hereafter cited as *A Bevy of Beasts* (New York: Simon & Schuster, 1980).

23 Giorgio Agamben, *The Open: Man and Animal* (Stanford, CA: Stanford University Press, 2004).

24 G. Durrell, *Beasts in My Belfry*, 98.

25 Ibid., 180–81.

26 David Grazian, *American Zoo: A Sociological Safari* (Princeton, NJ: Princeton University Press, 2015).

27 G. Durrell, *Beasts in My Belfry*, 115.

3 AFRICA

By the time Gerald ended his apprenticeship at the Whipsnade Zoo in 1946, animal collecting and zookeeping were clearly more than his hobby. "I went the rounds saying good-bye to the animals and men," he writes in *Beasts in My Belfry*. "I was sad, for I had been happy working at Whipsnade but, as I went round, each animal represented a place I wanted to see, each was a sort of geographical signpost encouraging me on my way."[1] The next logical step was to venture out into the field of the exotic animal trade, but time after time, collectors responded that only experienced collectors need apply. Zookeeping, working in a pet shop, and backyard collecting in Corfu did not qualify, but how could he get experience if no collector would hire an inexperienced assistant? Once again, no experience, no job—but no job, no experience.

Fortunately, on his twenty-first birthday, he inherited enough money to finance his own expedition. To Captain Beale's dire warning—"You'll be chuckin' money away, mark my words"—Gerald countered, "What about Hagenbeck?" "Those were the good old days," said the captain.[2] Beale spoke more truth than he knew, as Gerald was to discover after only a few years in the field. After mid-century, wild animals began to disappear at alarming rates—and replacement of improperly cared for zoo animals was only one of many pressures on wildlife.

But Gerald was obsessed, and his obsession was one expression of the complicated and contradictory social, political, and psychological pressures which had driven colonialism in the first place. Peter the Wombat drew him toward the "topsy-turvy continent of Australia"; the tigers, "their hides glowing a sunset-orange, were Asia." The polar bears pulled him toward the ice fields of the arctic and the buffalo herd to the prairies of North America. Whipsnade's gorilla, zebras, and flamingos spoke to him of Africa.[3]

The animals at Whipsnade yanked Gerald toward "the blank places on the map," just as Marlowe, the ambiguous hero of Conrad's *Heart of Darkness*, is mesmerized by a map of the Congo River, which snakes out of the heart of Africa. In a short story, "The Jury," Gerald resets *Heart of Darkness* in Guyana (at that time, British Guiana) probably because he had traveled by boat along its rivers. In this grim tale, isolation, drink, and a guilty conscience about his past role as a hangman in India conspire to defeat Menon, a minor official who hangs *himself* over a formal dining table in a sordid colonial river outpost. With a macabre twist, Menton channels Kurtz and his bizarre relationships with the "natives."

Gerald's travel books about Africa were by no means horror fiction, or self-conscious analyses of the psychological risks presented by imperial power. Still, it is impossible to ignore in Gerald's early writing the tension between the colonizer and the colonized parts of the earth's surface—the power and danger in claiming ownership of the exotic—so pervasive in cultural productions of the Global North. Although there is always a thread or two of self-parody, nevertheless, the parodies do not obscure what Mary Terrall calls the "metanarrative of courageous heroism," which characterizes stories told about European voyages of discovery during the Enlightenment, and certainly well past the early days of colonization.[4] Gerald's books, especially the early tales of Africa and South America, are very much in the tradition of hypermasculine, Eurocentric tales about risk, adventure, and scientific discovery. Gerald's early books also reveal his participation, as often as not unconscious, in what Bruno Latour calls the "long-distance" networks that supported colonial extraction of knowledge, natural resources (including animals), and wealth.[5]

The impulse to collect and own was also personal. What motivates collectors is no less complicated than the impulse to know the "other" and the "elsewhere" and is bound up with it. Sometimes, acquiring art, jewelry, wives, or exotic animals indicates a childhood of material, psychological, or social deprivation. Belongings can substitute for belonging. Gerald's childhood was rich in books, a worldly and kind family and friends, and a natural environment that was nourishment itself—rich groves, gardens and vineyards, an ocean of fish, the brilliant cookery of his mother, and friendly neighbors always willing to share what they had with a small boy and his dogs. But Gerald grew up with an existential awareness of contingency: everything could vanish in an instant. Animals, he felt, would always be there, as friends, objects of interest, and a focus of responsibilities.

So to Africa he went. When Gerald set out to capture animals in British Cameroon, he concentrated on the known animals zookeepers and what their public would want to see. In following imperial routes, Gerald not only benefited from colonial administrative and commercial contacts, he

62   THE EVOLUTION OF GERALD DURRELL

used existing descriptions and illustrations of the animals he wanted in order to enlist local help. He was assured of a market for any animals he could manage to send home alive and healthy. He began organizing the first of his three African adventures in 1947 and embarked to the Cameroons in January of 1948. These journeys challenged the young man in every possible way: acquiring the animals required a strategy of bargaining, buying, hunting, and catching—with predictable parasites, illnesses, and injuries to himself and his helpers. Feeding, housing, and transporting his creatures, as well as treating their illnesses and injuries, required the utmost patience and creativity. Red tape in country and back home was almost indescribably irritating to Gerald, and local politics in Africa were a puzzle.

A Zoo in My Luggage (1957), the tale of Gerald's third voyage to Cameroon, begins this way:

> From my seat on the bougainvillea-enshrouded verandah I looked out over the blue and glittering waters of the bay of Victoria, a bay dotted with innumerable forest-encrusted islands like little green, furry hats dropped carelessly on the surface. Two grey parrots flew swiftly across the sky, wolf-whistling to each other
> ... A flock of tiny canoes, like a school of black fish, moved to and fro among the islands.... Above, in the great palms that shaded the house, a colony of weaver-birds chattered incessantly as they busily stripped the palm fronds off to weave their basket-like nests, and behind the house, where the forest began, a tinker-bird was giving its monotonous cry, toink ... toink ...
> Dragging my attention away from a large, orange-headed lizard that had climbed on to the verandah rail and was busily nodding its head as if in approval of the sunshine, I turned back to my task of composing a letter.[6]

This passage reveals Gerald moved by scenic beauty, from his vantage point on the lower slopes of Mount Cameroon, riveted on animal life and resistant to writing. Vivid, active, adjectival, periodic sentences rise from the page with airy lightness. If Durrell's sentences challenge because the thought remains incomplete to the end, the details of those sentences seem irresistible. One pauses with pleasure to picture the "glittering waters" and "orange-headed lizard," while being swept along to the conclusion of the sentence—a structure bound with bolts of steel and brushed with iridescence. By all accounts, Durrell hated sitting down to

AFRICA **63**

write and resisted revisions, but childhood experience, voracious reading, fluency in naturally acquired languages, and literary instinct gave him a firm intuitive grasp of the deep structures of language.

The lizard was probably the rainbow agama, endemic to sub-Saharan Africa. As always, Gerald wanted to linger with the lizard in the moment, but the complicated writing dilemma in which he found himself had deep historical roots and required his attention. Victoria, the colonial port town where Gerald fretted about his letter, is now Limbe. The body of water he surveyed is now Ambas Bay. Limbe has become a tourist resort, thanks to its beaches and Korup National Park nearby. French Cameroon and the much smaller English Cameroon, where Gerald made three collecting trips between 1947 and 1957, are now one country. Cameroon, a nation slightly larger than California, is located exactly at the right angle where the northern part of the continent bulges out into the Atlantic Ocean.

Portugal was the first European country to stake a claim in the area, which had been settled for over two thousand years by three major ethnic

FIGURE 3.1 Agama lizard.

64 THE EVOLUTION OF GERALD DURRELL

groups—the Baka, the Bantu, and a little later, the Muslim Fulani people. Although Portugal's progress as a colonizer was impeded by malaria, the development of anti-malarial agents in the 1880s brought an end to the relative autonomy of the region.[7] Like other African countries, Cameroon still suffers from the effects of the nineteenth-century European race to colonize Africa. During this time, most of the continent was carved up into spheres of influence, colonies privately held by European monarchs, or areas such as the Cameroons, controlled by commercial enterprises combined with political bureaucracies. These divisions were imposed with little attention to ethnicity, languages, or local governance, mostly for the purposes of extractive mining, agriculture, wildlife hunting or collecting, and sheer political or military dominance within the Global North.

After Portugal, Germany dominated the area. The Fons, local rulers of a western grassland area called Bafut, resisted between 1901 and 1907, when they were defeated and brought under the control of the German protectorate.[8] After the defeat of Germany in the First World War, France and Britain divided the protectorate into English and French "Cameroons." Since the French and the English had been allies during that war, it is no surprise that Anglophone and Francophone people, both European and indigenous, got along reasonably well at that point. Although he preferred working in English Cameroon because of its biological diversity (and greater ease of communication), Gerald's collaborator collected some animals on the French side, where he, too, was met with cooperation. Since the many ethnic groups which make up most sub-Saharan African countries then spoke (and still speak) indigenous languages, pidgin languages arose, and Gerald was evidently fluent in English pidgin, but halting in French and French pidgin.

Things are different now. When French Cameroon led a rebellion from France in 1957, the English Colonial Office had to determine an official decolonialization policy. After independence, the area inhabited by the Fulani people integrated with Nigeria, reducing the size of what had been the English colony. (On Gerald's third African journey, part of his favorite collection area had become part of Nigeria and required Nigerian as well as Cameroonian permits.) Friction between those who wanted local control and those who seized control of a unified government resulted in violent conflicts between the Francophone majority and the Anglophone minority. Today, Cameroon is still divided by language and political affiliations, with the English speakers a disadvantaged minority.[9]

The Overloaded Ark (1953) is based on Gerald's first expedition to Cameroon in 1947–48, *The Bafut Beagles* (1953) on the second expedition, in 1949, and *A Zoo in My Luggage* (1960) on the third. Even on his first African expedition, Gerald could see some of the negative effects of extractive policies, which resulted in deforestation, an increasing human population, and depletion of wildlife—the unraveling of ecologies. His last journey to Cameroon, in 1957, was beset by minor inconveniences resulting from the turmoil. *A Zoo in My Luggage* recounts the 1957 expedition. When he wrote about his travels in Cameroon, and, a little later, in Sierra Leone, Gerald did not predict the degree of ethnic and political conflict or the deep environmental and political devastation which was to come in hot spots all over the world.

Although the danger signs were more pronounced when he struck out for Sierra Leone in 1965, an expedition narrated in *Catch Me a Colobus* (1972), only years later did Gerald entirely understand the connections between imperialism and degraded ecologies—the externalities, or hidden costs, of deforestation. That naivete emerges in his early bestselling books, but in fairness it must be said that during those years of the middle of the twentieth century, few people grasped all the environmental ramifications of colonial and post-independence policies throughout the Global South.

Instead, for Gerald, the 1947–48, African journey, especially, had a mythic quality: the lands he described were far away, presented as if lost in time. He was overwhelmed by beauty and beset by dangers, and always, always his travels were quests for exotic animal life. The cultural anthropologist Renato Rosaldo would call the tone of these early books "imperialist nostalgia."[10]

Gradually, Gerald's expedition narratives about Africa became less romantic, but as one reads them seven decades later, a profound disquiet underlies all of them: Gerald loved animals, but the methods by which he obtained these beautiful objects of desire sometimes destroyed them and, just as often, contributed to the degradation of their habitats and the fragile biological communities of which they were a part. He mourned those deaths and learned from them how to safeguard his beloved charges in the future. Even when he did not cause deterioration of the environment, he responded pragmatically to deforestation, or the acquisition of animals whose parents had been killed for convenience; this detachment could be considered complicitous. But even by the time he wrote about the expedition in Sierra Leone, his attitudes were shifting. The local people were not perfect stewards of the lands where they lived, but, in the middle of the twentieth century, the complex relationships among humans, animals, and landscapes were not well understood, least of all in foreign lands under colonial domination by outsiders whose presence was facilitated by colonial bureaucracies and infrastructures.

Gerald chose Cameroon, as he writes in his children's book *The New Noah*, because "it is a small, almost forgotten corner of Africa, which is more or less as it was before the advent of the white man. Here, in gigantic rain forests, the animals live their lives as they have done for thousands of years."[11] Although many tropical landscapes, especially, have now been converted to monocultures—mile after mile of banana and palm plantations, to the physical and economic detriment of the people and animals who live there—these industries were still at an early stage in Cameroon. The United Africa Company, which provided in-country help for Gerald's work, was established to oversee such enterprises in several west African colonies and continued operations for several decades after independence.

Gerald's first collaborator in Cameroon, John Yealland, was a skillful and established ornithologist (almost twice Gerald's age) who had already worked with Sir Peter Scott, one of the conservation giants of the twentieth century. Upon arrival, the two of them traveled all day from the coast through palm plantations—almost devoid of the bird life which should have been there—to a guesthouse in the town of Mamfe, about a hundred and fifty miles inland. From there, John went back to Bakebe, where he set up a base camp for his birds in an abandoned public works department storage shed.

Gerald went back through Mamfe, where he established a base camp for the animals he caught with the help of local hunters or bought from local residents. He also crossed the river to the village of Eshobi, where he enjoyed working with more local people and found some of his most interesting animals. Mamfe was literally the end of the road, so Gerald's travels from that point were on foot, alone, or with guides and bearers. This expedition in Cameroon, and two more in 1949 and 1957, followed a fairly straight road about two hundred miles, inland through the river port of Tiko, through Kumba and Bakebe, then with a westward turn to Mamfe and nearby villages. Gerald's second and third journeys to the country followed the same route, but extended farther inland to the traditional tribal area of Bafut, about three hundred miles by road from the coast.

Gerald wrote *The Overloaded Ark* for audiences back in England. As in all his early books, he dwells on the astonishing beauty and strangeness of his surroundings, which in the early days more than met his expectations. One of his most memorable experiences the first time out to Africa was a night walk on the slopes of N'da Ali, a mountain near the French Cameroon border, when he heard a "blood-curdling scream" followed by "spine-chilling gurgles of laughter."[12] Eventually he realized these sounds come from a chimpanzee troop. His own prickling scalp attested to his kinship with them.

Just as memorable, but for different reasons, was a visit to Soden Lake, near the town of Ndop, a little over two hundred miles inland, the farthest Gerald traveled from the coast during his first trip to Cameroon. Local missionaries introduced him to the beautiful lake, the village on a small island in it, and the abundant bird life around it. The water was free of deadly crocodiles, the culture apparently little touched despite the missionaries, and wildlife abundant. There were fish eagles, darters, several species of kingfishers, plovers, and crakes. Village boys caught as many specimens as Gerald could take back to John Yealland. One of the most remarkable incidents was an attempt to catch a four-foot-long soft-shelled turtle. He was saddened by the fact that an arrow had pierced the turtle through its neck, killing it. Most of the birds, however, fared well on the trek back along the winding path through the deep green forest, feeding on tiny fish Gerald had brought along in a large can.

Gerald's first two books set a trajectory for all his travel writing about Africa and South America: the animals in these books are primary characters, with agency, intentions, and personalities. Giant shrews, poisonous vipers, monitor lizards, pangolins, crocodiles, tall plantain-eating birds—all are individualized. They assert themselves by flight or painful bite, eating or refusing to eat, escaping or seeking out the company of those who care for them. Gerald always noticed the eyes: large, small, vacant or focused, black, golden, green, glittering. Almost every animal has a facial expression: proud, angry, puzzled, satisfied. One toad is "supercilious." Such a deep interest in the personalities of his catches contributed to his success in animal husbandry. Many specimens were new to him, without scientific descriptions, and with unknown diets or habits; yet most survived in his care.

The primatologist Hans Kummer has suggested that ethologists—scientists who study animal behavior and cognition—could be classified as hunters like Niko Tinbergen or herdsmen like Konrad Lorenz.[13]

68   THE EVOLUTION OF GERALD DURRELL

Tinbergen followed and observed animals in the wild; Lorenz tamed them—and is famous for the goslings that imprinted on him as if he were their mother. Gerald did both. He was literally a hunter in these early travels, with something of his brother Leslie's focused aggression, and he often carried a gun. He was a "herdsman," of course, once the animals were in cages. To keep them alive, he had to behave as they wished him to do. He tamed them by giving them what they wanted and needed, but they also tamed him to feed and shelter them, and even to amuse and stimulate them. As both a hunter and a herdsman, he had to enter their lives, their *Umwelten*, by discipline and stealth as well as empathy.

In *The Overloaded Ark*, the capture of the rare giant water shrew is a typical case of hunting: almost never did Gerald try to catch animals without the aid of expert local hunters, who often saw things that he could not because they had learned the search patterns needed in the forest. One night while walking down a water course with Amos, Elias and Andreia (he is shut out of their conversation in Banyangi), Gerald saw Elias suddenly drop into a stalking crouch as he tried to stop a creature the size of a small crocodile with the side of his machete (Gerald had just foolishly thrown away the catching sticks.) The creature eluded capture several times, finally retreating into a hole behind piles of boulders. After Andreia was bitten badly pulling the animal out, it required strenuous efforts by the others to release Andreia and shove the water shrew—two feet long, hissing, and trying to escape—into a cloth collecting bag. This adventure was the "zenith of our night hunting results."[14]

Ordinarily, Gerald consulted other travelers' tales only for practical information, but even at this stage in his career, he was conscious of competing with Yealland's mentor Peter Scott (and by the time of his third voyage to Cameroon, with television naturalist David Attenborough).[15] He was also eager to prove wrong Paul du Chaillu's sensational tales of jungle treks and wild animals—especially the fearsome western lowland gorillas that author claimed to have observed close up from a vantage point inside a cage—but Gerald had to admit that du Chaillu had been correct in his observations of the fighting giant water shrew. Unfortunately, Gerald was unable to travel far enough inland to catch sight of gorillas—and it would be many more years before he could bring lowland gorillas to the zoo in Jersey.

The water shrew episode demonstrates not only Gerald's commitment to the hunt, but also his other "ethological" skill: as a herdsman and future zookeeper, he had to keep the animal alive. It refused fish, purportedly the only thing giant water shrews eat, and a water snake, but finally accepted a crab . . . and then three more. Since an aquatic animal requires water in its habitat, and not just water to drink, Gerald sent porters eight miles back across the Cross River (now the Manyu River) from Eshobi to Mamfe for an oil drum, which he laboriously sawed in half, scraped, and washed over and over before it could become the shrew's swimming pool. The next challenge was to wean the animal from his accustomed diet (by this time, "it" is "he") by mixing foods that would be available in England and stuffing them into a crab shell. The ruse worked, and the animal continued to eat heartily, gaining weight and apparently in the full blossom of health.

To Gerald's delight, one of the villagers brought in a young female a few days after his dramatic capture of the male. At this early stage in his career, Gerald often kept single animals, but, even then, he recognized the value of bringing back a breeding pair. (Just a few years later, he released animals if he had little chance of insuring that they could reproduce.) But his captured male shrew died, for no apparent reason. A month later, the female died without warning. Captive animal death, especially unexplained death, became a perpetual nightmare for Gerald, even into the years when he seldom captured animals in the wild and devoted his attention to caring for animals in the zoo and *in situ*.

Neither of his water shrews lived long enough to have a name, although both certainly displayed forceful personalities. These might have been animals hard to love, but Gerald attended them devotedly, fascinated by the natural history they represented. The giant water shrew is "a warm-blooded, breathing, biting fossil," with only one relative that Gerald knew of, a small insect-eating animal in Madagascar, the *Geogale*, for which not even a fossil record existed.[16] (More recent investigations show the giant water shrew, or giant otter shrew, is related to a number of species of tenrecs in Madagascar.)

Animal death remains a concern throughout the collecting narratives, especially in the early years. Gerald no doubt learned from these deaths, some inexplicable, some because the animals were so rare that their habits were unrecorded, and many more from injuries the animals sustained when they were captured or transported to the camp. The duikers, lovely little antelopes, died for no apparent reason. A huge python, so long the seller who brought it to camp had crammed it into a basket with its tail twisted and bound to the outside, died of gangrene. Six pygmy flying squirrels died, one by one, the last one just before Gerald's ship docked in England.

At this stage in the game, even he and his hunters sometimes injured or even killed animals. Sometimes he smoked animals out of trees, a practice that could have led to considerable harm. Gerald himself fired a gun in a bat cave in order to capture bats. Although the damage this noise would have inflicted on the bats' sonar is well understood today, Gerald probably had no idea of the harm he was doing. He angrily resisted killing adult monkeys in order to retrieve the babies, but Gerald did describe killing adult hippopotami in order to catch an infant, which ultimately was eaten by crocodiles before it could be retrieved. Since his purpose was to amuse a reading audience, Gerald wisely omitted this incident from his published narratives, but he confessed it in a letter to Louisa.[17] He never again shot adults to capture the young. But he does omit the obvious likelihood that many of his charming baby animals came into captivity when, like the hippos, the adults were shot for food or to facilitate capture of infants for the pet trade. That was standard practice at the time, and bushmeat, including monkeys, was a staple source of protein for those who lived in the forest. (In the years after Gerald's last visit to Cameroon, bushmeat became a commercial rather than a subsistence commodity, and for upper-class city people, eating it became an illegal status symbol.)[18]

Many animals were brought to the camp by paid hunters, others by the villagers. Everyone was invested in the Durrell industry because it paid well. Some of his best agents were children; a tiny girl with a beautiful small bird in a handwoven basket was exemplary, and she was paid twice the going rate as an example to the rowdier boys who brought injured animals. Since Gerald had been a small, free-range child himself, he never underestimated how helpful village children could be.

Other animals were gifts or purchases from European and American owners who could no longer keep large unruly pets such as apes or big cats. On the first journey to Cameroon, one of his most interesting finds was George the baboon, who escaped one night from the camp to make his way down to a village dance. George entertained the crowd so successfully that they requested a return performance. Unlike the smaller monkeys, George had little fear of the reptiles in the collection (once he snatched up and ate a rare chameleon), and he protected the guenons from the mischievous drills, who took every opportunity to torment them.

Another character was Chumley the chimpanzee. Under the impression that he was very young, Gerald agreed to transport Chumley back to England as a gift for the London Zoo. But when he was delivered in a large cage, with a chain around his neck, it was instantly clear that Chumley was rapidly approaching adulthood. He smoked (and lit his own cigarettes), drank sugared tea from a mug, and generally behaved with confidence and aplomb. Both the baboon and the chimpanzee had been pets, left with Gerald when their owners could no longer take care of them. (In later voyages, he would accept five more pet chimpanzees, more than one of them named "Chumley" or "Cholmondely.") With one of the Chumleys, the Durrells developed a lasting relationship. Back in Bournemouth, while the family searched for a zoo location, he lived in Margo's house, lounged in the front windows, wore Fair Isle sweaters and tams against the cold (knitted by Louisa), traveled around the countryside with Gerald, and selected a favorite pub, where he was entertained with orange juice and crisps and the indulgent attention of the bar tender. Chumley was eventually donated to the London Zoo, where later on he was shot after escaping twice—an incident which contributed to a downward spiral in Gerald's relationship with the zoo he had loved during his childhood months in London.

Chumley's life ended in tragedy, and in all likelihood, it began the same way. Like many of the animals Gerald received and transported back to England, both George and Chumley probably came into captivity as orphans. How George's life ended, Gerald does not say.

Despite animal deaths, the overwhelming tone of these books is hilarity. Some jokes are at the expense of the laconic, buttoned-up Yealland, who was from time to time caught unaware muttering soft sentiments to Gerald's animals as well as his own birds. Both Gerald's African helpers and local colonial officials sometimes looked ridiculous, and Gerald was his own target even more often. Once, after he and the hunters spent hours clearing brush from around a dead tree trunk, staking and partially burying mesh nets around it, building a fire at the base, and waiting, and waiting some more, only one "disdainful" pygmy chameleon eventually emerged. Elias slapped his thighs "in excess of mirth," Durrell observes, and refused to let the joke die: "Massa we done catch big beef to-day."[19] The sentence is in pidgin, but it is telling: the young Durrell, his caged animals, and his foreignness made for good entertainment, not just some extra cash. Sometimes the jokes on Gerald himself were more dangerous, and he admitted being foolhardy or stupid, especially when dealing with poisonous snakes.

From the second African narrative, recorded in *The Bafut Beagles*, Gerald came away with more chimpanzees (Chumley the second and Sue, whose parted straight hair suggests that she might have been a bonobo), snakes, amphibians, monkeys, pygmy flying squirrels, beautiful little Red River hogs and hairy frogs, several species of mongoose, snakes, and a precious golden cat.

A hyrax, a small gray-brown herbivorous mammal weighing less than ten pounds, turned out to be one of Gerald's most challenging opponents. He and his helpers set off from the town of Bafut one morning to walk through small farms and grassy fields toward the mountains where these "rock rabbits" lived in a valley at the base of sheer cliffs. Despite their genetic relationship to elephants, hyrax are quick and agile. The team struggled up through the boulders to set their net over a hole in the rocks, where Gerald had located one of the animals with his field glasses. They succeeded in smoking out two babies before the mother, "a corpulent beast in a towering rage," appeared on a ledge, knocked down a hunter with a single leap, fastened her teeth into his leg with the tenacity of a bulldog, and almost succeeded in tangling the equipment beyond use. All the while, she emitted "loud and terrifying 'Wheee' noises through her nose."[20] After much stress and trouble, the hunter was released from her angry jaws, all three animals were captured and sorted out, and a male hyrax was netted. Durrell had a breeding group.

Many of the characters, human and animal, are hilarious, although Gerald sometimes over-reaches. His chief helper in Mamfe, Pious, was evidently modeled in part on Wodehouse's Jeeves, as Gerald's caricature of himself sometimes resonates with Bertie Wooster. Gerald invariably presented Pious as reliable and competent. However, *The Overloaded Ark* and *The Bafut Beagles* also includes numerous stories about the African people—observations that Gerald admits are an "anthropological survey of the Bafut people."[21]

Most of the Africans in these early books were seemingly less thoughtful than Pious. Sometimes, Gerald let his imagination run away, hoping for "intrigue ... witches and magic potions full of leopard whiskers."[22] Instead, soon after this thought, he got a realistic dose of local color, combining danger and humor, when an elderly woman, fat, chuckling, wearing only the briefest of garments, presented a snake in a calabash. As she panted and wheezed from exertion, Gerald dumped the snake out. The elderly woman moved quickly away, but Gerald followed his usual pattern of dismissing native caution and so was bitten when he grabbed it. The snake turned out to be venomous, and though his servant Jacob administered first aid, both knew he really needed antivenin, which could only be obtained from a doctor (if the doctor had any) thirty miles away along a rough road (if the ailing kit car didn't break down). Gerald's arm swelled and he feared the worst, but luckily, the car arrived safely, and the doctor had the serum. When Gerald returned the next day, the old woman, smoking her pipe, "waddles" toward him: "Masa never pay me for dat fine snake I done bring."[23]

This incident, which shows Gerald not only being extremely sexist, but also reckless in handling the snake and also foolishly drinking spirits along the way, represents the kind of skewed ethnographic perspective which can be observed in such nineteenth-century European phenomena as Hagenbeck's zoo, which included both animals and "exotic" people in native dress, with "primitive" accoutrements, carrying on what was supposedly their normal way of life. (Hagenbeck dropped the practice when he realized that his actors went out after working hours, wearing ordinary street clothes, and sometimes asking locals for cigarettes.)[24] However quickly Gerald developed as an animal collector, zookeeper, and conservation specialist, as an anthropologist, he remained an amateur. Decades later, he would realize this disadvantage.

Features of the colonial "other" in cultural works by the colonizer include mimicry, exaggeration, and representations of their study subjects as opaque, with seemingly unknowable intentions. As usual, when reporting his conversation with the old woman, both she and Gerald speak pidgin, but since the rest of the text is written in the Queen's English, Gerald's mimicry reinforces the stereotype of colonized people. *Can* the subaltern speak? In this book, not very well, although in other episodes the subalterns could well be pulling the European's leg about believing in his juju. As the Finnish social scientist Jopi Nyman points out, Durrell's works *do* contain "their own critique."[25] Every aspect of the old woman's non-English physical appearance is described, and her intensions are obscure. Gerald evidently knew nothing, as he revealed nothing, about how she obtained the snake, what she knew about it, or whether she wished him well. Compliant as they might have seemed, the Africans he encountered were clearly more intentional, shrewd, and self-serving than the laughing, dancing, obsequiousness he often portrayed in these early narratives.

Gerald's encounters with the Fon of the semi-autonomous Bafut region reveal the same uncertainty. Historically, the Fons were friendlier to the English than the Germans, French, and Nigerians. Achirimbi II, who ruled from 1932 to 1968, seems to have been entirely friendly to Gerald (although Gerald never gives his name). After all, Gerald was a prepossessing young man, accustomed to communicating freely with his elders, who fell in with the Fon's vivid lifestyle and paid his subjects cash for animals and services. In short, for many in the village, he was a source of profit and entertainment. Once the animals were caught, the Fon enjoyed the opportunity to observe area wildlife in their cages. Sometimes there were awkward moments, as when the Fon insisted that Gerald marry one of his daughters, but he accepted the explanation that, in England, Gerald is allowed only one wife. The older man remained hospitable and helpful.

The Fon and the English District Officer did not always see eye to eye, however. The Fon was seemingly obeyed at all times by everyone, and energetic enough to drink and dance all night. The D. O. characterized him as a "sort of Nero of the region," "a delightful old rogue,"[26] but this colonial officer evidently misunderstood that the Fon's many formal powers were checked by a council of elders, an organization of all Fons in the region, and time-honored precedents. Although the Fon's power was not hereditary, there were formal advisory roles for his male relatives. As for the Fon's attitude, he seems simply to have found the D. O. tedious.

Although Gerald's descriptions of Bafut and its ruler have become valuable sources for historians and anthropologists, Gerald himself seems to have had an oversimplified view of the Fon's role. So it is helpful to read between the lines, from a postcolonial perspective. Although the Fon occupies a prominent place in the narrative of Gerald's second and third outings to Cameroon (*The Bafut Beagles* and *A Zoo in My Luggage)*, only the Fon's title, not his name, appears in the books about Cameroon. Achirimbi II was impressive: he seems to have understood juju, or personal power, better than Gerald, who sometimes claimed European juju in order to get what he wanted. (It is difficult to be sure how Gerald understood this term: according to the ethnologist R. K. Engard, one meaning of "juju" in the Bafut area is the aura of strangeness surrounding an outsider until the outsider is integrated into the community.)[27] The Fon's ceremonial robes were voluminous and ornate, sometimes white, as if to contrast with the vivid robes of the elders. Gerald was presented with a robe, as well. (The Fon's elaborate elephant hair headdress can be seen in a photograph in the exhibition on Gerald's life and work at the Jersey Zoo.) The Fon was several inches taller than Gerald and powerfully built. When he was away from the palace overnight, his children sang there to keep it "warm."

Clearly, the Fondom of Bafut was bound together by powerful, multivalenced rituals. But Gerald described the flamboyant ruler's role in village celebrations without reaching conclusions about their cultural significance. The grass ceremony, with its practical purpose of gathering materials to replenish the thatch for the houses, including the Fon's compound, evidently had, in addition, a community-building function. Gerald witnessed and participated in a number of traditional dances, without mentioning that they, too, were profoundly important. These were special occasions, marked by beautifully wrought ceremonial clothing and accessories. Although Gerald does not say so, one dance, in which the Fon was a central figure, was a structured interaction reinforcing a bond of trust between him and his wives, who caught him when he threw himself into their arms at the climax of the dance. Another dance, with a conga rhythm, describes a spiral. A few years later, after the Smithsonian Institute collected video footage of these ceremonies, Engard identified the spiral dance as the Abin e Mfor, an annual celebration of renewal.

The one time when Gerald seemed sure of the Fon's power was when the older man managed to procure a much-coveted golden cat, the evening before Gerald had to close his camp. The African golden cat is red-gold with faint spots, its ears almost as pointed as those of domesticated cats. Smaller than a serval, and larger than the Maine coon and Norwegian forest cats, the golden cat is so fierce that Gerald was unable to convince any of his hunters to search out one for his collection. When the Fon arrived late in the evening at the guest house where Gerald was encamped, Gerald immediately saw the hunters' point. When he untied the collecting bag in which the Fon presented the animal, the cat's yowls sent chills up his spine, its mouth opened in a snarl, and he noticed its eyes, the color of "leaves under ice."[28] After carefully caging the animal and sawing through the cords around her feet with a knife attached to a pole, he presented her with a small chicken, which she was able to pull through the bars with her powerful claws.

Even though the Fon encouraged the farmer who caught the cat to explain why and how he caught her, the timing of this capture remains something of a mystery. But like all the other acquisitions, the golden cat involved a business transaction, and the Fon nodded approvingly as Gerald handed over a generous sum to the farmer.

So why the writer's block, as Gerald sat on the veranda a few years later, in 1957, overlooking the Victoria harbor, trying to decide how to ask the Fon's permission to return?

To Gerald Durrell, almost everything could be turned to comic purposes. Gerald subjected the villagers, the Fon's prodigious alcohol intake, and his relationships with his many wives with the same broad humor he meted out to his own family. Gerald might have been charming, but he was not tactful, and the colonial office, even when retreating from Cameroon, was still concerned about how Gerald's published accounts might be perceived. The D. O. had a point, but just as Gerald did not grasp some of the complexities of the deteriorating colonial situation, or the African people who assisted in his collecting activities, the officer did not understand Gerald's brilliance in choosing helpers, cultivating personal relationships, and having fun.

It was also more than likely that the D. O. failed to understand the Fon and his particular power in this semi-autonomous region of the country. Gerald found these British officials useful, but his caricatures of them are as ludicrous as his treatments of anyone else, including the Africans who helped him. One autofictional sketch in *Fillets of Plaice*, "A Question of Promotion," is a case in point. Martin, the District Officer of Mamfe, is frantic because, on a previous visit, his superior fell into a badly constructed outdoor water closet. Martin expects to be demoted and sent deeper into the interior. Unfortunately, he truly is incompetent in every way except administering his formal duties. These he discharges to the entire satisfaction of both the six white inhabitants of the district and the "ten thousand vociferous Africans."[29] So everyone, including Gerald's right-hand man Pious, cooperates to make the visit successful, to the point of resurrecting a broken ceiling fan, now home to numerous wild creatures, including a highly venomous green mamba, who lands on the dining table just as dinner is being served. And "in that irritating way that snakes have," the mamba slithers toward the District Commander in charge of the District Officer's fate.[30] Everyone cooperates again to repair the damage, and, to his delight, Gerald's animal collection increases by one green mamba and a few smaller creatures. With the description of the local crowd, greedy for entertainment, the grinning, good-natured African stereotype is reinscribed, but so is the stereotype of the fumbling colonial administrator.

The 1957 expedition described in *A Zoo in My Luggage* differs in several ways from the earlier Cameroon journeys: this time, Gerald was accompanied on a mission to collect animals for his own zoo by his wife, his secretary, and a young naturalist, Bob Golding. A secondary purpose of the expedition was filming. This part of the project complicated Gerald's established methods, but it also provided significant financial support for supplies and equipment, including the ciné camera supplied by Varley Dry Accumulators, Ltd.

Between the second Cameroon expedition and the third, Gerald had married Jacquie Wolfenden, the daughter of a hotelier in Manchester, where Durrell was taking animal orders from the zoo in preparation for the second Cameroon venture. She was won over when she observed his care and attention for the individual animals before turning them over to the zoos for which they had been collected. Unlike other animal collections, Gerald's did not stink! Gerald's collecting accounts show her to be a quick study, whose assistance in caring for the animals through dicey moments during voyages could mean the difference between success and failure, and her impressions, if phrased differently, are similar. Since she did not have to win over a reading audience, sometimes she was even more explicit. Just before the couple eloped, as Gerald had started to prepare for his third expedition to Africa (and a zoo of his own), he explained that the rationale for any zoo had to be as a "last sanctuary for wild things" as humans encroached on their homes. In *Beasts in My Bed* (1954), Jacquie remembered:

> He told me how whole herds of wild game were being shot in a misguided tsetse fly campaign in Central Africa. Elsewhere, dams were being constructed and vast areas flooded that were the natural feeding grounds of many wild creatures. It was inevitable that when the interests of man conflicted with those of wild life, the animals would go to the wall.[31]

Passionately attached to his charges, Gerald ran into one obstacle after another as he searched for a zoo location. When Bournemouth and other neighboring towns evinced insufficient interest in the project, it was Jackie who suggested that they might find space in the Channel Islands. Indeed, Botting's reading of the Durrell letters, and his extensive interviews suggest that without pressure from Jacquie, even the books might not have been written. Collecting adventures might pay for themselves, but they did not pay the cost of living in between trips, or organizing the zoo, and since Gerald's expertise was the sort which could not be certified in official ways, finding employment—especially interesting employment—was difficult. But Jacquie remembered thinking, "If one Durrell could write, and make money at it, why should another one not try? So began Operation Nag."[32] Without the income from the books and, a little later, lectures and television programming, the collecting trips could not have continued, and the zoo itself would not have survived the early years.

This would be Jacquie's first trip to Africa, but her second collecting trip with Gerald, and she had learned a thing or two about the business. At Jacquie's suggestion, preparation included contacts with numerous businesses in England, which provided subsidies in return for a mention in the Acknowledgment section of the book. The list takes up three pages. Even though the D. O. scornfully identified Gerald as "that animal maniac," the list of colonial and corporate officials, missionaries, and shipping companies upon whose help the Durrells depended takes up two more pages. His collecting and zookeeping practices remained embedded in the official and unofficial imperialism of the twentieth century.

The last Cameroons account is more sober than the previous African adventures. Gerald was eight years older. The zoo did not yet exist, except in imagination, as a goal. His six-month stay in Cameroon yielded a needle-clawed bushbaby, Demidoff's bushbabies (both members of the Galago family), mongooses, snakes, various monkeys, and pottos. With uncertainty about where the animals would live once they returned to England, and the weight of years and added stress, he was ill and worn out by the time the party headed home.

Perhaps because they remain relatively unedited, the extracts from Gerald's diary included in *A Zoo in My Luggage* reveal more about his relationships with the animals than the rest of the narrative—how he cared for them, his discoveries about behaviors, and his emotional investment in their well-being and individuality. The most moving portion of the book consists of a two-day section about a chimpanzee after he was caught in a trap intended for antelope:

April 2: Young male chimp, about two years old, brought in today.... The palm of the hand and the wrist were split open and badly infected with gangrene. The animal was very weak, not being able to sit up, and the colour of the skin was a curious yellowish gray.... Drove it to Bemenda for the Dept. of Agriculture's vet to look at it, as did not like ... curious lethargy in spite of stimulants.... Have done all we can but the animal appears to be sinking fast. He seems pathetically grateful for anything you do for him.

April 3: Chimp died. They are a "protected" animal and yet up here, as in other parts of the Cameroons, they are killed and eaten regularly.[33]

This passage shows more than a glimpse into Gerald's writing process and, too, the way in which he reconstructed care and feeding routines for the animals he brought back to England. The brief diary notes about this chimpanzee, whose fate is not mentioned elsewhere, suggest the beginnings of an anger which could not be absorbed into the cheerful books he was writing at the time for a public enthralled by comic adventure stories. The chimpanzee died the day after Gerald's last attempt to save him.

In spite of obstacles, the mission was a success. As it turned out, for the Fon, publicity was publicity—and more useful than not. He welcomed Jacquie warmly and, as before, encouraged Gerald in his mission. Hundreds of animals, large and small, were collected for the new zoo. There was still adventure: Gerald and Bob almost captured a large python from its refuge in a shallow cave, and one day as they ventured down the Cross River, they narrowly escaped having their small boat capsized by hippos, who had developed this aggressive habit shortly before Gerald's arrival and managed to kill a few humans.

From Mamfe, Gerald also returned to Eshobi, where he caught up on gossip, caught sight of the rare *Picathartes* (or "rock fowl," much coveted by the London Zoo), and acquired a bush baby for the collection. There were fewer excursions into the bush, but just as many animal acquisitions. With limited time, Gerald also created realistic sets in the compound for filming, and his 16mm footage was later combined with studio sequences for a BBC series, *To Bafut for Beef* ("beef" being pidgin for wildlife). On the way back to the coast, Jacquie and Gerald took charge of separate parts of the collection and returned by different routes. Gerald drove the larger and sturdier animals along paved roads on the French side, with Jacquie and Sophie transporting the more delicate creatures along the English side of the border. Once again, the United Africa Company came to the rescue with two large trucks.[34]

The narrative ends back in Bournemouth, where the primates, in particular, created havoc when they were temporarily housed in the

FIGURE 3.2 Gerald and Jacquie Durrell with Animals in Bournemouth.

basement of a local department store as a special Christmas exhibit. Some would end up in the zoo at Paignton and some in Margo's back garden (with Chumley in her house) until some months later, when Gerald, Jacquie, and some of the animals finally found their permanent home on the Isle of Jersey.

Gerald's fourth and final African expedition was to Sierra Leone in 1965, four years after the country's independence and six years after the founding of the zoo. He wrote about Sierra Leone in the longest section of *Catch Me a Colobus*. This account is bookended first by descriptions of (mostly) human behavior at the zoo, and after the Sierra Leone narrative, another section about settling the animals he collected into their new homes. The final section of this book describes an excursion to capture volcano rabbits in Mexico. This book, published in 1972, is marked throughout by outrage.

Gerald's contacts with the BBC helped fund the 1965 journey to Sierra Leone, another former British colony, in which British commercial interests and regulatory infrastructure remained. Once again, these holdovers from empire smoothed the way. Housing, servants, transportation, and some of the supplies were furnished by government and commercial agencies. Permits to collect animals were easier to obtain in Sierra Leone than the paperwork required to bring them through or into the United Kingdom. Employing his previous tactic of advertising, with permission of village chiefs, Gerald was able to accumulate what he wanted, mostly small creatures.

Animals still occupy center stage in *Catch Me a Colobus*, with the primates providing the most entertainment. Gerald observed that the patas monkeys engaged in lively structured dances. Georgina, a pet baboon, enjoyed startling passers-by by jumping out of hiding places, deftly disrobing unwary victims, and breaking into the camp shower stall while it was occupied. Another Chumley enjoyed rousing Gerald from his sleep by pulling his hair and touching his feet with cold hands. Minnie, the female chimpanzee purchased from a Dutchman living in a nearby village, entertained visitors to the camp with a song, her cage serving as a drum.

But most of the hijinks are gone, and the lyrical descriptions of the landscapes are almost altogether missing. Gerald's descriptions of the Africans, as well as his team and the BBC film crew that accompanied them, are tamer and less hyperbolic. What unifies the book is not so much a sense of place, but as a sense of helplessness at animal endangerment and human carelessness.

Sierra Leone, about the size of North Carolina, lies in far west Africa, with Liberia to the south and Guinea to the north and east. Freetown, the capital, is a port city, and Kenema, near where Gerald and John Hartley set up their base camp, lies about two hundred miles to the southeast of Freetown. The areas that became Sierra Leone had been involved in the Atlantic slave trade until the trade was abolished within the British Empire in 1807, and freed slaves living in England emigrated to establish a colony at Freetown. Like Cameroon's borders, Sierra Leone's were created by colonial powers, with little regard for the ethnic boundaries already in place. Since before independence in 1961, mining has been a mainstay of the economy.

When Gerald arrived, British commercial enterprises were still in place, active, and sometimes detrimental to local environments, societies, and economies. Agriculture, which included subsistence crops such as rice, and export crops such as bananas and cocoa, suffered during the ethnic conflicts that followed independence.

The all too common objectification of zoo animals Gerald had already observed in his own zoo was akin to the carelessness he was beginning to observe all over the world. Failure to enforce wildlife protection laws in

82 THE EVOLUTION OF GERALD DURRELL

Sierra Leone was akin to the bureaucratic sluggishness in Mexico City that almost prevented Gerald from capturing endangered volcano rabbits from the slopes of Mount Popocatepetl. People are outraged about two thousand human highway casualties in Great Britain, he noted, but no one seemed to care that two million birds suffered the same fate on those highways (1972 figures). The same attitudes led, in North America, to the extinction of the passenger pigeon and the near extinction of the bison. All these events reveal an attitude, common throughout the world, that Gerald would fight against for the rest of his life.

This early post-independence situation made Gerald's collecting work easier, of course. Permits for capturing and exporting animals were still required, but, with the new government, Gerald encountered no more obstacles than he had done in his third expedition to Cameroon. In fact, an officer of the Sierra Leone Army, coincidentally an animal lover who (as "Uncle Ambrose") hosted a children's show on Sierra Leone Television, provided military trucks for transporting the animals to their ship for the voyage home. Multinational corporations also helped. Housing built for the administrators of the chrome mines was abandoned when the mines were depleted, but still new and available as a relatively luxurious camp. Company officials gave Gerald's team and the BBC film crew who accompanied them free use of the area, which soon became known as the "beef mine." By this time, the Trust had been created to support the zoo and its conservation projects; a trust member with connections to the Diamond Corporation of Sierra Leone provided transportation out to the town of Kenama, the center of Gerald's collecting activities, and other assistance.

In the early 1960s, when Gerald wrote his account of Sierra Leone, he did not connect all the dots. Conditions would become far worse, not only for the animals, but for their human neighbors. When the book was published, few would have predicted that "blood diamonds" would fuel civil war in the decades that followed, or that piecework, or "artisanal" mining by individual miners, rather than mechanized mining, would have a detrimental effect on the local economies in the south and east of the country. Gerald cannot be blamed for making use of available resources without foreknowledge of the way these international corporations would operate in the future, but, as in so many other ways, everyone who benefited or benefits from the extractive commercial enterprises on former colonies is implicated in it. (That includes almost every twenty-first-century user of smart phones, which depend on cobalt and tantalum mined in Africa.)

He did not need a crystal ball to predict what would happen to the animals, however. The disquiet informing Gerald's description of the monkey drive reveals not only his own ambivalence, but the mixed feelings of many conservationists working in environmental hotspots from the late twentieth century into the present. In Gerald's account, he explains how, at regular intervals in the planting and growing cycles of the cocoa plantations, local people were paid by the government to drive monkeys away from the plantations and kill them so that they would not destroy the crops. Some monkeys—guenons and Diana monkeys—do feed on the cocoa, making the drive "necessary," according to the plantation owners and the local workers. Several other monkey species in the area are commensal; that is, they socialize with the guenons and Dianas. However, since ordinary people did not distinguish clearly among these species, all monkeys caught in this hunt were usually dead monkeys. Gerald was distressed at both the loss of animal life and the destruction of trees for the hunt and the planting that followed.

He wanted the large colobus monkeys, who did no harm at all to the cocoa trees. At that time, these monkeys were numerous, but difficult to trap. The many species of the colobine genus are large monkeys with a wide range in Africa and the Indian subcontinent. Instead of fruits and nuts, which most monkeys prefer, the colobines eat leaves, bark, vines, and various tiny critters they pick up in the treetops, where they spend most of their time. They are fully adapted to this life, with complex digestive systems and huge bellies, and their locomotion is so dependent on brachiation that their tiny thumbs, which would be a nuisance as they swing through the branches, cannot grasp objects as most primate thumbs are able to do. Only big cats comfortable in trees, or a chimpanzee hunting party, would have access to such monkeys.

Early during his stay in the country, Gerald observed a group of red and black colobus monkeys arriving at a treetop just down the hill from the guest house where he was staying. He was astonished at their beauty:

> They had rich, shining, chestnut-red and coal-black fur, and in the morning sun they gleamed as if they were burnished.... There must have been a dozen or so with a couple of babies, and it amused me the way the babies would use their parents' tails or the branches of a tree indiscriminately, as a means of hoicking themselves from one place to another.... They were, without doubt, some of the most beautiful

monkeys I'd ever seen, and I was determined that we were going to add a few to our collection, come what might. They stayed in the tree, feeding quietly and uttering little cries to each other, until Sudu suddenly arrived on the veranda with a great rattling tray of teacups. When I looked back, they had all disappeared.[35]

Before he left Sierra Leone, Gerald had acquired enough of these monkeys for a breeding group, and enough black and white colobus for another. Although the red and whites were picky eaters and presented culinary challenges in the camp and during the voyage home, all survived.

This descriptive passage about the monkeys is typical in many ways. Gerald was always moved aesthetically and emotionally by animals. He watched closely and with great patience. He was annoyed by the demands of daily life, in this case by a servant's delivery of afternoon tea—as so many of his quotidian needs were handled in the colonies and former colonies.

The off-season drive was organized so that Gerald could capture the colobus monkeys occurred at Bambawo, a village near the town of Kenama, headed by the paramount chief of the area. The chief understood that since Gerald's time was limited, he could not participate in the regularly scheduled drives, however much he might have liked to do this, so that some of the driven monkeys could be spared. The drive also had to be scheduled later in the morning than usual, when there would be enough light for filming. Following their normal procedure, with explicit instructions to capture but not kill, a number of village men, spaced in a circle in the forest, drove the monkeys to a tall tree located at a central point, where scores of them climbed up and congregated. After the surrounding trees and large branches were cut down and propped up against the tree trunk, some of the villagers produced a saw and began to cut, or at least pretend to cut down the monkeys' refuge. Despite Gerald's skepticism, the monkeys appeared to believe the tree would be felled, so they climbed down into the "coop" of brush and branches at the base of the trunk. There, Gerald and his helpers could pull them out with ease, without injuring them, and pop them into the row of cages assembled at the edge of the clearing.

It could have been worse. The film crew could have experienced bad weather. The villagers could have accidentally killed monkeys. Perhaps Gerald's captures would have been killed in a later drive. The trees were scheduled for felling anyway for another cocoa plantation. Still, even as he rejoices in the fulfillment of his collector's greed and his conservationist goal, there is much to worry about: the two species of Colobus are vulnerable during monkey drives, despite legal protections:

> It was the same situation that I had seen all over the world and which always sickens me; governments ready to pay out millions of pounds for airy fairy schemes, but not a penny towards animal conservation. So you get the situation where three thousand monkeys are slaughtered per annum, half of which have committed no crime against the cocoa crop and which could, in fact, be a valuable tourist asset.[36]

Gerald would return to the theme of human carelessness, greed, and cruelty throughout the rest of his life. Although no monkeys were killed this time, Gerald used an extractive colonialist enterprise to collect monkeys that were not endangered at that time—but they are now, from hunting and deforestation for agriculture. In Sierra Leone, colobus monkeys are now locally extinct. One suspects that some of the rage against these practices, expressed even more emphatically in later books, was fueled by his own participation, however removed from actual destruction, in an unsustainable system. Now, almost all wild primates are endangered.

Other adventures in Sierra Leone were less disturbing. Gerald's humor almost returned in full force when he described attempts by the English film crew to capture the natural behaviors of the animals he caught. All film is fiction, he comments, including wildlife film. Limited time and resources meant that the crew could not always follow him about in the forest while he (or his various helpers) tracked and caught wildlife. The answer was to create stage settings in the forest, surrounded by nets, in which to release and film individual animals, doing what they might normally do. Captured on film were a water chevrotain, pouched rats, a Woodford's owl, and several snakes. Bob's accidental release of the green mamba into a crowd watching the procedures produced screams and laughter and might have inspired the climax of Gerald's short story about the promotion of the inept district officer.

"Natural" was never natural, and expected behavior was often long in coming. For example, the "acting" of the potto, a mild little primate in the loris family, resulted in can after can of wasted film because it refused to run along a branch, as it was expected to do. The potto's normal defense is to run, and then cover its head with its hands and turn its back, adorned with sharp spines, to potential predators. On this occasion, it simply sat still for a long time before running in an unexpected direction, away from the cameras. The pouched rat was an equally unwilling actor. Like the potto and the rat, the lovely water chevrotain refused to exhibit "natural" behavior. She sat in her large water dish, but refused to sit in the more naturalistic set Gerald had created. He had to rely on tiny bits of film and clever editing, along with more mundane footage of animals in cages, for the fakery that is wildlife documentary. If the efforts to film were frustrating, at least they were good for comic episodes in books.

The crew got lucky when a pair of half-grown leopard cubs escaped from their temporary confinement in a toilet shack and had to be recaptured. Gerda and Lokai, as they were called, came to Durrell from Joe Sharp, a tall, lanky American Peace Corps volunteer, on his way back to the United States. Joe wasn't sure where they came from or how old they were, but he thought they were littermates because they were about the same size and comfortable with one another. (In all probability, they were taken when their mother was killed.) Unfortunately for Gerald's team, Gerda, especially, wasn't comfortable with anyone except her brother and Joe Sharp. Even feeding the pair of them was a challenge. One swipe of a paw, even in play, could inflict a serious injury. When the two went missing from the toilet shack, Gerald and Long John (a new acquaintance Gerald's party had met in country), each with a helper, rounded up Gerda and Lokai separately by slipping ropes under the collars they still wore and luring them little by little back into confinement. When the ordeal was over, Gerald and John were sweating and covered with scratches.

"That was a marvelous sequence," one of the film crew sang out. "Blast the BBC" was the response.[37] (One wonders about the exact choice of words.) In any case, more marvelous to Gerald and his companions was the return to Jersey, where the leopards quickly adapted to their zoo quarters and enjoyed playing with John Hartley, apparently without rancor.

The film crew planned to accompany the Jersey team all the way home in order to capture film along the way and as the animals settled into their new home at the zoo. In Freetown, Uncle Ambrose added one more animal to the collection—Blossom, a tiny, beautiful, voracious Red River hog; in Gerald's opinion, this animal is the most beautiful member of the pig genus.

The rigors of the voyage back, though, were considerable, as always on Gerald's collecting trips: many hours of travel along rough roads (or none) in a caravan of assorted vehicles with animals whose experience had certainly not prepared them for vehicular travel or a sea voyage that lasted weeks. As usual, Gerald also faced a challenge in feeding them, and the equally frustrating challenges of paperwork when returning to England. This time, he encountered another obstacle. Just before leaving the relative luxury of the chrome mines in Kenama. As he sat on the tailgate of a truck as it jolted along a bumpy road, he suffered painful broken ribs and back injuries which prevented him from lifting or bending down to care for the animals. A complicated series of communications brought Jacquie to his side—a detour from her own return from a separate collecting trip in Argentina.

Her welcome gift from her husband was an infant squirrel in a small cardboard box lined with cotton wool. It was a Sierra Leone striped squirrel. Descendants of the squirrels Gerald brought back from this last African journey now live in the London Zoo.[38] Such gifts, she wrote in *Beasts in My Bed*, "at least prevent me from having a stockpile of bottles of perfume and other unwanted gifts."[39]

When colonizers traveled from Britain to the colonies, they were said to go "out." This would be the last time either Gerald or Jacquie would go out to Africa. But there were other adventures in store, more causes for worry, and more inspiration in beautiful, endangered lands.

Notes

1 G. Durrell, *A Bevy of Beasts* (New York: Simon & Schuster, 1980), 244.

2 Ibid., 240.

3 Ibid., 245.

4 Mary Terrall, "Heroic Narratives of Quest and Discovery," in *The Postcolonial Science and Technology Studies Reader*, ed. Sandra Harding (Durham, NC: Duke University Press, 2011), 84–89.

5 Bruno Latour, *Science in Action* (Cambridge, MA: Harvard University Press, 1987).

6 G. Durrell, *A Zoo in My Luggage*, 14.

7 BBC, "Cameroon Profile—Timeline." https://www.bbc.com/news/world-africa-13148483

8 Mathias L. Niba, "Bafut under Colonial Administration 1900-1949," *Paideuma: Mitteilungen zur Kulturkunde*, 41(1995), 63–72.

9 Chimamanda Ngozi Adiche, "Carnage in the Cameroons," *New York Times Sunday Review*, September 16, 2018, 10.

10 See Renato Rosaldo's classic essay "Imperialist Nostalgia," *Representations* 26, no. 2 (1989), 107–22.

11 G. Durrell, *The New Noah*, 13–14.

12 G. Durrell, *The Overloaded Ark*, 176.

13 Hans Kummer, *In Quest of the Sacred Baboon: A Scientist's Journey* (Princeton, NJ: Princeton University Press,1995), 82–82.

14 G. Durrell, *Overloaded Ark*, 102.

15 Maria Lindgren Leavenworth suggests that a few decades later, most travel writers engaged more actively than Gerald with their sources, using their predecessors not only for travelogues, but to compare and contrast their own insights and conclusions with previous texts. Gerald's work was not so consistently and consciously intertextual. He argued only with a few authors who presented oversimplified and negative views of animals. See Leavenworth's "Footsteps," in *The Routledge Research Companion to Travel Writing*, ed. Alasdair Pettinger and Tim Youngs (New York: Routledge, 2020).

16 G. Durrell, *Overloaded Ark*, 100.

17 Botting, *Gerald Durrell*, 165.

18 The modern trend in bushmeat consumption is well documented, most interestingly, perhaps, by Vanessa Woods in *Bonobo Handshake: A Memoir of Love and Adventure in the Congo* (New York: Gotham Books, 2010).

19 G. Durrell, *Overloaded Ark*, 128–29.

20 G. Durrell, *Bafut Beagles*, 59.

21 Ibid., 65.

22 Ibid., 126.

23 Ibid., 135.

24 Nigel Rothfels, *Savages and Beasts: The Birth of the Modern Zoo* (Baltimore, MD: Johns Hopkins University Press, 2002) describes the conception and failures of Hagenbeck's people shows.

25 Jopi Nyman, "Gerald Durrell and the Colonial Animal," in *Postcolonial Animal Tale from Kipling to Coetzee,"* ed. Nyman (New Delhi: Atlantic Publishers and Distributors, 2003), 122. Nyman is one of Gerald's fiercest critics—a position based apparently on a narrowly postcolonial reading of the early books. This perspective is important, but so is the context of Gerald's whole body of work, including the later books and the conservation projects.

26 G. Durrell, *Bafut Beagles*, 10.

27 Ronald K. Engard, "Dance and Power in Bafut (Cameroon)," in *Creativity of Power: Cosmology and Action in African Societies*, ed. W. Arens and Ivan Karp (Washington, D. C.: Smithsonian Institution Press,1989), 129–62.

28 G. Durrell, *Bafut Beagles*, 140.

29 G. Durrell, *Fillets of Plaice*, 88.

30 Ibid., 127.

31 J. Durrell, *Beasts in My Bed* (London: Collins, 1968), 11.

32 I 30.

33 G. Durrell, *Zoo in My Luggage*, 104–5.

34 J. Durrell. *Beasts in My Bed*, 91.

35 G. Durrell, *Catch Me a Colobus*, 117.

36 Ibid., 119.

37 Ibid., 105.

38 "Sierra Leone Striped Squirrel 1976." https://www.zoochat.com/community/media/sierra-leone-striped-squirrel-1976.338617/ [accessed July 18, 2023].

39 J. Durrell, *Beasts in My Bed*, 183.

4 SOUTH AMERICA: THE HUMAN FACTOR

Gerald's tutor George succeeded brilliantly in teaching him geography: "We would draw giant maps, wrinkled with mountains, and then fill in the various places of interest, together with drawings of the more exciting fauna to be found there." Every clime was dramatically illustrated, and "Our oceans were anything but empty . . . fur-clad Eskimos pursued obese herds of walrus through ice-fields thickly populated by polar bears and penguins. They were maps that lived . . ."[1] Sometimes, the pair wandered down to the shore, where they made gigantic maps with flotsam along the water's edge.

And here he was in 1950, sitting with his companions around the table in a bar, studying a map of British Guiana. They needed to choose a base of operations. "I stared at the map, tracing the courses of the rivers and mountains, gloating over such wonderful names as Pomeroon, Mazaruni, Kanuku, Berbice, and Essequibo."[2]

A few reviewers of the earliest books have asked why Gerald Durrell failed to see his own collecting missions as complicit with contemporary wasteful zookeeping practices, or why he represented African speech in pidgin, a literary practice which reinforced negative stereotypes, however innocently intended.[3] The reason lies partly in his age—he was barely twenty-three when he first when out to Africa, and only two years later did he began writing. Not until many years later did Gerald's grasp of geography extend to global structures of domination, exploitation, the extractive practices of colonialism, or his own complicity with those forces.

True to form, in Guyana, Gerald's second destination after Cameroon, in 1950, he followed the routes of earlier travelers, beginning with Walter Raleigh, the poet, courtier, promoter, and pirate. Raleigh's *Discovery of Guiana* (1596) established in the British colonial mind the "Guyanas"

(Guyana, Surinam, and French Guiana) as the mythic El Dorado. This region spans a section of the Caribbean coast of South America, from Venezuela in the west to Brazil in the south and east, and just north of the Amazon basin. It is a challenging landscape of wetlands, mountains, ancient dunes, and almost unnavigable rivers.

British travelers who went out to South America followed a set of rules and priorities different from those governing British behavior in Africa. Unlike Cameroon, which offered strategic advantages during the age of empire, Guyana was valuable principally for its timber and potential for cash crops. It became the only formal British colony in South America, wrested in 1652 from the control of Spain, the Netherlands, France, and before them, the Caribe Indians. A century after Raleigh, it became obvious that, not gold, but the European addiction to sugar, would be the source of New World wealth for the British.

European powers fought over the Caribbean coast of South America until the early decades of the nineteenth century. In *A Description of British Guiana*, an official 1840 report commissioned by the British government, Robert Schomburgk notes that at that time, sugar, cocoa, and indigo were the commercial successes of the area. Additionally, he believed the colony could serve as an outlet for manufactured goods from the home country. Schomburgk also recommended shipping a large labor force from the Indian subcontinent and diversifying the local agriculture to raise grains, much needed in England. At the date of his report, the slave population which made sugar production on such a scale profitable had been freed. The former slaves became a less reliable work force as they found new ways to make a living. But with newly imported labor from the eastern rim of the empire, sugar remained king there and in the rest of the region after the formal end of slavery in 1833.

The externalities for the sugar industry were high: establishing and running the plantations had first depended on enslaved Africans and, later, other imported labor. Indigenous people were displaced and biodiversity significantly diminished, as in Africa. Schomburgk presented generous tabular renderings of the demographics, lamenting the gradual disappearance of the South American Indians, who originally numbered "in the millions."[4] The premier European explorer of his day, Alexander von Humboldt, had predicted the environmental decay of South America much earlier. In spite of Schomburgk's clarity on this point—like Humboldt's—he nevertheless urged further development of agriculture and deliberate attempts to populate the region, not only with East Indians, but with working-class Europeans to develop the commercial sector needed by the great plantations.

Such blind spots are all too common in the imperial mindset—and at first Gerald was no exception. However, by the time he published *The Whispering Land* (1961), recounting a third expedition to the continent, he had begun to see that labor in the cane fields and the sawmills that processed the lumber to make way for them were "soul-destroying."[5] He had an inkling, as well, that in the vast tracts given over to ranching and monoculture, native flora and fauna were under a siege they might not survive.

Even during his first venture, in British Guiana, Gerald treated the South Americans he encountered more sympathetically than he depicted the Africans in Cameroon. His South American travel writing no doubt reflects different underlying British attitudes about Latin America: the stereotypes of native Americans and the mestizo population were not as ingrained in the British imagination as racist stereotypes in discourse about Africa and Africans. However, in his first Latin American venture, in 1950, Gerald seems to have been almost oblivious to his own role in depleting Guyana of its natural wealth—the animals, the only kind of wealth that mattered to the young collector. If the kingdom of Bafut was to him an enchanted land, at first untouched and untouchable by time, the Guyana landscape, though rich, was so forbidding that in his early travels, he could not see it as vulnerable at all. In the early 1950s, he failed to mention the invisible cost of collecting animals in either place to repopulate zoos, which had poor records on animal health and reproduction. Not quite yet.[6]

Gerald's initial colonialist pathways were figurative, depending on the early travel literature, and geographical. Conditions on the ground determined where, when, and how he could travel once he arrived in the country. Schomburgk followed Humboldt, who explored the region in 1800. As part of a second exploratory wave (or third, if Raleigh is credited as the first), Schomburgk was a promoter: he praised the "majestic scenes of nature" and defended the climate against claims that it was unhealthy for Europeans by climbing the mountains of Guyana himself, recording temperature, barometric pressure, and rainfall.[7] However, even he represented the difficulty of exploring the interior of the country. Transport along the rivers was possible, he noted, only during the rainy season, when the increased flow rose above the rapids to allow boat travel.

Given the geography of the colony, it is not surprising that *Three Singles to Adventure* (1954) begins and ends in Georgetown, the colony's capital. At first, the rainy season confined the party to the coast. In Guyana, a watery coastal plain extends inland between twenty and forty miles, where a range of great sand hills begins. Most of the agriculture and some cattle ranching occupy part of this coastal belt in Guyana.

Part of the Essequibo River Valley, too, supports cattle ranching, but east-west mountain chains farther south have restricted transportation since Europeans first occupied the area. Schomburgk noted that where the major rivers of Guyana cross the mountains, large cataracts course down the mountainside.[8] He suggested that the height and direction of these mountains made fixing and defending the southern border of the colony difficult—and even the most current map published by the National Geographic Society shows a section of territory still disputed by Guyana and Surinam, formerly Dutch Guiana. Between these rivers and the east-west mountain chains are savannahs.

Like Raleigh over three centuries earlier, Gerald at first avoided the Guyanese interior, venturing finally past the mountains and into the savannah to the large cattle operation of Tiny McTurk at Karanambo. Small planes to the savannah left only once every two weeks, and that part of Gerald's expedition would be planned in a hectic burst of activity at the last minute, after the collecting party explored the coastal region.

Travels along the coast, up the first twenty or so miles of the Essiquibo River, into the "Creek Lands," and across the challenging sand ridges on foot were easier to arrange. With Robert Lowes (an artist hoping to paint the Amerindians), Ken Smith (an old friend from the Whipsnade days), and the general factotum Ivan, who advised the party about local wildlife and customs "with the traditional air of Jeeves choosing a suit," Gerald traveled west along the coast, "by road, rail, launch, and steamer" to a nearby little village with the happy name of "Adventure."[9] This outpost, inland a few miles on the west side of the river, appears nowadays on few maps, but, as a gateway for his first Latin American collecting venture, it lived up to its name. Ivan quickly found a small, typical stilt house adequate for the party's activities, a guide named Cordai, and a small band of hunters, Black, Chinese, and East Indian, reflecting the ethnic diversity encouraged by official policy.

Before striking out on his own, following a practice he established in Cameroon, Gerald spread word among the local community around Adventure that he would buy animals, and creatures started to appear— an angry escape-artist anaconda constrictor, a coatimundi, some beautiful lizards, five squirrel monkeys, and Cuthbert the curassow, a large, unusually tame bird who "peeted" incessantly. Cuthbert knocked over bottles of ink, defecated on travel notes, and, because he was constantly under foot, caused Bob to tangle the three hammocks suspended in the expedition's tiny living space. As in this (and all of Durrell's other collecting narratives), the animal becomes not just a specimen, but a "character," whose story includes comedy, drama, and conflict. The curassow got his just deserts for being a pest when the monkeys reached through the bars of their cage, where he decided to roost, to pull out his tail feathers.

The longer the party stayed in Adventure, the more specimens the locals presented—opossums, reptiles, birds, monkeys, and a rare two-toed sloth, described by Ferdinando de Oviedo, in a passage in *Purchas His Pilgrimes* which Gerald excerpts. Gerald clearly did his homework in researching the species he wanted to collect, and he differed with Oviedo about the right relationship between beast and human in general—the sloth, or *cagnuolo*, in particular. Useless, slow, heavy, dull, and completely helpless on the ground, for the sixteenth-century European, these animals, are "altogether brutish, and utterly unprofitable, and without commoditie yet knowne to man."[10] The authoritative eighteenth-century natural historian Compte de Buffon, Gerald noted with annoyance, made even grosser errors, describing the sloth as "a gigantic error on the part of nature." Gerald corrected the record by reporting the sloth's cleverness in repeatedly escaping from its cage and pointed out that the sloth is fitted for its arboreal life by physiological features adapted to the trees where it lives and moves. Oviedo concluded that because sloths "are of no use to man they are of no use at all. The belief that all animals were placed on earth purely for man's convenience . . . still lingers on today." Persistence in such a sentiment is merely proof of human arrogance.[11] Well, Oviedo also believed that sloths lived on air.

Gerald also wanted to meet the Amerindian villagers who lived in Santa Maria, a village on Capoey Lake. Not only was he curious about them, he also believed they could help him find more animals. Although the lake lies in the coastal plain quite near the sea, and near the town of Adventure, the journey took more than a day on foot and involved trekking through forest, wetlands, and the loose sand of ancient dunes.

The challenge of meeting the villagers, who could only be hailed by shouting for several hours across the lake, turned out to be as difficult as the journey to the lake. When a youth appeared in his canoe to paddle them across, they discovered that most of the villagers had moved on. Only one family remained, polite but wary. Although the family agree to sell Gerald any interesting animals they found, he did not insist on protracted conversation.

> When you consider the history of the South American Indian, starting with the refined and Christian cruelties of the Spaniards and working down to the present day, when the Amerindians, their country wrested away from them, are forced to live on reservations so that they may be better protected from the blessings of civilization ... it is astonishing that white people can come into any sort of contact with them at all.[12]

Although this view was not universally shared, it was not new. Here Gerald echoes Schomburgk, who reported in detail on the demographics of the region, commenting that the native population had already declined precipitously.[13] Dispossessed from their land, they have "wandered from their ancient homes"; they are "all but annihilated," he continued, by internal feuds, European vices, and the incursions of slave-takers from Brazil.[14]

Schomburgk failed to recognize the irony of his own recommendation to increase agricultural production by importing labor from Europe and East India. Likewise, Gerald failed to recognize a similar deep historical pattern. It would be several years before he understood that the same voracious capitalist forces which drove the native Americans out of sight and depopulated this once populous land were similar, if not identical, to the forces which depleted the South American and African landscapes of the animals he loved. Even so, the representation of subject peoples in *Three Tickets to Adventure* is more thoughtful than his view in *The Overloaded Ark* and *The Bafut Beagles*. He was beginning to connect the dots.

Even though they failed to enlist the Amerindian family in their search for animals, during this short excursion, Gerald and Bob caught soldier rats which were "not even rare," Bob complained, by entangling the beasts in their clothes.[15] Still naked (except for their hats) they jumped into the lake—until warned about piranhas. The pair also managed to trap a brown tree snake and caught sight of rare tanagers. In Gerald's memory of the trip, irony competed with "startling beauty" which held him "spellbound." On the returning to Adventure, he paused, the gleaming sand reefs on one side, and on the other a woodland that reminded him of England. In their branches he saw, for the first time, a troop of howler monkeys, their fur the colors of chocolate, copper, and wine. "The old male was the most vivid of the lot, and he sat in the topmost branches of a tree, in the direct rays of the sun, so that his coat shone as though it were on fire." For the young Gerald Durrell, such beauty elicited a powerful desire to possess "one of those glossy, fantastic monkeys, even if I had to pay a king's ransom to get it."[16]

The next stop was Karanambo, a ranch in the cattle country of Rupununi, an interior settlement which, in Schomburgk's time, would have been accessible only to the most intrepid travelers on foot. In many ways parodies of heroic travel books, Gerald's narratives are always interrupted by zany scenes. The second side-trip in *Three Singles to Adventure* involves a small, groaning plane with a motley crew of human and canine passengers—missionaries, East Indian immigrants, and a young native boy, among others. The flight—over two hundred miles—took them across white sand reefs, mountains, rivers, and forests, "a thousand different shades of green, looking . . . as tight and curly as a rug of green astrakhan," and finally, to the grasslands.[17] After their host, Tiny McTurk, collected Gerald and Bob at the airport, he zigzagged in his jeep at breakneck speed across potholes, red clay, and grass tussocks to reach the ranch, at this season populated largely by hordes of tiny but ferocious kaboura flies.

The other animals of the region, including electric eels and caimans, are almost as fierce, and Gerald and Bob innocently lounged in riverside holes made by stingrays until McTurk warned them away. After two weeks at Karanambo, they returned to Adventure with a giant anteater, unruly capybaras, armadillos, tortoises, and pocket toads, who incubate eggs in tiny capsules in the skin until the metamorphosis of tadpoles into fully formed toads is complete. Gerald was devastated to learn that they had to abandon a large strong caiman, which he had foolishly tried to yank over a bluff single-handedly—until Bob joined him in the struggle. Equally foolish was the belief that there would be room for it on the plane.

The last excursion from the coast was to "a scattering of houses" called Charity, situated in the creek lands near the Orinoco River, which separates Guyana from Venezuela.[18] Once again, the territory was familiar through books. Raleigh had explored the region. According to his narrative, the Amerindians conducted a robust trade in foodstuffs, durable goods, and gold throughout the Caribbean. Now, Gerald of course wanted only the animals. He noticed that the children, especially, kept many tame birds, monkeys, and other less common animals. Many households had boas—so much better for catching vermin than cats would be and, in Gerald's opinion, more decorative.

The guide for this part of the journey, a Mr. Khan, was a great teller of tall tales about his encounters with caimans, jaguars, and anacondas. (The *miles gloriosus* or some version thereof became a standard fixture in Gerald's stories.) By enlisting delighted schoolchildren in the village, Gerald came away with a crab-eating raccoon, agoutis, boas, and a fleet peccary who terrified Mr. Kahn. To redeem himself, Khan tried to capture a desirable carpenter bird, only to kill it in the process. When the children's schoolmaster sent the party on to another village, Gerald encountered more Amerindians whose love of animals seemed to rival his own, despite the difficulties of their subsistence livelihoods. Their skills with animals contrasted with Mr. Kahn's clumsiness. Soon, back to Adventure the party went with all their acquisitions, including the latest—a tree porcupine and a tiny arboreal anteater. At the end of their stay in Guyana, they now had five hundred specimens.

It would be three years before Gerald returned to South America, traveling the next time to Argentina and Paraguay with Jacquie. Jacquie had first choice of the destination, but it is surely no accident that the couple followed in the footsteps of Lawrence and his second wife Eve, who in 1947 had been sent by the British Council to Argentina. Jacquie's practical contributions to the second South American enterprise were critical, as they were in Africa. If primitive conditions in Guyana had taxed Gerald and his friends, conditions during the Durrells' six-month stay farther south in 1954 ranged from the primitive and even dangerous—when they were almost entirely isolated from communication with the outside world by an unexpected revolution in Paraguay—to the sumptuous, with every gradation in between. Gerald wrote about the trip in *The Drunken Forest* (1956). Already, Gerald noticed evidence of looming extinctions. One imminent loss was apparently the viscacha, a striking little rodent with "charming" habits, who lives, like the prairie dog, in colonies of around forty. Not one could he find during this six-month stay. "The farmers went to war, and the viscacha has been harried and slaughtered and driven away from most of his old haunts."[19]

After the middle of the nineteenth century, British financiers and merchants established a lucrative trade infrastructure in South America which was both extractive and developmental. As Britain's economic hold on Argentina began to fade, the British Council, founded in 1934, sent ambassadors like Lawrence to strengthen Britain's cultural hegemony. The mission was "to create in a country overseas a basis of friendly knowledge and understanding of the people of this country, of their philosophy and way of life, which will lead to a sympathetic appreciation of British foreign policy, whatever for the moment that policy may be and from whatever political conviction it may spring."[20] Lawrence and Eve began and ended the sojourn in Córdoba with time spent in Buenos Aires.

"The history of Buenos Aires is written in its telephone directory," Bruce Chatwin remarks in his famous account of Argentina, *In Patagonia*. "Pompey Romanov, Emilio Rommel, Crespina D. Z. de Rose, Ladislao Radziwil, and Elizabeta Marta Callman de Rothschild—five names taken at random from among the R's—tell a story of exile, disillusion and anxiety behind lace curtains."[21] As the lace curtains suggest, this polyglot assemblage of surnames also indicates, for some, privilege within international colonial and postcolonial commerce.

Through the Argentine writer Enrique Revol, the Lawrence Durrells met Monono and Bebita Ferreyra, a wealthy and generous couple. Equally fluent in Spanish and English, the Ferreyras belonged to a cosmopolitan elite which included Theo. Monono and Bebita entertained Lawrence and Eve in the city and on their ranch, where Lawrence rediscovered his childhood excitement about horseback riding. Monono helped Eve negotiate financial paperwork and facilitated introductions to other illuminati, including the writer and diplomat Edouardo Mallea, composer William Walton, and Jorge Luis Borges. Lawrence's ultimate posting, though, was Córdoba, over four hundred miles west of Buenos Aires, where he delivered a series of lectures about English poetry. In his memoir of Lawrence, published in a special 1987 Durrell issue of *Twentieth Century Literature*, Monono recalled him as so bored with the conservative high society types at a party that he took "his shoes off and improvise[d] a toe dance. It was a good party."[22]

Although Córdoba had much to recommend it, including the first university established in Argentina, and although the lectures were well received, Lawrence and Eve disliked the climate of the country, including Buenos Aires, as well as the architecture. "Sorry!" wrote Monono. "Many people think of Buenos Aires as a damn beautiful town."[23] (The "many" included Gerald, who, in *The Whispering Land*, describes the "tall and elegant buildings" of the city, which "seemed to gleam like icebergs in the sun" along broad avenues lined with jacaranda trees.[24]) But Lawrence had the family genius for friendship, as well as insatiable curiosity. While visiting the Ferreyras, he was also writing an essay on Freud's contemporary Georg Groddeck. Monono credited Lawrence with introducing him to a body of psychological inquiry which helped him cope with tuberculosis: "I have always held Larry responsible for saving my life!"[25]

In addition to waves of settlers from the British Isles, "British capital investment" between 1880 and the First World War "was one of two basic factors, the other being immigration from southern Europe, which led to Argentina's swift transformation from an unknown primitive appendage to the world periphery into one of its foremost producers and exporters of agricultural and pastoral products."[26] And though Great Britain began to loosen its grip on the economy during the great depression and the Second World War, it remained an important trading partner until the time of Lawrence's Durrell's posting in Córdoba and Gerald's collecting expeditions. The British continued to import produce (mainly beef, sugar, and grain) in exchange for manufactured goods.[27] As he wrote about these expeditions, Gerald began to see the effects of this commercial exchange.

Although Gerald did not consider his venture in Argentina as diplomatic, the time he spent there among the power elite was a turning point in his understanding of the damage done by economic development to South American environments and local, traditional ways of knowing. Most obviously, he realized that when zoos took animals from the wild (or, worse still, when animal populations were deliberately destroyed for some perceived benefit to commercial ranching and farming) these practices contributed to population depletion. However, the parallels between extractive industries such as sugar plantations and *ingenios* (on-site factories) and the destruction of animals in those same locations remained elusive for him until his interests shifted toward the Indian Ocean years later, when he was able to work out the processes of island biogeography.

In 1953, Gerald had even more reasons to plan a collecting venture to Argentina than he had when venturing into British Guiana. In Argentina he again followed routes laid down before him by explorers, merchants, imperialists, and, this time, his cosmopolitan older brother, although Lawrence is not mentioned in Gerald's tales. Larry had come back with tales of a bad climate and bad architecture, but the prospect of physical discomfort would have made no impression on Gerald.

The appeal of the country was obvious. In his role as the naturalist on a ship exploring the commercial potential of South America, Darwin had found the country fascinating. In addition to finding animals, Gerald's goal was to trace Darwin's travels as much as possible through Patagonia, and Jacquie caught his enthusiasm. Larry had bequeathed him ready-made friends. The British diplomatic infrastructure would be helpful.

It would be only a slight exaggeration to say that the entire British establishment and international community seem to have been involved in organizing the Durrells' expedition. In *Beasts in My Bed*, Jacquie noted that, to her own confusion, their mission was considered "official," and they were expected to attend official functions.[28] Gibbs, from the British Embassy, arrived as they disembarked to smooth the way with customs. Bebita Ferreyra enlisted friends to lodge them, feed them, care for the animals they collected, and escort them on excursions to the south and east of the city. The first of these shorter trips, to Los Ingleses, the *estancia* belonging to the Boote family, yielded bird specimens for the London Zoo—guira cuckoos, oven birds, and great screamers, large flocking birds persecuted by Argentinian farmers for destroying field crops. From a neighboring *estancia*, the Durrells added a pair of hairy armadillos.

As it turned out, air travel to Patagonia turned out to be impossible within the time they had allotted for the venture because the available flights were already booked, so the Durrells quickly changed plans, traveling to Paraguay instead, exploring not one country, but two. Another friend of Bebita, Rafael De Soto Acebal, agreed to accompany the Durrells as a translator there for two months. The adventures Gerald describes in *The Drunken Forest* (*palos borrachos*, or "drunken branches," in English, the silk floss tree) far exceeded anything they expected.

They flew to Asunción, the capital of Paraguay, with the understanding that a British rancher in the country would lend his private plane for some of their travel within its borders. The La Plata and Uruguay Rivers suggested a good route back again to Argentina after collecting animals in Paraguay. Their base in this central part of the country was a village oddly named Casado, "married," and their plump, vociferous, housekeeper was the local madame. Since she knew everyone in town, Paula turned out to be a powerful ally in their collecting operations, which eventually yielded a faun and many reptiles, amphibians, birds, and armadillos. Some became characters rather than just specimens—a douracouli monkey, a crab-eating raccoon, and Sarah Huggersack, an affectionate anteater.[29]

These animal characters are more individualized and fully developed than most of the humans Gerald encountered in Paraguay. The sojourn in that country was abbreviated when an unpredicted revolution trapped the party until their one lucky chance was provided by an American with a small plane. With the Durrells, back to Buenos Aires, came the crab-eating raccoon and Sarah Huggersack, whose public appearances later in

England made her famous. But few of the animals could be evacuated. Gerald's account of leaving them is heartbreaking: days went by before the ones left behind consented to leave their cages and the cottage where the party stayed. The whole expedition was marked by fits, starts, stops, and changes of plan.

This time back in Argentine, they traveled almost to Patagonia, but not quite. (The Patagonian adventure would have to wait four years more.) Bebita stepped in again to arrange the Durrells' final weeks on the continent, another spontaneous plan to fill in for the collapse of the expedition to Paraguay. Gerald and Jacquie had two weeks to travel by train to the village of Monasterio, some forty miles from the city, where Rafael's brother Carlos collected them for the short trip to Secunda, the De Soto family's *estancia*.

Even in 1953, rhea flocks were already scarce in Argentina, but the De Soto family's estate had been hospitable to these birds. There, Gerald was able to film a spectacular rhea hunt across the pampa by the gauchos, who brought the birds down with traditional *boleadoras* before releasing them. The pampa teemed with birds early in the morning. Most of the party ventured out on horseback, with a cart to carry the filming equipment through a purple mist of thistle. First the gauchos identified a female with chicks but did not pursue her (only the male rhea incubates and cares for the young, so they probably saw a male). The hunt began when some of the horsemen spotted rheas over a mile away, but still visible across the plain, and began chasing them toward Gerald and the rest of the party, with their film equipment. The birds ran so fast that Gerald barely had time to set up the camera in its cart, and the birds were apparently so terrified that they nearly collided with it. The boleadora jumped out from the horseman's arm, encircling the rhea's neck and legs so that it fell, in a flurry of wings and kicking feet, with lethal claws. Although Gerald reports that the bird ran away unscathed when it was freed from the ropes, historic footage of these South American hunts is violent and difficult to watch.

This last adventure before the Durrells had to leave the country ended with a nostalgic note, which is becoming familiar in Durrell's travel books. Plovers call in the distance: "I could hear the voice of the pampa, the shrill warning to all living creatures that lived there . . . 'Tero . . . tero . . . tero . . . teroterotero . . .'"[30]

Like his awkward letter to the Fon at the beginning of *A Zoo in My Luggage*, published a few years later, Gerald's acknowledgments note not only the generous help of the Ferreyras, but the possible offense he has given to Bebita. Beautiful, generous, and capable, she spoke beautifully but with a decided lisp, which crept into every utterance Gerald recorded in his story. "I have repaid her very uncharitably by portraying her in the foregoing pages."[31] Although the Ferreyras' nicknames might have inspired Gerald's less than generous characterizations ("Mono," meaning "monkey," sounds a bit like Monono's name, and "Bebita" means "little baby"), the Durrell family vices of caricature and idiolects apparently remained irresistible. The pattern continued in the next South American adventure story, *The Whispering Land*, in which Gerald devotes an entire episode to his frivolous, feminine, and very obese seatmate en route to the province of Jujuy.

Nevertheless, the 1961 narrative of Gerald's long-awaited journey in 1958 to Patagonia and the far western tropical and mountainous paradise of Jujuy is one of Durrell's kindest and most genial stories. In contrast to the earlier story about Argentina and Paraguay, which races from one spicy episode to the next, *The Whispering Land* is meditative, leisurely, and lyrical. The narrative arcs are longer, both animal and human characters are developed over time, and for the most part, the human characters are treated with sensitivity and tact. This story is altogether more intimate and more mature than Gerald's previous books. *The Whispering Land* marks a turning point in his perception, or at least his account, of diminishing animal populations in parts of the world which had previously been sparsely settled. In this volume, he also begins to suggest conservation strategies.

As before, the story begins in Buenos Aires, where friends and officials generously came once again to the Durrells' aid, extracting from customs their caging materials (though, inexplicably, their technical equipment was more easily released), "entertaining us lavishly and acting as drivers, translators, guides, carpenters and cooks, on our behalf."[32] Still others housed the constantly increasing number of animals, with some inconvenience to themselves.

The goal, expressed eloquently in Gerald's headnote, taken from Darwin's *Voyage of the Beagle*, would be to follow Darwin's geographical route as closely as possible along the coast and into the interior, as well.

In calling up images of the past, I find the plains of Patagonia frequently pass across my eyes; yet these plains are pronounced by all to be wretched and useless. They can be described only by negative characters; without habitation, without water, without trees, without mountains, they support merely a few dwarf plants. Why, then, and the case is not peculiar to myself, have those arid wastes taken so firm a hold on my memory?

Carmen de Patagones, "where Darwin had stayed for some time" was the first stop on the way to Puerto Deseado, which "resembled the set for a rather bad Hollywood cowboy film."[33] Arrangements there and in the surrounding area were easier than might have been expected: the town was home to a substantial community of British expatriates and their descendants.[34]

But an area near Puerto Deseado, the site where a million penguins gathered each year in November to breed and raise their young, suggested possibilities for filming. With the help of a local resident, Captain Giri, who directed them to the *estancia* of his friend Señor Huichi, Gerald, Jacquie, and two friends from Buenos Aires located and filmed the colony for three weeks. Huichi's hospitality included a magnificent traditional *asado*—a party with gallons of red wine and an entire beef barbecued for hours in an open pit—and extended to taking the wheel of the Land Rover as it lurched across a forbidding landscape, the home of giant tortoises, armadillos, and Patagonian hares, as well as the penguins.

Unlike larger and more southerly species, these Magellanic penguins dig burrows into grassy tussocks and stand guard at the entrance. The

FIGURE 4.1 Magellanic penguin.

adults bray at one another (and other intruders) from time to time and keep up a constant stream of traffic back and forth between their burrows and the sea, where they forage far and wide before returning to share parental duties—as do other penguin species (in contrast to the rheas). For several days, Gerald filmed adults as they commuted, up and down dunes and tussocks, noting that they often had to stop and rest. Penguins have no pronounced fear of humans, but the two families he watched closely became so accustomed to his presence that they allowed him to come even closer to their burrows than most of the others.

After Gerald's team intimately observed two penguin families and filmed the whole colony for two weeks, Huichi joined them for a meditative rest and a search for artifacts left by the Patagonian Indians. Huichi himself, whose ancestry probably included the Tehuelches, kept a collection of these artifacts, superior to any Gerald had ever seen pictured in a museum:

Each piece was a work of art, beautifully shaped, carefully and minutely chipped, edged and polished, constructed out of the most beautiful stone the maker could find. You could see they had been made with love. And these, I reminded myself, were made by the barbarous, uncouth, savage and utterly uncivilized Indians for whose passing no one appeared to be sorry.[35]

Gerald had read his Darwin, perhaps including *The Voyage of the Beagle.* In this travel narrative Darwin described the settlers' horrifying tactics against the Indians of this area (including femicide) and protested to one of the perpetrators. "What can be done?" the man responded. "They breed so!"[36] During the eight months he spent in Patagonia and the far western provinces of Argentina, Gerald was learning to grapple with his own place within the global webs of knowledge, extraction, privilege and power. Like so many other details in Durrell's work, the awe he experienced in considering Señor Huichi's collection is self-enclosed, emotionally but not narratively connected to the rest of the book. In Gerald's books, explicit connections between environmental destruction and these webs of knowledge would come later.

The Deseado episode ends with a spell of meditative quiet as the party bade farewell to the penguins, looked out over the sea, and looked to the sand at their feet for arrowheads. Gerald found a beautifully preserved skull, which he buried once more in the sand instead of following his first impulse—to take it back to England. Huichi found artifacts as if by magic, but Gerald himself found a bone knife, carved more for beauty than utility, and a rare harpoon head made of seal bone, which he gave to his host the next day. "It broke my heart to part with it, but he had done so much for us that it seemed very small return for his kindness."[37] The familiar nostalgic note creeps into the tale, and, with it, the suggestion of greater understanding for indigenous peoples who occupy the lands of Durrell's beloved animals.

Filming rather than collection was also the purpose of the party's trek northward again, where they searched for breeding colonies of fur seals and elephant seals. Peninsula Valdes, which juts out into the Atlantic south of Punta Colorada, is almost an island. Its rich wildlife includes "a wonderful cross-section of the Patagonian fauna"—armadillos, Patagonian foxes, Darwin's rheas, flocks of large birds known as "martinetas," and small herds of guanaco.

At one time, foxes were shot there as predators of small domestic animals, and guanaco because ranchers believed they competed with sheep for grazing. Still, it seemed to Gerald that on the peninsula, there was a greater chance of controlling landowners' predatory practices and winning them over to the concept of conservation. Again, this passage, in Chapter 4 of *The Whispering Land*, is an expression of an idea that becomes integrated into the author's life work, if not in this particular narrative:

> It was almost as if the peninsula and its narrow isthmus into which all the wildlife of was a *cul-de-sac* into which all the wildlife of Chubut had drained ... I wish that it were possible for the Argentine Government to make the whole peninsula into a sanctuary, for which it seems to have been designed by nature.[38]

Provincial protection of the area indeed began two years after Gerald's visit. Much later, in 1999, the idea became reality, and the peninsula is now both a wildlife refuge and a UNESCO World Heritage site. According to UNESCO's online description of the area, it is the most important breeding ground for the Southern Right Whale and offers protection for both elephant seals and sea lions on their way to Antarctica. Beach refuges for seals and sea lions at the base of steep cliffs are inaccessible to land predators, but on display here are unique feeding behaviors of the orcas of the south Atlantic. During breeding seasons of the pinnipeds, orcas patrol the shores. Hurling their bodies onto the shingle beach, the orcas snatch pups, wring their necks, and shuffle their own huge bodies back toward the water until they are again safely afloat. Life for all these creatures is lived on the edge, but the refuge now protects them from human predation and carelessness.[39]

In 1958, the main business for Gerald and his team was observing the seal colonies. The party filmed fur seals while they camped, with scant creature comfort, inside and under the Land Rover. Durrell was charmed by these animals—beautiful, sexually dimorphic in the extreme, and playful. As an added bonus, he was awakened one morning by the rustling sound of two foxes playing with a roll of bright pink toilet paper:

> they danced and whirled on their slender legs, hurling the toilet roll to and fro, occasionally taking streamers of it in their mouths and leaping daintily into the air ... their agile bodies were well set off against the green sky, the yellow-flowered bushes and the pink paper. The whole camp was taking on a carnival air.[40]

Following the practice established at the penguin colony, the crew filmed the entire seal colony at times, but chose a focal group (a bull and his "wives") and a pup they called Oswald. Over the two-week course of filming, they observed elaborate mating games, battles between the bulls, and Oswald's mischievous antics—typical of almost all young animals and many of Gerald's favorite creatures through the years. When not battling for female attention, the bulls sometimes tossed frantic pups into the water repeatedly, apparently to make them strong swimmers. It would be an adaptive behavior. Under watchful parental eyes, they were certainly being toughened up for a life of evading fierce predators in the ocean around them.

The elephant seal colony turned out to be more elusive. It was late in the breeding season, and further south, Huichi had steered them only as far as the fur seals. To make matters more difficult, the elephant seals were strangely camouflaged by their lassitude and their resemblance to boulders on the beach, enhanced by the habit of flipping sand onto their backs, much as elephants scatter dust, for sun protection. Their eyes are huge and beautiful. Only when someone on the team popped a cork for consolation did one of these creatures open a liquid eye, revealing its identity.[41] In his surprise, Gerald became pedantic, indulging in a lecture on seal behavior which might well have been boring to his companions watching these very creatures: "Did you know that the intestine of an adult bull can reach six hundred and sixty-two feet?"[42] Still, his lecture becomes an interesting thread for readers interested in the book's natural history.

The climax of the episode came when, hoping for movement they could film, Gerald threw pebbles at an old bull until, who in desperation reared his upper body into the air before taking to the sea, as "great black tears ooze" from his eyes.[43] In a panic, the rest of the colony followed. In the coming years, Durrell no doubt learned that disturbing wildlife can be potentially harmful as the animals' energy budget is stretched in self-defense.

The Whispering Land has two equal parts. The first narrates Gerald's travels in Patagonia, where Señor Huichi stands as an emotional center, even though the episode in which he figures is relatively short. After the Patagonian adventure, Jacquie and other members of the team returned to Buenos Aires. The second part of the adventure takes place in Jujuy, a lumber and sugar-producing area in the far northwest, between the Andes and the jungle, cornered by Chile, Bolivia, and the Argentine province of Salta. The Andes rise sharply along the western and northern border of the province. The population is largely Quechuan, and the landscapes are varied and beautiful.

Calilegua, Gerald's base in the province, was "primarily a sugar-producing estate," where tropical fruits were also grown for the Buenos Aires market:

> It was a flat plain that lay in a half-moon of mountains that were covered with thick, tropical forest. It was curious how suddenly you came upon this lushness ... We left the airport and ... drove through a desiccated landscape of semi-arid hills, sun-baked, scrub-covered, dotted here and there with the great swollen trunks of the *palo borracho* trees ... and here and there you saw one of the giant cacti rearing up. Then we sped round a couple of corners, down a hill, and into the valley of Calilegua, and the vegetation changed, so suddenly that it was almost painful to the eye. Here were the vivid greens of the tropics, so many shades, and some of such viridescence that they make the green of the English landscape look grey in comparison. Then, as if to assure me that I was back in the tropics, a small flock of parakeets swooped across the road. ...

Small groups of Indians appeared on the streets, and "After being among Europeans so long ... the Indians, the parakeets, and the vividness of the country ... went to my head like wine."[44]

The emotional center of Part II is a local peasant, like Huichi, of uncertain ethnicity. If Huichi is thematically and otherwise tied to the Indians driven to extinction by the deliberate policy of European settlers, Coco is tied both to the birds he studies so passionately and the indigenous human populations under stress.

Typically, Jujuy's economy within the vast sugar commercial networks developed in the eighteenth and nineteenth centuries was built on the exploitation of cheap labor. Here, atypically, new railways made possible the development of the *ingenios* for sugar production, vast plantations which included factories, with a built-in labor supply. These plantations and factories occupied land the Indians had formerly worked as herders and small farmers. After a failed rebellion in 1874–75, the former occupants of the land were forced for the first time to pay rents.[45]

> This system worked like this. In the *latifundos* [land grants, originally made by royal charter, roughly the size of a typical county in the United States] which had been rented by the   *ingenios*,   the Indian *arrenderos* [share-croppers] became the *ingenios'* sub-tenants . . . the Indians' rental payments were transformed from payments in money or goods into payments in labour . . . working for six months as cane cutters in the *zafra*.[46]

Instead of producing their own livelihoods on land they owned, they also now bought at exorbitant prices from company stores, to which they were perpetually in debt.

In 1946, with Juan Peron's rise to power, the system began to deteriorate, and by the time Gerald traveled in the area, labor in the *zafra*, or harvest, was supplied largely by Bolivian seasonal migrant workers, and local people who had no other recourse labored in the factories for very low wages. If the Peronistas had made a difference in the sources of labor, they brought about little improvement in the standard of living for ordinary people in the sugar regions of Jujuy or, indeed, in the lives of imported laborers. So, by 1958, when Gerald visited Jujuy, the *ingenio* system was largely still in place, although labor was technically not forced.

Within a short time, Gerald bought owl monkeys, collared peccaries, owls, coatis, Brazilian rabbits, and macaws, including a rare Tucuman macaw whose conversation was enlivened by calling everyone "*Hijo de puta*." (The owner felt this speaking talent merited a higher price until Gerald's assistant pointed out the obvious—that *what* the parrot said rather diminished his value.) Gerald continued to add birds to the collection and had good luck locating members of the cat family. A rare, spectacularly beautiful Geoffrey's cat, or *gato montes*, soon appeared at Gerald's door, carefully transported in a straw hat. By his estimate the kitten was barely two weeks old, but already too fierce to handle until he found a domesticated tabby kitten to keep and feed with the Geoffrey's kitten.

Early in Gerald's Calilegua stay, he found a pleasant, competent helper attached to the *estancia* of his hosts; Luna had contacts for animal purchases in neighboring villages, and his deep knowledge of folk music made life more joyful for everyone involved in the expedition. Luna never appeared without his guitar, and when not talking, he was usually singing. In Oran, Luna's home village, where every backyard, no matter how poor the owner, "was neat and full of flowers," Gerald bought a beautiful, healthy puma from the owner of a roadside zoo.

He made another cat purchase from the backyard of a man "with beady eyes that were alternately cringing or cunning."[47] For the first time in Gerald's published work, he allowed his rage to burst through the comic surface of his prose: this backyard was filled with weeds, junk, and a tiny cage into which a half-grown ocelot had been crammed. When the owner "hauled" her out, Luna and Gerald could see that she was filthy, injured, and malnourished. When Luna translated Gerald's bargain and his comments on the man's character as a "bloated illegitimate son of an inadequate whore" (somewhat softened in translation), the owner "giggled feebly," and the cat changed hands. Perhaps the macaw's *palabrones* opened the door for Gerald to introduce profanities of his own.

The daily lives of all these cats are woven into the narrative fabric throughout the rest of the book. The puma throve, and the Geoffrey's kitten started to eat when it saw the tabby kitten doing so. Soon, the two young cats were playing games, and they slept in one another's arms all the way back to England. Despite Gerald's fears, a sawdust bath, penicillin shot, and gradually increased diet restored the young ocelot to health.

The emotional energy of these animal stories sweeps into an echo chamber near the end of the Jujuy section of *The Whispering Land*. Days before leaving Jujuy and Argentina, Luna heard about a man named Coco in a village near Calilegua; his neighbors called him *loco*, because of his love for animals and devotion to pets. Gerald's encounter with Coco serves as a climax to *The Whispering Land*. Despite the fact that this village was economically depressed, this poor man spoke good English, lived in a small house with a spotless garden, and kept a tiny, well-organized study.

In order to put food on the table, Coco worked at the local sawmill, which was indirectly related to the sugar industry. A 1928 study of agricultural regions in the country by Clarence Jones noted that in this region "Each sugar estate is a large clearing in the forest.... The harvest labor consists largely of Chaco Indians; some 6,000 temporary immigrants arrive each year between March and June; occasionally whole tribes migrate."[48] And more recently, Larry Sawers has argued that profits gained in ranching, logging, and export-crop production produce deforestation:

> This deforestation forces the poor into compensatory efforts to expand production on marginal land, intensify existing production, or diversify into cash crops. All of these reactions place further pressure on the environment, further reduce the incomes of the poor, and reinforce the downward spiral of poverty and environmental destruction. Thus the wealthy degrade the environment directly but also indirectly by worsening the plight of the poor.[49]

This was the economic and environmental context in which Coco worked, in an occupation that exploited his labor, while compromising the lives of the wild creatures he loved, to care financially for a family. When Gerald asked Coco (one wonders why) how he liked the sawmill work, Coco responded, "Like it? . . . *like it?* Señor, it is soul-destroying."[50]

Under these circumstances, Coco studied, cataloged, and painted the birds of the region, which he felt were unknown and ignored, even in Argentina. "Here was work that was almost up to the standards of some of the best modern bird painters," Gerald writes. "It was done with meticulous accuracy and love, and the bird glowed on the page." And with sensitivity unequaled in any of his earlier writing, he continues,

> Here was a man—a peasant, if you prefer the term—who worked in a saw-mill and lived in a house which, though spotless, no so-called 'worker' in England would be seen dead in . . . to find him here in this remote, unlikely spot, was like suddenly coming across a unicorn in the middle of Picadilly.[51]

However much he wished it, Gerald understood that offering Coco money for the paints he needed or the ciné-camera he so much desired would be deeply insulting.

All Gerald could give was some aid in placing Coco's paintings. All he was able to do later was send some natural history volumes from his own library which he thought Coco might like. Unlike Darwin—or, for that matter, Hugh Lofting's Dr. Dolittle, who took his friend Long Arrow's records back to England—Gerald does not mine Coco's knowledge or his lovely paintings to suit his own needs,[52] just as he recognizes that artifacts of the Indians driven to extinction or assimilation in Argentina belong there, with their descendants.

This episode suggests maturity. In the books Gerald wrote about his earliest African adventures, the style is untethered, African stereotypes abound and are potentially damaging, and his perspective is privileged by race and alliance with the British Empire. Surely in Africa he met individuals who shared his interest in animals, but he did not often distinguish them from other local people. In contrast, the books about South America, written a few years later, reveal a new sensitivity toward local people, especially Señor Huichi and Coco, who shared his love of animals.

Gerald could never quite forgive the damage done to wildlife or habitat by desperately poor people, and he would never relinquish the broad humor, exaggeration, or jokes at the expense of his companions of all races, genders, and ethnicities. Nevertheless, this human turn in perspective in *The Whispering Land* would become indispensable as his work evolved from collection to protection.

In the conclusion of the book, Coco's trusting hospitality is echoed and doubled by the unselfish efforts of Gerald's hosts in Jujuy, Charles and Joan Lett; his most energetic helpers, Luna and the Vorbach family; and even strangers on the train back east, as they worked tirelessly to help him, unaccompanied this time, transport his treasured creatures back to Buenos Aires, and, from there, back across the Atlantic to the Isle of Jersey and the new zoo.

Notes

1 G. Durrell, *My Family and Other Animals*, 59–60.

2 G. Durrell, *Three Tickets to Adventure* (New York: Berkley Publishing Company, 1964), 11. [Published in the UK as *Three Singles to Adventure*. For the sake of accurate documentation, I consistently use the titles available to me.]

3 Botting, *Gerald Durrell*, 206-07.

4 Robert Schomburgk. *A Description of British Guiana, Geographical and Statistical* (Reprint of 1840 ed) (London: Frank Cass & Co., 1970), 48.

5 G. Durrell, *The Whispering Land*, 194.

6 In *The Touch of Durrell: A Passion for Animals*, "Foreword" by Lee Durrell (Sussex: Book Guild Publishing, 2009), 237–38, Jeremy Mallinson quotes this passage from Botting's Amazon diary of October 27, 1965, when Gerald was already an experienced traveler in the region: "The most interesting encounter was the first thing at the hotel with a young Englishman who is wandering through the Amazon region alone on a recce mission on behalf of a cause known as animal conservation. Nice, bright, committed chap. I hope he'll survive the trip—but I don't suppose he will." (The date given for Botting's diary entry is probably incorrect: Gerald had already published three books about South America by 1961, the description certainly more likely applied to Gerald on his first journey to Guyana in 1950.)

7 Schomburgk, *Description*, 29.

8 Ibid., 4.

9 G. Durrell, *Three Tickets*, 54.

10 Qtd. *Three Tickets*, 60.

11 Ibid., 61.

12 Ibid., 46–47.

13 Ibid., 42–52.

14 Schomburgk, *Description*, 42–52.

15 G. Durrell, *Three Tickets*, 39.

16 Ibid., 48.

17 Ibid., 71.

18 Ibid., 125.

19 G. Durrell, *The Drunken Forest* (New York: Berley Publishing Corporation, 1964), 41.

20 British Council, "Our History," https://www.csiro.au/en/About/History-achievements/Our-history [accessed October 14, 2020].

21 Bruce Chatwin, *In Patagonia*, "Introduction", Nicholas Shakespeare (New York: Penguin, 2003), 4.

22 Monono Ferreyra, "Durrell in Cordoba: Jorge Ferreyra Remembers," *Twentieth Century Literature*, 33, no. 3 (1987), 330.

23 Ferreyra, "Durrell in Cordoba," 329–30.

24 G. Durrell, The *Whispering Land*, 15.

25 Ferreyra, "Durrell in Cordoba," 330.

26 David Rock, ed., "Introduction," *Argentina in the Twentieth Century* (Pittsburg, PA: University of Pittsburgh Press, 1975), 2.

27 See Ian Rutledge, "Plantations and Peasants in Northern Argentina: The Sugar Cane Industry of Salta and Jujuy," *Argentina in the Twentieth Century*, ed, David Rock, 88–113. See also Colin Lewis, "Anglo-Argentine Trade, 1945-1965," *Argentina in the Twentieth Century*, 114–34.

28 J. Durrell, *Beasts in My Bed* (London: Fontana Books, 1967), 44.

29 G. Durrell, *The Whispering Land*, 82.

30 G. Durrell, *The Drunken Forest*, 194.

31 Ibid., 205.

32 G. Durrell, *The Whispering Land*, 215.

33 Ibid., 29, 34.

34 J. Durrell, *Beasts in My Bed*, 119.

35 G. Durrell, *The Whispering Land*, 58.

36 Charles Darwin, *The Voyage of the Beagle* (New York: Barnes & Noble Books, 2004), 105.

37 G. Durrell, *The Whispering Land*, 62–63.

38 Ibid., 87.

39 For descriptions of the Valdes Peninsula and orca predation behaviors, see the title essay in Diane Ackerman's *The Moon by Whale Light* (New York: Vintage, 1992). See also "Peninsula Valdes," "Peninsula Valdes." https://whc.unesco.org/en/list/937/ [accessed July 18, 2023].

40 G. Durrell, *The Whispering Land*, 89–90.

41 Ibid., 96.

42 Ibid., 98.

43 Ibid., 100.

44 Ibid., 113–14.

45 Rutledge, *Plantations and Peasants*, 94.

46 Ibid., 99.

47 G. Durrell, *The Whispering Land*, 148.

48 Clarence F. Jones, "Agricultural Regions of South America. Instalment II." *Economic Geography*, 4 no. 2 (1928), 175). https://www.jstor.org/stable/14027 [accessed: August 22, 2018].

49 Larry Sawers, "Income Distribution and Environmental Degradation in the Argentine Interior." *Latin American Research Review*. 35, no. 2 (2000), 6.

50 G. Durrell, *The Whispering Land*, 194.

51 Ibid., 194–95.

52 Hugh Lofting, *The Voyages of Dr. Dolittle* (New York: Frederick A. Stokes Co., 1922).

5 ISLOMANIA

There are two kinds of islands: continental and oceanic. As the word suggests, oceanic islands rise from the ocean floor, most of the time as a result of volcanic activity. The Galapagos Islands are an archipelago consisting of twenty-one such islands, in addition to reefs, atolls, and seamounts—volcanoes that don't quite reach the surface. These islands lie on the eastern edge of the Pacific Ring of Fire, a volcanic zone along the seams between several of earth's tectonic plates. Such small, relatively new oceanic islands can give rise to tiny populations of bizarre creatures, adapted for the peculiar climatic and geological areas they inhabit, and to each other. In *The Amateur Naturalist*, a field guide for children, Gerald includes pictures of four finch varieties Darwin found there, with dramatically different beaks for different diets, but Darwin's finches are only the best known of innumerable possible examples.[1] The small islands Gerald explored in the 1970s and 1980s, Mauritius and the Mascarenes, are dispersed along the western boundary of the ring of fire.

Continental islands, such as Corfu and the Isle of Jersey, where Gerald established his zoo in 1959, were once part of the same land mass as nearby continents. Their plants and animals are similar to or indistinguishable from those on nearby mainlands, but if a continental island is separated long enough from adjoining land masses, its life forms will also diverge into new forms.

As Gerald came to understand during his childhood in Corfu, there are also islands within islands. In *Prospero's Cell*, Lawrence describes geographical differences between the mountainous "bare northern reaches" of Corfu and the "southern valleys, painted out boldly in heavy brush-strokes of yellow and red."[2] Not only do the two regions offer distinct micro-climates, Lawrence found cultural distinctions, as well. The peasants of the northern region dressed in blue and black. In the south, their clothing was vivid and multicolored. In the south, the paddy fields left from old

Venetian days added more varied foodstuffs to the tree crops found everywhere on the island—olive, fig, citrus, and pine. Sheep were—and still are—everywhere on Corfu. Every garden has a citrus tree or two, and almost everyone has olives, which are harvested after the fruits ripen and fall to the ground. This method is unique to Corfu, and, as any taxi driver will tell you, the green house shutters are unique in Greece, as well—an architectural theme also left from the days of the Venetian occupation.

Most continental islands, including Corfu and Jersey, have been separated from the continent by sea level rise. In contrast, Australia and New Zealand, Gerald's destinations after his last South American venture, became islands as the tectonic plates of a giant land mass that geologists call Gondwanaland (one of four supercontinents) drifted apart, so many millions of years ago that their fauna and flora are quite different from the biotic suites on other continents.

There are, of course, degrees of insularity. The northern and southern regions of Corfu are different, but not extremely isolated from one another. In contrast, when Gerald visited New Zealand, Australia, and Malaysia in 1962, even his insatiable reading had not prepared him for the strangeness and vulnerability of the animals and plants he met there, especially in New Zealand and Australia, so different from the creatures he had met in Europe, Africa, and South America. "Islands are havens and breeding grounds for the unique and anomalous. They are natural laboratories for extravagant evolutionary experimentation," writes David Quammen in his long, lyrical narrative account, *The Song of the Dodo: Island Biogeography*.[3]

The journey alerted Gerald to two important things. The first concerned evolution, the evidence of which he saw first-hand, the way Darwin saw it in the Galapagos. Gerald's own ecological theory began to coalesce along the same lines as those of official academic science. Second, witnessing the careless destruction of all these unique creatures, Gerald was struck with volcanic force by the reality of anthropocentric greed and ignorance. Here, he preaches the gospel of environmentalism in the "Summing Up" chapter of *Two in the Bush*:

The attitude of the average person to the world he lives in is completely selfish. When I take people around to see my animals, one of the first questions they ask (unless the animal is cute and cuddly) is 'What use is it?' . . . Does a creature have to be of direct material use to mankind in order to exist? By and large, by asking the question 'What use is it?'

you are asking the animal to justify its existence without having justified your own.[4]

Like his acquaintance with Coco in Jujuy, Gerald's first-hand observations of the challenges faced by island species, habitats, and conservationists who cared about them was a decisive point in his own evolution. Deeper understanding created a sense of urgency.

From childhood, Gerald had participated in an ecology of knowledge. His understanding of natural selection and speciation came from his own lived experiences, of course, but also from studying. He grasped ecological relationships first by rambling around the hills, valleys, and shorelines of Corfu, as well as from reading and conversations with Theo. In *The Amateur Naturalist*, Gerald describes the small library he owned in Corfu, which contained, among other books, the works of Darwin and Fabre. Gerald's early studies also included the work of Gregor Mendel, the eighteenth-century memoir of Gilbert White, who for decades kept detailed observations of his own garden, and nineteenth-century naturalists Humboldt, Thoreau, and Wallace.[5]

Fortunately for the particular niche Gerald occupied (and still occupies) in wildlife conservation, he always had one foot in the amateur world of the Victorian naturalist and the other foot in academic, or official, science. In the 1980s, he met the elderly pioneering limnologist Evelyn Hutchinson, the very model of a naturalist, whose conversation ranged from giant tortoises to the blue blood of king crabs, to the possibility that the English poet William Blake had met some South American monkeys. Often called "the father of modern ecology," Hutchinson contributed the term "niche" to the field, as it was developing in the 1930s, to explain the positioning of floral and faunal species within ecological systems, and he trained many other well-known scientists in the field.[6] For Gerald, Hutchinson's attitude was just as important as his science: "nothing escapes Professor Hutchinson's attention or disrupts his deep interest and reverence for the world around him."[7] The ecologist Thomas Lovejoy, who wrote Hutchinson's obituary, would become Gerald's friend and a fundraiser for the Durrell organization in North America. Gerald was at home in the wide world, but sometimes it was also a small world.

Of special important for twentieth-century and twenty-first-century ecology and conservation—and for any student of islands—is the theory of island biogeography. A diagram in "An Equilibrium Theory of Insular

Zoogeography," the foundational study first published by MacArthur and Wilson in 1967, looks simple, but it describes a complicated theory of interlocking parts. The version below is simplified from the original, and the theory itself has been modified since these scientists created the original. Still, the original conception of speciation and extinction has remained generally true, and useful.

The diagram illustrates the theory that the larger the island and the closer it is to other land, the more quickly species richness increases. Likewise, the smaller the island and the farther it is located from other land, the higher the probability of extinction increases. Wilson and MacArthur proposed that islands are populated in two ways: (1) immigration of species from outside (one of their examples is the arrival of a spider, floating on strands of web carried by air currents) and (2) speciation *in situ*, or evolution of several distinct species from a common ancestor; these new species may take advantage of different niches within the ecosystem (for example, Darwin's finches). Some species will become extinct as new species arrive or evolve, but over time, they argued, an undisturbed island, or isolated area, will relax into equilibrium.[8] The terminology has evolved since the early days when Wilson and MacArthur proposed the theory (for example, the term "equilibrium" implies permanence and minimizes both inputs and stochastic events such as hurricanes). And more often these days, the field has become an important theoretical building block for "conservation biology." No matter the refinements of the basic theory, Quammen explained why the study of small populations on small islands and other isolated areas will continue to be relevant. Here is his imagined image of the last dodo as she died on her island home of Mauritius:

> In the dark of an early morning in 1667, say, during a rainstorm, she took cover beneath a cold stone ledge at the base of one of the Black River cliffs. She drew her head down against her body, fluffed her feathers for warmth, squinted in patient misery. She waited. She didn't know it, nor did anyone else, but she was the only dodo on Earth. When the storm passed, she never opened her eyes. This is extinction.[9]

The flightless dodo's plight—a result of her evolution on a small island with no predators— was the reason Gerald chose the dodo as the symbol

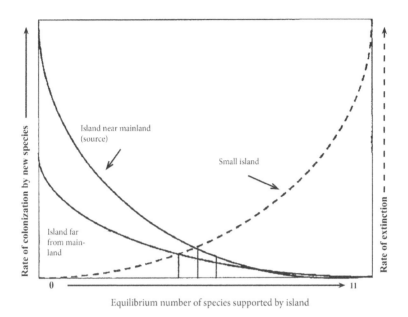

FIGURE 5.1 Wilson and MacArthur's Theory of Island Biogeography.

for his zoo and the motto of the entire Durrell project: "saving animals from extinction."

Islands aren't just bits of land surrounded by water: plants and animals in an area completely surrounded and isolated by radically different topography are functionally island species. Lovejoy, whose work in this field followed that of Wilson and MacArthur by about twenty years, persuaded ranchers clearing forest in the Amazon to leave isolated patches he could study, in one of the longest running experiments of its kind. Elaborating on the initial theory, he collected data showing that species usually disappear more quickly from small forest patches than from larger ones, as predicted by the model, all other variables being equal.[10] But Lovejoy's study also identified details about the processes contributing to the reduction of species diversity in these Amazonian patches. Drying edges of the forest patches, interruption of migrations and fragmentation of the gene pool in fragmented habitat, and the cumulative effects of both would eventually lead, he discovered, to "ecological collapse." The smaller the insular area, the more rapidly this collapse would occur—*all other variables being equal*. (It must be noted that, despite the science, despite the obvious devastation to the biosphere and the indigenous Amazonian peoples, the destruction of the Amazon has continued unabated. Many climate scientists and ecologists believe this vast region, "the lungs of the world," has already reached a tipping point.)

Although the multiplicity of variables in isolated patches have meant that island biogeography is less predictive than its original developers foresaw, the field continues to provide important models for understanding the linked processes of speciation and extinction.

Gerald discovered, not surprisingly, that as a boy, Lovejoy had read his books about Africa and South America.[11] Just as Gerald's work contributed to official knowledge by influencing scientists, official scientific knowledge strengthened Gerald's participation from the margins and fortified his position within the international wildlife conservation community. Official knowledge coincided with Gerald's thinking about extinction and speciation. He understood the world intellectually, emotionally, and viscerally: his grasp of islands and island species was even deeper after his feet touched the ground in New Zealand, Australia, and Malaysia in 1962 and Mauritius in 1976. Lovejoy and Gerald started collaborating in the 1970s to establish an arm of the Durrell trust in America; shortly thereafter, Gerald met Hutchinson and some of the scientists he trained.

By the end of the 1970s, Gerald was writing out his own theory of island biogeography in a comic novel entitled *The Mockery Bird*, published in 1981. *The Mockery Bird* describes a fantasy island rather like a relatively undisturbed Mauritius, which Gerald first visited in 1976.

Gerald's credibility and his understanding of both the probabilities of extinction and specific details about animal habitat would become essential as his conservation projects spread outward from the zoo into environmental hot spots around the world. His solutions to the difficult political climate for wildlife conservation would be intensive studies of the species involved and intensive management, at first through captive breeding in the Jersey Zoo and *in situ*, later by careful (and rare) reintroductions of captive bred animals into original or restored habitat. Whenever possible, he tried to strengthen wildlife protections in at-risk animals' native habitats so that extreme measures would not be necessary.

The rescue of the Mauritian kestrel is a case in point. In *Song of the Dodo*, Quammen notes that several wildlife funding agencies became leery of supporting Welsh population biologist Carl Jones's long-shot project to save to save a razor-thin population of these birds, but the

Durrell foundation apparently supported Jones's successful work by engaging in all these strategies.[12] By some counts, Jones had only four birds to work with, by some, seven. In any case, by the time of his project, the kestrels' range had been reduced by introduced species and agricultural cash crops (at that time dependent on the application of DDT) to a tiny area of the Black River cliffs. That much was clear. And yet Jones brought them back from the edge, in large part because of Gerald's help.

If, as Quammen suggests, Gerald was attracted by the sheer zaniness of Jones and his project, it is also apparent from Gerald's written accounts that he understood genetics in small populations that evolve in small places. On a small island, evolutionary pressures operate in a shorter time. Population bottlenecks often occur within a few generations after immigration and continue through a few generations more. In this way, non-adaptive traits can sometimes be eliminated in a species that manages to persist long enough to evolve. In the future, most of Gerald's conservation work would be devoted to such species, not only because he loved islands and felt at home on islands, but because island species were most at risk—and in some ways the most likely candidates for captive breeding. Indeed, the avian ecologist Stanley A. Temple suggests in a 1986 study that the kestrel's evolutionary history, including its rescue, may be an exemplary case of this phenomenon.[13]

In 1962, after settling the last animal shipment from Argentina into the Jersey Zoo, becoming a best-selling writer and popular public figure, and making more solid contacts with the BBC for wildlife film contracts, Gerald began to look farther afield. Commonwealth countries were a logical place to study and "collect" animals on film, just as they had been for live captures. As neo-European settler colonies with strong ties to the empire, New Zealand and Australia offered administrative clarity and more advanced conservation strategies than those he had seen in Africa and South America, although not, Gerald discovered, much understanding among the general public in those places of why conservation was necessary.

It turned out that these landscapes, especially in New Zealand, were no easier to navigate than those through which he had trekked in his earlier travels. Many of the animals were even harder to find here than in Africa and South America because of pressures on populations that were rare to begin with, and because specialized adaptations for unique and confined habitats confined some of these animals to islands within islands.

In New Zealand, Gerald saw extinction in progress. New Zealand separated from Australia around a hundred million years ago to become an archipelago of continental islands with Pacific Rim volcanic features. Until he visited the country in 1962, Gerald's island experiences had been limited mostly to Corfu and Jersey. The native biotic community of New Zealand is fundamentally different: it includes descendants of ancestral species from the supercontinent Gondwanaland, as well as newer arrivals by air and water, and their descendants. All these animals and plants had settled into relatively peaceful coexistence before human arrivals—first the Moa Hunters, whose impact was definite but not devastating. Next came the Maori, around 1350 AD; they killed off most of the moas (and the Moa Hunters) and destroyed some of the forest. Finally, the Europeans arrived, a little more than three hundred years ago.[14]

The changes made by Europeans were the most profound of all. Gerald complained that the country looked too much like England to be appealing, Unfortunately, the unique and vulnerable biota that developed during the eons after New Zealand's separation from Australia and the supercontinent existed within a climatic zone so familiar to northern Europeans that they cut down native forests within a few decades, allowing accidentally introduced European weeds to flourish, along with the plants and animals the Europeans really wanted. The new settlers brought passerines, non-native black swans from Australia, several species of deer, possum, sheep, and, inadvertently, rats that devastated large areas of the country and put at risk or extinguished dozens of native species, just as surely as if the settlers had deliberately harvested them. A forested paradise with no major predators quickly became a beautiful but deadly trap for the native species that remained. The last wave of settlers also diminished the power and population of the Maori.

New Zealand and Australia

Between them, the Maori and neo-Europeans have been responsible for the extinction of almost fifty bird species (including ten species of moa), ten reptile species, and an assortment of insects, fish, mollusks, reptiles, and amphibians.[15] The landscape has been changed beyond repair. There were no mammal extinctions simply because there were no indigenous mammals to kill off.

To record and help save what was left, Gerald and Jackie came to New Zealand, Australia, and Malaysia with a BBC film crew for a television series, *Two in the Bush*. Gerald's book by the same title appeared four years later. Some of his anecdotes reflect the popularizing mission of the whole project. For comic relief, he included a story of Jacquie, instructed to stand close to a geyser just before it erupted a few seconds later and of the whole crew nearly trapped during a storm in an isolated valley. Another comic episode describes the movement of the whole crew and their equipment in a net dangling from a crane, across crashing waves onto "White Rocks," an island bird sanctuary in the Wellington region of the north island. Gerald and Jacquie met with such situations during the entire trip, but the heart of the narrative is serious. The beautiful but deadly black swans—millions of them, crowding out native waterfowl—were so spectacular that the film crew couldn't resist them, but the focus was on the tiny populations typical of island species. The film would be Gerald's first significant foray into conservation to the exclusion of collecting.

Even in 1962, Gerald found the keas (parrots), New Zealand pigeons, and tame, inquisitive wekas, significantly threatened—and hard to locate. Once found, these birds were sociable, trusting, and entertaining. On Kapiti, a small island sanctuary off the west coast of the North Island, the wekas had so little fear that they flocked to the filmmakers' equipment, pecking and peering to see what it was all about. If the animals could trust humans here, mused Gerald, the "whole world" could or should be a Kapiti. The crew also filmed the Cook Strait blue penguin and king skag. (Since the 1980s, other species, including the little spotted kiwi, the smallest of the order, have been relocated there.)[16]

Later, on a peninsula off the South Island, they filmed yellow-eyed penguins and an albatross colony, endangered by "morons" who seemed to enjoy breaking eggs and killing the parents.[17] Like many other animal species perceived as competitors by their human neighbors, these birds were persecuted by fishermen who justified killing them because of their reputation as fish eaters.

Although the Galapagos were Darwin's evolution textbook, it is now generally understood that almost any island or island group (especially volcanic islands) could have served as a foundation for evolutionary theory because any isolated plant or animal evolves into a unique form to fit its niche. White Rocks, a pair of tiny New Zealand islands, is a case in point. On White Rocks, the tuatara are numerous, but since the animal is a specialist, it is endangered to the extent that the habitat is limited and must be protected. Quammen mentions this creature in passing; Gerald gives it almost a whole chapter—"The Three-eyed Lizard." The name comes from the tuatara's "third eye," or visible forehead pineal gland, and the ridge of white points on its back made it an interesting species to film. Its phlegmatic nature made filming relatively easy. To all appearances a lizard, about two feet long and two pounds in weight, it is in fact the only survivor in an order that mostly disappeared two hundred million years ago. Tuataras are older than dinosaurs.

In the entire Durrell enterprise, as in wildlife conservation universally, the requirements of needy species must be balanced with those of charismatic animals easy to love. Since Gerald loved all animals, this balancing act seemed to come naturally. The attractive kea (one of three indigenous parrots) is "a gay and wicked clown."[18] A lizard-like creature might be harder to admire, but Gerald singled out an individual tuatara, "majestically stroll[ing] through his moonlit kingdom like a dragon. Presently he paused . . . looking at me haughtily—but the effect was spoilt, for nature has designed his mouth in a half smile. . .".[19]

In the section of *Two in the Bush* about his New Zealand adventure, Gerald recounts how he left this strange land and all its creatures with a nostalgic vignette of

> Mount Cook wearing a tattered hat of pink snow; wisps of morning mist drifting languidly along the mountainsides . . . covering the scars made by recent landslides; and flying against it, arrow swift and eager, a group of Keas, their wings flashing in the sun, their joyful shout of 'Kea . . . kea . . . *kea*' echoing and ringing among the ancient rocks.[20]

And so, on to Australia aboard the ship *Wanganella*.

In the 1960s, conservationists in New Zealand and Australia faced much the same obstacles that conservationists worldwide still face today: agricultural and commercial interests, official ignorance, and human carelessness or violence. Gerald's anger leaks through the prose in this book, tempered only slightly by his wit and charm. In the final "Summing Up," he wrote, even before climate change was widely perceived,

> We have inherited an incredibly beautiful and complex garden, but . . . [W]e have not bothered to acquaint ourselves with the simplest principles of gardening. By neglecting our garden, we are storing up for ourselves . . . a world catastrophe as bad as any atomic war, and we are doing it with all the bland complacency of an idiot child chopping up a Rembrandt with a pair of scissors. We go on . . . creating dust bowls and erosion but cutting down forests and overgrazing our grasslands, polluting . . . water with industrial filth, and all the time we

are breeding with the ferocity of the Brown Rat. . . . We now stand so aloof from nature that we think we are God. This has always been a dangerous supposition.[21]

If New Zealand struck Gerald as too close to England for comfort, dusty Australia enchanted him from the moment he encountered its citizens and caught sight of a eucalyptus stand.

The particulars of the Australian landscape were another reminder of the evolutionary processes which created biological forms so different from the animals he knew. About a hundred million years ago, Australia separated from Gondwanaland during the early Cenozoic period, some forty million years after New Zealand had already separated from Australia and drifted eastward. In geological terms, Australia is an anomaly—isolated enough to behave as an island, but large enough to be a continent, with the biodiversity of a large land mass.

When Gerald filmed *Two in the Bush*, the point was to understand, protect, and delight in what remained, but understanding depended on a foray into ecological history. Australia has its own vast, unique suite of reptiles and amphibians, insects, birds, fish, and mammals; plants; and radiations—that is, ecological patterns of biota as they fill ecological niches. In Australia, marsupials have filled niches occupied on other continents by ungulates and their predators. Among the most familiar examples are kangaroos, who are grazers; the extinct thylacine, or marsupial wolf, was a top predator. Gerald noted that niches filled in other places by squirrels are here filled by possums and phalangers (the sugar glider is one of these). The wombat (one of his old friends from Whipsnade days) takes the place of the badger. The island continent was also hospitable to monotremes, egg-laying mammals like the duck-billed platypus.

Like New Zealand, Australia has flightless birds—emus and cassowaries. Gerald encountered an enormous white emu which, to his delight, sat on a nest, displaying unique male reproduction strategies. Male emus philosophically but somewhat lethargically mind the eggs; the nesting male Gerald met allowed Gerald to hoist him off his nest without complaint, even though the bird could have killed him with one well-placed kick. Among other birds found only in Australia, Gerald filmed the kookaburra, famous in a campfire song, and a lyrebird the locals called "Old Spotty," who tried to engage female interest with extravagant feathers and elaborate dancing.

Among the possums, Gerald was most charmed by the delicate, endangered Leadbeaters; two of them fit together in his palm. In *Two in the Bush*, as usual, Gerald played his wounds for laughs—as would Steve Irwin, the Australian Crocodile Hunter and defender of wildlife, decades later. Gerald was severely bitten while lending a hand to the Wildlife Service agents who managed the Koala population, once critically endangered by aggressive fur hunting which coincided with a deadly virus. In the twenty-first century, habitat destruction still threatens the koala. In 2019 and 2020, habitat for almost all Australian wildlife and millions of the animals themselves were destroyed in fierce record-breaking wildfires. Day after day, news reports featured burned, orphaned, and frightened koalas.

As always, in *Two in the Bush*, Gerald described his subjects as individuals, keeping in mind the challenges faced by the species. Many of the animals he met were known to the rest of the anglophone world, although their unique biology was not; some who have achieved name recognition now, thanks in part to the Durrell project, were not known in

FIGURE 5.2 Leadbeater's possum.

1960. If Gerald's principal mission for filming in New Zealand seems to have been alerting his audience to ongoing extinction events, an equally important mission in Australia was introducing new or misunderstood animals. Following the lives of animals in each film episode allowed his audience to be fully engaged and therefore more open to his urgent conservation message.

Another goal of the book and the series was to educate his audience about conservation biology:

> Before you can control any wild animal, you have to know something about its basic biology; a simple policy of slaughter—quite apart from its threat to the survival of that particular species—is liable to do untold damage to the whole ecological structure of the country. An unbiological approach in different parts of the world to problems of this sort have, in the past, proved disastrous.[22]

After a century or more of pulling threads out of "the tapestry of life," Australia did develop a better approach with the creation of the CSIRO (Commonwealth Scientific and Industrial Research Organisation), which became fully operational in 1926, only after the extermination of the thylacine.[23] To the wildlife officials of this federal agency, Gerald owed some of the most interesting details of the BBC program and the book.

At the height of the ranching expansion, "the 'kangaroo menace' came into being" because kangaroos and wallabies competed with sheep for forage (or so the ranchers thought) and seemed to appreciate the wells drilled for sheep and cattle. And so these animals occupy a prominent place in *Two in the Bush*. Kangaroos are uncanny animals, both familiar and strange. The kangaroo, with her convenient pouch for the Joey, has been familiar in zoos, literature, and popular culture since before the days of *Winnie the Pooh*. (Amazon alone markets scores of plastic and plush mother kangaroos with their babies.) But the actual biology of that pouch and its role in reproduction is to most people alien.

In *Two in the Bush*, Gerald shared his own astonishment when he watched a kangaroo give birth—an event rarely if ever witnessed, until CSIRO wildlife biologists observed it in 1960. Pamela the kangaroo alerted her keepers to the impending birth by cleaning her pouch, a process that took hours. Eventually, after looking "uncomfortable," she dug a hole next to the fence of her enclosure, lowered her substantial tail across the hole, sat on her tail, and leaned back. After some time, a "pinky-white, glistening blob no longer than the first joint of my little finger" "dropped out on to Pamela's tail and lay there."[24] In a few minutes, the baby, "no more than an embryo," made an arduous climb across its mother's belly to the pouch, apparently unaided. Gerald was startled to learn from the research team that a kangaroo can become pregnant while one baby is in the pouch and another is hopping along beside its mother but still nursing. This episode suggests that kangaroos must be protected not because they resemble the Kanga and Roo beloved by Cristopher Robin, but because they occupy a niche in a natural landscape, they offer a real-life window into the animal uncanny, and because all animals have a right to their own lives and ways of being.

Pressures on other Australian wildlife included hunting by humans; habitat destruction, especially by overgrazing; competition with introduced species; fragmentation of migratory routes; and even infrastructures intended to mitigate the unintended consequences of the above. One of the best-known Australian mammals, of course, is the dingo, probably introduced by the aboriginal settlers. Along with the foxes introduced by the English for sport, dingoes threatened native species by eating them. Foxes and dingoes are true canids, in contrast to the thylacine, which evolved along with other indigenous species until it was harried into extinction in the early twentieth century. Sheep contributed to the decline of indigenous species in two ways: directly, by relentless grazing, and indirectly, by human intervention such as kangaroo persecution to protect the flocks against perceived threats. As much as sheep, introduced rabbits overran the continent to the extent that in the early twentieth century, the Public Works Department began to build a rabbit-proof fence to run the entire length of Western Australia from south to north, to protect pasture lands for commercial livestock. In ecological terms, of course, fences never make good neighbors! (Eventually, the fence became obsolete when myxomatosis was introduced.)

Threats to indigenous wildlife were by no means past history when the Durrells visited Australia in 1962. It was too late to eradicate unintentional and intentional threats from foxes and rabbits—or to bring back species already extinct. But Gerald was appalled by current threats that could be managed: deliberate slaughter of wildlife and habitat destruction.

In addition to bounties on the thylacine and the frequent killing of kangaroos, Gerald learned first-hand about the routine shooting of wedge-tailed eagles when he saw twenty-eight birds strung from a fence with wings outstretched, as if they had been crucified. The number, it turned out, was considered "nothing" by the locals, for whom a "good bag" would be fifty. As the largest birds of prey in Australia, wedge-tailed eagles can take lambs and young kangaroos, along with their diet of smaller creatures and road kill, but "Although at the moment the Wedge-Tail is fairly common, if this sort of slaughter increases, what chance of survival does the bird have?"[25] Very little, it turns out: by the twenty-first century, the species had become endangered.

An even more intransigent problem was overgrazing. Gerald deliberately sought out the mallee fowl, which was preyed on by foxes and had to compete with rabbits and sheep for forage. As Gerald puts it, "the sheep was more important to man" than native fauna.[26] Grazing land was a limited resource, and large herds presented the same kind of threat to the bush that ranching did to the North American prairies. But grazing was not the only threat. Up until 1960, this unique landscape in New South Wales and Victoria, dominated by "islands" of eucalyptus and home to many species found only there, had been considered too barren for human use beyond grazing. (Gerald compares these clumps of forest to the Galapagos, where isolated species evolved into new, unique species.) But new chemical fertilizers were now enabling farmers to plant wheat. Like the sage grouse in North America, the mallee fowl was threatened because its habitat eventually became useful to humans—in more ways than one. The species is now classified as vulnerable.

Despite the looming threats, the team were able to locate and film these birds, about the size of turkeys, but with very different habits. Cock birds dig large holes, or "incubators," flinging the dirt into a surrounding berm sometimes twelve feet in diameter. The hole is filled with rotting vegetation, covered with sand, and left to generate heat that helps hatch the eggs, which are layered with the vegetation. The cock guards the nest, turning his eggs to keep them at 95 degrees until they hatch. When they hatch, the chicks must climb up through the nesting material to the top, much as the baby kangaroo must climb up the mother's belly. Although exhausted, they learn to fly within a day. Gerald's detailed account of this bird's behavior and habitat ends with the hope that both will be protected. It may not be enough, but several decades later, almost eight square miles of Malee scrub are now protected in the Bakara Conservation Park.

Malaysia

Malaysia was the third stop on this BBC expedition. Like Australia, Malaysia is megadiverse. That is, the ecological tapestry here is rich in species numbers, and rich in species endemic to it. The two largest land masses of the country are on the Malay Peninsula and the large island of Borneo. Many of the animals who inhabit these two large land masses are related, but genetically distinct. For example, the siamang, a gibbon which evolved on the peninsula, differs from the white-handed gibbon and Mueller's gibbon, which evolved on Borneo.[27]

The geography of Malaysia illustrates a Durrellian principle: that human-drawn geographical borders are unnatural and irrelevant for nature, especially animals. Like its neighbor Indonesia, Malaysia might be more accurately called a region instead of a country. The vivid human history of the entire region is one of colonial domination by the Chinese, Portuguese, Dutch, and British. On the Malay peninsula, a border with Thailand was established in 1909. On the island of Borneo, the British established a strong presence in the early eighteenth century, the Dutch ceded the northern part of the island to Britain in the 1820s, and Sir James Brooke established the separate kingdom of Sarawak in 1841. The southern part of the island retained by the Dutch is now part of Indonesia, and the small nation of Brunei has been chopped out of the northern coast. Malaya, the section of Malaysia located on the Malay Peninsula, became independent from Britain in 1957, and a Malayan Union, including other territories in the region, was formed. In 1965, the borders of the Malayan Union were adjusted again to the present conformation. Maylasia includes over eight hundred islands, large and small.[28] It sounds confusing, as political boundaries tend to be when they do not follow natural features of land and sea.

Following the lead of other scientist explorers and predicting Gerald's own approach to the study of wildlife, Alfred Russel Wallace explored this region between 1854 and 1862 and, in a path parallel to Darwin's, came to many of the same conclusions. (The two men collaborated on a paper published a year before *The Origin of Species* appeared in 1859.)[29] For better and for worse, the travel, wildlife research, and conservation enterprises of the Global North in environmental hotspots are always entangled with imperialism. Imperialist extractive practices have left environmental devastation and contributed to species endangerment to a degree impossible to calculate. Gerald was part of the entanglement, trying to undo some of the damage and forestall damage in the future.

Unlike New Zealand and Australia, which were settler colonies, this region had served as a source of extracted wealth, particularly rubber, through the British East India Company. Political instability was a long-term result, and "the picture of conservation ... was distressingly familiar."[30] In fact, when Gerald visited Malaysia in 1962, relative calm in the newly organized country, especially in the jungles, had been established only recently after the "Malayan Emergency" during the period from 1948 to 1960. This messy conflict was Britain's lesser-known version of the French and American engagement in Viet Nam. Some of the British colonial bureaucracy was still in place when Gerald arrived, a convenience which might have influenced his decision to go there and certainly was still felt in local conservation activities. Located on the southeast corner of the peninsula, the oldest and largest national park was originally established as a colonial game reserve in 1929. In 1939, it became King George V national park and, a few years later, Taman Negara.

The area Gerald visited is distinctive geologically and in terms of biodiversity. In our current geopolitical climate, that biological diversity also makes the park an environmental hot spot. Although the peninsula is not an island, a glance at the map shows that it is connected with mainland southeast Asia by a narrow strip of land, as little as forty miles wide at one point, in shape somewhat like the Valdés Peninsula in Argentina. The area is isolated and rich in species because of its proximity to the equator and, consequently, environmentally fragile. In part because many of the floral and faunal species found here are endemic, rare, vulnerable, and endangered, the park was designated a World Heritage Site in 1984. Plant species number over 3,000. The park is home to 470 bird species, 150 mammals, 67 snakes, 57 amphibians, at least four turtles, and several lizards.[31]

Gerald's Malaysian exploration began here: in *Two in the Bush*, he entitles this episode "The Vanishing Jungle" because, even in 1962, it *was* vanishing. The park was newly open for recreation, and Gerald's introduction to it was an invitation for a "tiny drink" with a local fishing party. As usual, when Gerald was not angry about some human carelessness with animals, he found humans fascinating and peppered his prose with hilarity about human behavior: this time, the all-night drinking party conversation was a thorough and erudite colloquium on homosexuality. The last word came from a man who had been silent throughout: "what *I* say is that every man should have his hobby."[32]

In addition to the eccentric humans, Gerald describes some of the most charismatic animals in the park. He and a companion unwittingly, and fortunately, manage to frighten a king cobra into vacating the premises—just before they sat directly in its path. (Leeches were the most worrisome foe, it turned out.) Gerald saw fruit bats during the day, hanging upside down from a leafless tree by the river "like badly made umbrellas." In the evening, they moved, "honking and flapping . . . towards their feeding grounds."[33] The bovine seladang, tiny mouse deer, tree shrew, slow loris, binturong (commonly known as the bearcat), and several fish species also emerged from rest and hiding.

Gerald even had the gift of making plants charismatic. Some of the flora became characters in Gerald's story of life in this jungle: the leaves of an unidentified vine, for instance, "delicate, pale-green, fern-like" and apparently so fragile that one brushes them gently aside. But the vine has "curved, needle-sharp hooks" on the underside and "sinks these vegetable grappling-irons into your flesh . . . and the more you struggle, the more involved you become" to the point of bleeding like "an early Christian martyr."[34] Gerald probably knew that the first rule for anyone exploring a tropical forest is to refrain from touching anything you can't identify—so you wear gloves. But his attention was continually drawn to the marvels around him, so he evidently forgot from time to time.

Four creatures, in particular, receive the most attention in the Malayan episode of *Two in the Bush*: the *Draco volins* (flying lizard), leatherback turtle, elephant, and siamang. The curious flying lizard, who glides from tree to tree by means of a membrane attached to its ribs, was rarely seen, even in 1962, but after glimpsing one in the forest, Gerald searched for them, eventually finding several in the garden of an Englishman who had stayed in the area after the formal end of British rule.

The "flying" lizards (actually, they glide, as flying squirrels do) had to be thrown into the air for the film crew to capture the behavior. After hours of attempts, they salvaged only fifteen seconds of film. If filming the flying lizard had occurred after the captive breeding operation at the Jersey Zoo developed and the trust began publishing *The Dodo*, a journal devoted to zoo practices, Gerald might have convinced the film crew not to use the animal in this way, or at least would have acknowledged the problem.

The endangered "leathery turtle," or leatherback presented fewer challenges, although these animals can only be seen when the females come onto the beach at night to lay eggs. The massive size of these animals—nine feet long, according to Gerald's account—inspired the chapter title, "The Giant's Nursery." In the early 1960s, it was thought nesting for this species was limited to Ceylon, Puerto Rico, and Dungun, in Malaysia, where the film crew arranged with local officials for a night filming. The government, supported by the Malayan Nature Society, had just instituted a conservation project, which included relocating nests into protected and guarded areas, collecting hatchlings, and moving them out past the shoreline, where the majority are typically caught by predators. Local villagers were paid for their help, and for the loss of income the eggs would have provided.

This project ultimately failed, and the turtles are functionally extinct in Malaysia. However, additional nesting grounds were later discovered—mostly in tropical zones.[35] Conservation projects (now protecting nests rather than moving eggs or transporting babies beyond the breakers) have better succeeded elsewhere. However, because of ever more plastic refuse, and ever larger fishing nets, and because the leatherback's eggs were (and still are) regarded as a delicacy and an aphrodisiac in many parts of the world, the leatherback is still endangered throughout its range.

Part of the appeal of all Gerald's books come from the vivid descriptions of individuals and groups of animals. In Taman Negara, an entire herd of elephants moved almost silently through the forest (except for the rumblings of their stomachs) until they encountered water, which they "adore." Then they seemed to lose all self-control. With the film crew, Gerald observed a particular mother and juvenile elephant playing in a stream:

> She stepped into the shallow water and paused, musing to herself, as if to test the temperature . The baby, who had had a certain difficulty in negotiating the steep bank of the stream, arrived at the water's edge and gave a ridiculous squeak of delight, like the noise of a small, falsetto tin bugle. . . . Having reached his mother's side, he scrambled out onto her wet flank, giving little squeals of pleasure to himself. He then evolved a game which I could only presume to be the elephant equivalent of submarines. Disappearing beneath the water, he circled round and round his mother, attacking her from different angles under the surface until she reached down into the water with her trunk and hauled him up by his ear. We watched them for an hour or

so, until it was too dark to see, and the baby was still indulging in his underwater game with undiminished vigor.[36]

This pastoral description, even in 1962, was at odds with the plight of the elephants outside the park, where they were systematically oppressed. Decades later, outside the park, at least a third of all Asian elephants are captive to forestry interests, ceremonial uses, and tourism. Along with their African cousins, they are persecuted and killed as crop raiders when agriculturalists take over their traditional habitat. Worldwide, elephants with tusks are slaughtered for ivory, and those without tusks for their meat. According to World Wildlife Fund estimates, fewer than 500,000 elephants—Asian and African—were alive in 2018, and more are killed each year than are born.[37]

Gerald was also enchanted by the "Singers in the Trees," as he called siamangs. At around twenty-five pounds, these black and white apes are the largest of the gibbons. Males and females share dominance in monogamous pairs and larger social groupings, and they have been known to socialize sometimes with other species of gibbons or even other apes in the wild or in captivity.

Like other gibbons, the siamangs are almost entirely arboreal, so their characteristic locomotion is brachiation, but Gerald was not the only one to find their most striking feature to be their voices. In *The Great Apes*, his 1929 textbook, the pioneering primatologist Robert Yerkes reproduced records of siamang song which had been transcribed in musical notation in 1841 and 1865.[38] Males and females often perform duets which can carry over a mile through the jungle canopy. In their native habitat, these duets are one way the siamangs define their territory. In *Two in the Bush*, Gerald described a large family, including a large male, a female, two juveniles, and an infant, listening with rapt attention to the complex vocalizations of the patriarch, and sometimes joining in. "It was nice to feel," he remarked in closing the chapter, "that in this enormous section of protected forest, there would always be groups of Siamangs singing happily to each other in the bowers of green leaves."[39] Of course, this was a note of unusual optimism.

"The Vanishing Jungle," Gerald's title for the Malaysia section of *Two in the Bush*, alerts his readers to the cold comfort offered in this beautiful place. The equilibrium does not hold. Currently, there is some evidence that limited agricultural clearing within the Malaysian jungle allows sunlight into the forest floor, and that the resulting small meadows create extra browse for elephants. However, at the same time, these clearings inhibit the siamangs, who travel almost exclusively through the canopy. Too, if the population of elephants in Taman Negara has remained steady or, according to some estimates, has increased, these numbers may be the result of increasing pressures from outside the park: habitat destruction and conflicts between humans and elephants have risen in recent years.[40] Outside the park, numbers of free Asian elephants in Malaysia have declined steadily for decades. The same is true for the singers in the trees, protected in this forest but endangered in Malaysia and Indonesia generally. Habitat loss, killing, and capture for the pet trade and other commercial uses have earned these lovely animals a spot on the Endangered Species list. If elephants and siamangs sometimes seem to compete, that is because they are always under pressure from their human neighbors.

What should be done to protect the animals Gerald observed in their peaceable kingdom on the Malay Peninsula, and others he did not write about: several felids, wild canid and cattle populations, bats, tapirs, and mountain goats? It is too late for the Sumatran rhino, among others, who lived on the peninsula as well as Sumatra. It was hunted to extinction by 1932.[41] Habitat area and connectivity must be maintained. Direct human interactions because of farming, the pet and entertainment trade, and slaughter for animal products must be monitored and controlled. Legal protections must be taken seriously and vigorously enforced.[42] These mandates align with what is to be done for other floral and faunal species in other environmental hotspots—that is, areas of the greatest biodiversity and the greatest threats to that diversity.

What was true for the Malaysian species Gerald encountered was also true for the endangered species of New Zealand and Australia. In 1962, as the British Empire was disintegrating, and the damage to ecosystems wrought by imperialist and capitalist practices was manifestly clear, Gerald's impassioned response to this crisis echoes the political rhetoric of the time:

> Unlike us, animals have no control over their future. They cannot ask for home rule, they cannot worry their M.P.s with their grievances, they cannot even get their unions to strike for better conditions. Their future and their very existence depend on us. The Jersey Wildlife Preservation Trust has created a sanctuary ... a sort of stationary Noah's Ark. The need for such work is terribly urgent. In the case of

many animals, help in five or ten years will be too late—they will have vanished.[43]

Extinction is a slow-moving, continuous disaster. The urgency of Gerald's request at the end of *Two in the Bush* reflects not only his sense that the pace of extinctions worldwide was escalating, but that his own efforts to slow the pace were in jeopardy.

Gerald was not the first to attempt captive breeding and reintroduction. However, his observations of such projects in Australia, where wildlife officials bred kangaroos to understand and protect them, and in Malaysia, where he saw the leatherback project in action, he was inspired as he carried out similar projects himself. He took these lessons back to the zoo, and from the zoo a few years later into other projects on other islands, even more at risk than those he explored in the South Pacific.

Notes

1 G. Durrell and Lee Durrell, *The Amateur Naturalist*, (New York: Knopf, 1989), 13.

2 Lawrence Durrell, *Prospero's Cell: A Guide to the Landscape and Manners of Corfu* (NP: Open Road. Kindle Edition, 184).

3 David Quammen, *The Song of the Dodo: Island Biogeography in an Age of Extinctions* (New York: Simon and Schuster, 1997).

4 G. Durrell. *Two in the Bush*, 250.

5 G. Durrell, *The Amateur Naturalist*, 11–14.

6 Ibid., 23. Hutchinson's students included the congenial Allison Jolly, a lemur specialist who later worked closely with the Durrell Foundation before and after Gerald's death. Robert MacArthur, whose collaboration with E. O. Wilson resulted in the foundational essay on island biogeography, also studied with Hutchison. The ecologist Thomas Lovejoy wrote Hutchinson's obituary, "George Evelyn Hutchinson": 13 January 1903 17 May 1991." *Biographical Memoirs of Fellows of the Royal Society*, 57 (May 17, 1991).

7 G. Durrell, *The Amateur Naturalist*, 23.

8 One of the clearest explanations of the speciation process for the lay reader can be found in E. O. Wilson's "Krakatau" (Chapter 2), *The Diversity of Life*, Revised ed. (Eastbourne: Gardners Books, 2001).

9 Quammen, *The Song of the Dodo*, 275.

10 See Lovejoy, *Lessons from Amazonia* (New Haven, CT: Yale University Press, 2001) for the scope of Lovejoy's project and the work of numerous other scientists who contributed to it.

11 See Botting, *Gerald Durrell*, 388–92, for Gerald's acquaintance with Lovejoy.

12 Quammen, *The Song of the Dodo*, 558.

13 Stanley A. Temple, "Recovery of the Mauritian Kestrel from an Extreme Population Bottleneck," *The Auk*, 103 (3), July 1986, 632. https://academic.oup.com/auk/article/103/3/632/5191477 [accessed July 19, 2023].

14 G. Durrell, *Two in the Bush*, 200.

15 "Extinct Species of New Zealand." nhc.net.nz/index/extinct-new-zealand/extinct.htm [accessed July 27, 2019].

16 "Little Spotted Kiwi." https://www.doc.govt.nz/nature/native-animals/birds/birds-a-z/kiwi/little-spotted-kiwi/

17 G. Durrell, *Two in the Bush*, 53.

18 Ibid., 118.

19 Ibid., 81.

20 Ibid., 118.

21 Ibid., 250

22 Ibid., 180.

23 CSIRO's latest estimates, published in March 2023, suggest that the thylacine might have endured longer than previously assumed.

24 G. Durrell, *Two in the Bush*, 194.

25 Ibid., 171–72.

26 Ibid., 179.

27 Jean-Jacques Petter and François Desbordes, *Primates of the World: An Illustrated Guide* (Princeton, NJ: Princeton University Press, 2010), 134–39.

28 Jeffrey Hays, "British in Malaysia." Hays, Jeffrey. "BRITISH IN MALAYSIA". Facts and Details, https://factsanddetails.com/southeast-asia/Malaysia/sub5_4a/entry-3619.html#chapter-5 [accessed 19 July 2023].

29 For a detailed and generous account of Wallace's time in Malaysia, see Quammen's chapter "The Man Who Knew Islands," in *The Song of the Dodo*.

30 G. Durrell, *Two in the Bush*, 250.

31 "National Park [Taman Negara] of Peninsular Malaysia." https://whc.unesco.org/en/tentativelists/5927/#:~:text=The%20National%20Park%20(Taman%20Negara,was%20gazetted%20in%201938%2F1939 [accessed July 19, 2023].

32 G. Durrell, *Two in the Bush*, 203-4.

33 Ibid., 207.

34 Ibid., 214–15.

35 "Leatherback Sea Turtle (*Dermochelys coriacea*)." https://www.google.com/search?q=%E2%80%9CLeatherback+Sea+Turtle+(Dermochelys+coriacea).%E2%80%9D&rlz=1C1CHBF_enUS934US934&oq=%E2%80%9CLeatherback+Sea+Turtle+(Dermochelys+coriacea).%E2%80%9D&gs_lcrp=EgZjaHJv

bWUyBggAEEUYOTIICAEQABgWGB4yCAgCEAAYFh [accessed July 19, 2023].

36 G. Durrell, *Two in the Bush*, 211–13.

37 Jeffrey P. Cohn, "Elephants: Remarkable and Endangered," *BioScience*, 40, no. 1 (1990), 10–14. *JSTOR*, www.jstor.org/stable/1311233 [accessed July 19, 2023].

38 Musical notations of siamangs were made separately by William Charles Martin in 1841 and S. R. Tickell in 1865. Quotations from both are included in Robert and Ada Yerkes, *The Great Apes* (New Haven, CT: Yale University Press, 1929), 75, 78. Now, the songs are easily available on YouTube and worth hearing. See the example of a "Siamang Duet" recorded by the Palm Beach Zoo and Conservation Society on August 22, 2013.

39 G. Durrell, *Two in the Bush*, 224.

40 Clements et al., "Trio Under Threat: Can We Secure the Future of Rhinos, Elephants and Tigers in Malaysia?" *Biodiversity and Conservation* (2010).

41 N. Manokaran, "An Overview of Biodiversity in Malaysia," *Journal of Tropical Forest Science*, 5 (2), 271–90, 281.

42 Manokaran, "An Overview," 274 and elsewhere.

43 G. Durrell, *Two in the Bush*, 256.

6 MADAGASCAR AND THE MASCARENES

"Pink Pigeon Valley," announced Dave McKelvey, who operated a small captive breeding center for the endangered pigeons and Mauritian kestrels at Black River . . . "Took me an age to discover it."[1] The valley is an island within an island: despite the protection it offers to its rare residents, by the mid-1970s, a total of only thirty-five pigeons remained. These birds persist in this small place, and nowhere else. Down the "precipitous slope" and into "a mixed assortment of plants to groves of cryptomeria trees, at first glance looking rather like a prickly species of pine tree, dark green with heavy bunches of needles" stumbled Gerald, McKelvey, and the zoo's reptile keeper John Hartley. Few trees of any sort were left on the island, which, after a succession of Portuguese, Dutch, French, and English invaders, was devoted to vast monocultures, mostly of sugar cane. The original conversion to sugar represents a common and familiar intersection between natural disaster and human disaster: the labor of clearing land and cultivating cane was done by enslaved Africans, transported to this small island and managed with cruelty.[2] The slopes of this particular valley were too steep for felling, and that is why a few trees remained to shelter the pigeons.

Loss of habitat was not the only threat, however: for some now unfathomable reason, Portuguese sailors introduced crab-eating macaques in the sixteenth century.[3] Large, smart, and aggressive, these monkeys worked their way into this hidden valley, where they took the pigeons' eggs and fed on the young.[4] In addition, the macaques were among the few animals able to scale the volcanic cliffs of Black River Gorge, the favorite nesting ground of tiny Mauritian kestrels, whose numbers were reduced in the mid-1970s to the edge of extinction. With the help of ornithologist Carl Jones, who revived the kestrel population a few years after the pink pigeon venture, the pigeons have made great progress after Gerald and other conservationists started breeding and re-introducing them to their native home.

Mauritian history is a classic example of the way evolutionary process in an isolated geographic space has produced specialist species without defenses against invaders— pathogens, aggressive plants or animals, or humans with guns and greed. Mauritian kestrels, pink pigeons, and the famous dodo evolved in the absence of significant predation and with plenty of the resources they needed. Gerald found the pigeons beautiful, but too complacent and phlegmatic for their own good. Similarly, the dodo has been accused of naivete—not a particularly derogatory term for a bird who has never encountered significant threats in its entire evolutionary history. The dodos were easily destroyed by sailors, who bundled them by the thousands onto ships to be eaten *en route* when they had nothing better. Neither the kestrels nor the pigeons are said to make good eating, but, like their predecessor the dodo, likely extinct by 1690, they are ill equipped to fend off threats from primate invaders. The pigeons and kestrels have held out a little longer. Still, although cliffs and tall trees may be good defenses for flying creatures, monkeys can climb them. The situation becomes infinitely worse if the boundaries of the animals' habitat are relentlessly pulled into an ever-tightening noose by constant land clearing.

Like monkeys, humans can chase and climb if they must, and that is how Gerald and his companions managed on the 1976 expedition to capture an adult pigeon and, a bit later, one juvenile; finally, they acquired an egg, which was hatched by a domesticated pigeon. With these small contributions to Dave McKelvey's breeding colony, the party felt enough optimism to return the following year, when they captured eight birds, left three in Black River, and returned to Jersey with the rest, a viable pink pigeon breeding colony.

The capture and relocation of macaques might relieve the pressure for kestrels and pigeons, but let's be clear: macaques in Mauritius are not the villains. They were removed originally from Southeast Asia, where they lived as part of a balanced ecosystem. Soon after Gerald's work with the pink pigeons was carried out, many of the macaques descended from those early transported monkeys were caught as a breeding population for biomedical research. Supplying these animals became a growth industry for the island. Using primates in biomedical research raises other ethical questions, but taking them from a habitat where they do not belong saves creatures who do belong there.

Mauritius is part of the Mascarene group of volcanic islands in the Indian Ocean, about seven hundred miles east of Madagascar. Within the last four centuries, the original flora and fauna of these islands have been drastically depleted. In human terms, this island group is one of the most densely populated areas of the globe. Rodrigues, the third largest island of the Mascarenes, has lost virtually all its forest to agriculture and human expansion, which has been even more aggressive here than in Mauritius. The Rodrigues solitaire was a distant relative of the dodo and, like its cousin, hunted to extinction by humans. For the same reasons, the domed tortoise and the saddleback tortoise, both endemic to Rodrigues, also became extinct around 1800.

There is almost no fruit in Rodrigues. That was the word to Gerald and his crew as they planned to go island-hopping around the Mascarenes after their work with the pigeons on Mauritius. And no wonder, since there are no trees. There was fruit, actually, a tiny patch of mangos which was just about to fail at the end of a two-year drought. The Rodrigues fruit bat depended entirely on the mangos. The plight of these little mammals was exemplary: extinction looms for small populations of rare animals who have evolved in isolated areas, especially when a stochastic event such as drought coincides with loss of habitat and the resources their habitat is supposed to provide. Saving them was the second emergency Gerald's crew found in 1976 and 1977. Like the pink pigeons of neighboring Mauritius, the bats had probably managed to hang on for three hundred years after human settlement because no one wanted to eat them. Failing to protect fruit bats is especially short-sighted because they are major pollinators of many tree species. Maybe the island's trees had been felled, but who was to say that fruit cultivars would never again make their appearance?

For any impassioned wildlife conservationist, the "use" of an animal is beside the point. The bats were beautiful, endangered, and endowed with the right to exist for their own sake. The Durrell team endured the usual tangles of red tape, mud (the two years' drought broke only hours before their small plane landed), clouds of mosquitos, and the work of transporting lavish bat baits from Mauritius. The weight limit for the small plane meant that boxes of fruit were loaded before clothes, which became expendable. The outcome was a feast for both fruit bats and mosquitos, who feasted on the bare arms, legs, and torsos of those who had also given up their shirts. As usual, Gerald tries to smoke and joke through miseries endured by the humans in the story:

"It's a form of conservation program, really," I said. "You can imagine how many mosquitos we have saved from starvation.... the World Wildlife Fund will probably erect a posthumous Golden Ark on this spot to commemorate our contribution to nature."

"It's all very well for you to joke, said Ann bitterly. "You don't seem to be affected when they bite you ...".[5]

Although Gerald's later narratives tip over more frequently into the elegiac mode, he always, at some point, managed to find comedy in bickering, pratfalls, and general human frailty. Most horrific of all was the protagonist (or antagonist) of this episode in *Golden Bats and Pink Pigeons*, a jackfruit. Jackfruit is a watermelon-sized relative of fig and breadfruit, with highly nutritious yellow flesh popular these days as a meat substitute in delectable dishes such as vegan tacos. Told on Mauritius that the Rodrigues bats particularly enjoyed it, Gerald and his crew packed an over-ripe one, carefully wrapped. "It tastes good," the head of forestry, Wahab informed him, "if you like that sort of thing."[6]

FIGURE 6.1 Rodrigues fruit bats.

The official could have been more forthcoming about the obnoxious fruit, but his help was indispensable. After loading and unloading the small plane twice, and waiting all night before it was allowed to take off, they found the giant fruit's "effluvium" overwhelming, as did passers-by at the airport and fellow passengers on the plane.[7] Food and clothes were steeped in the scent, which was impossible to escape for days thereafter. (One suspects they actually got hold of a durian, a similar fruit which exudes an intense, sickeningly sweet odor and has a viscous texture. Not quite as large as the jackfruit, the durian is still big enough to cause trouble.) In any case, whatever its true name, the bat-bait fruit caused infinite pain and trouble before it was finally hacked to bits and served, in a wire basket attached to the mist nets strung up to catch the bats.

It was not the first time Gerald's most outrageously funny character was a plant: remember the cruel, devious vine in Malaysia. Once in the field, the team's sandwiches were attacked and largely consumed by giant, omnivorous land snails, so many and so heavy that they almost brought down the roof of the party's hut. After enduring two wakeful nights in the company of land snails, mosquitos, hungry rats, and awkward manipulations of themselves and their equipment, Gerald and his companions had secured enough individuals for a successful breeding colony in Jersey. When they released the redundant males on the last day, the bats struggled against the stiff wind blowing down the valley, and Gerald wondered, "how they would fare in a cyclone lasting three or four days, or a week."[8] Comedy is sometimes hard to sustain.

Back to Mauritius they went, where Gerald snorkeled by himself in a dream-like trance above the spectacular reefs—an experience he would share with Lee on a return trip. Decades later, even these reefs would be dying, although he did not know this. But for now, there was still more work to be done.

"Desert island" is usually a misnomer since it means an island with no humans. Brand-new volcanic islands are desert islands in the true sense, but only for the very short period it takes for life to arrive on currents of air and ocean, to settle and emerge into new forms. Round Island, one of the smallest of the Mascarenes, is a volcanic dome which, until goats and rabbits were introduced, supported a unique suite of flora and fauna. It almost became a "desert island" in the true sense. Predictably, the introduced herbivores ate all they could, weakening the substrate so much that tropical cyclones in the early 1960s washed away the topsoil and most of the remaining trees. The underlying volcanic tuff eroded into great gullies, and the animal populations dropped drastically, until Gerald's crew visited the island as part of their larger project in the Mascarenes.

During the 1950s and 1960s, colonial officials Robert Newton and Jean Vinson became alarmed about the island and sought aid from the international wildlife conservation community. They were especially concerned about the seabirds who nested there—tropic birds, petrels, and shearwaters—easy marks for casual hunters.[9] The Durrell Trust answered the call during the excursion to Mauritius and Rodrigues, to capture endangered animals for captive breeding. During a second visit in 1982 they captured more. Gerald concentrated on the reptiles, less visible and more vulnerable, and in *Golden Bats and Pink Pigeons*, he noted a small, lovely Bottle Palm, one of several endemic and endangered plant species on the island.

In 1976 and 1977, Round Island was the site of hair-raising adventures for Gerald and his friends. Their visits began with attempts to disembark at the one spot on the islet where that was possible—a large rock, to which visitors had to leap, hoping for the best. Fortunately, they succeeded. (Years later, they enjoyed rides in a net lifted by a crane, as they had done to reach the island refuge of the tuatara "lizard" in New Zealand.) The sides of the dome are so steep that climbing to the "Picnic Tree," the only spot on the island shady enough to relax without being completely seared by the tropical sun, was strenuous. Loss of footing on the rough terrain could result in major abrasions—exactly what happened to Gerald at one point as he made his way back down. Pitching tents was predictably challenging. A false step near the island's steep sides would precipitate you headlong into the sea, and rescue would be difficult or impossible.

The risks were worthwhile. By searching inside the flared leaf bases of palm trees, the team found infant, juvenile, and adult specimens of the shy and secretive Round Island boas to bring back to Jersey for breeding. The burrowing boa, a species which, as its name implies, stays mostly underground, was more difficult to locate. With these snakes, they had less luck and worried that they might be too late. However, they were successful with the lizards, including Gunther's gecko and the Bojeri skink. The large, iridescent Telfair's skinks practically begged to be captured, climbing into their laps as they ate and taking food when they could.

John Hartley speculated that the snake populations suffered from predation by the Telfair skinks. If he was correct, pressures on this tiny island ecosystem from the introduced rabbits and goats disrupted the food chain, to the extent that one endemic species might well have been the agent of the other's destruction: ecological collapse. Forty years after Gerald's team worked on this island, balance has been almost restored with the removal of the goats (by the New Zealand Navy) and rabbits (with the development of a specialized poison recommended by the New Zealand Wildlife Department). Again, introduced species almost destroyed an entire ecosystem because they had been removed from where they belonged. But had these interventions not occurred, the Telfair's skinks might have eaten all the other snakes and lizards until they themselves died of starvation. As the Round Island expedition drew to a close, Gerald realized

> that here was a unique, miniature world that had, by a miracle of evolution, come into being and was now being allowed to bleed to death. . . . While everyone argued over what to do about the rabbits, and got no forrader, this unique speck of land was diminishing day by day. It seemed to sum up in miniature what we were doing to the whole planet, with millions of species being bled to death for want of a little, so little medicare.[10]

The next stop in the southern Indian Ocean was Madagascar. The pilgrimages to Madagascar in 1981–82 and 1990 were the culmination of Gerald's mission. In geographical terms, Madagascar was perhaps the most fascinating island of all, and the clearest example of what Gerald had learned about island biogeography over decades of study and experience. In ecological terms, the Madagascar projects were more focused on what would be possible and necessary for the Durrell Wildlife Trust to undertake. Fortunately, the film projects were also generously funded by the local Jersey station, Channel Television. Finally, if Gerald had a favorite animal, it was the aye-aye, a tiny, rare, and strange member of the lemur clan with great round, orange eyes and bizarre hands.[11] On Madagascar, he found the aye-aye and kindred species, rescued individuals from markets, cooking pots, backyard kennels, and degraded habitats, and brought them back for captive breeding in the Jersey Zoo. By the time of his last few voyages, Gerald was also fully and deeply aware of the historical and political forces which brought the animals to such a sorry pass.

If the Madagascar journeys were more successfully focused on practical results for wildlife conservation, they were also the most emotionally conflicted.

Madagascar is a large continental island, a chunk wedged, some two hundred million years ago, between Africa and the Indian subcontinent, all part of Gondwanaland. Alison Jolly, a lemur specialist who also wrote more broadly about Malagasy history, flora and fauna, called the island a "micro continent."[12] Even a cursory look at a map shows that Madagascar's western coastline roughly mirrors the coastline of Mozambique, over three hundred miles away—a graphic illustration of continental drift. However, the climate of the island differs from that of Africa, as does its culture. For almost a hundred million years, the island has been separated from India and Africa, and isolation gave rise to a unique group of plants and animals, found nowhere else, undisturbed by busy humans. In deep time, our species arrived only a few seconds ago.

Descending from a few ancestral species from before the time of the island's separation from the continent, and a few more species likely to have arrived early on via flotsam, the biotic suite of Madagascar is even more complete and—subjectively speaking—stranger than the plants and animals found on other islands. Jolly estimated its youngest "founding stocks" as at least fifty million years old.[13] There are Malagasy reptiles, fish, birds, marsupial mammals, and placental mammals similar to those found on continents other than Australia before human settlement. Madagascar's fauna and flora provide some of the world's most striking examples of adaptive radiation, that is, the evolution of an original species into a multiplicity of related species within a small area. Although Gerald's heart belonged to the animals, his sympathy extended to the threatened plants—unique flowering plants, mosses, ferns, conifers, and over a thousand species of orchids. All these species co-evolved into ecological balance until human settlement, less than two thousand years ago. Human presence has upset this balance irrevocably.

The baobab is exemplary. These trees (Gerald counted nine species) evolved to thrive in dry, nutritionally poor soil in the western, northern, and southern parts of the island, Each Malagasy species of this tree has specialized for conditions within a distinct ecozone. Baobabs capture and store water in huge, pot-bellied trunks, with branches, leaves, and flowers only at the very top, where they are protected from fire and other threats. Gardening websites advise that if you want to plant baobabs, the distance between them should be about forty feet, a span which would protect the leaves to a degree even from sifakas, the striking, mostly white lemurs known for their effortless leaping ability. Although an individual baobab tree can survive in harsh conditions for thousands of years, baobabs are now under threat because humans are harvesting them for a variety of products and, Gerald noted in *The Aye-Aye and I*, as an emergency water source for zebu cattle during droughts and the dry season. The radiation represented by the baobab, its oddity, its rarity in other parts of the world, and its vulnerability—ironically due to the very adaptations which allowed it to evolve and thrive in the dry forests of Madagascar—typify the speciation and extinction patterns explained by the principles of island geography.

There were, as well, distinctive birds, brilliantly colored chameleons of all sizes, beautiful and bizarre tortoises, harmless endemic boas, tenrec mothers who called their babies by shuffling their spines, and giant jumping rats. Madagascar's top predator, the fossa, resembles a large cat but is related to the mongoose. Locating these creatures was not easy because, even in the 1980s, many parts of Madagascar were ecologically devastated, but persistence paid off. Gerald's party found most of the animals they sought for collection and filming.

Madagascar has for almost a century beckoned wildlife conservationists and primatologists specializing in prosimians, that is, primates whose lineage was the first to split from our family tree, followed by the simians—New World and Old World monkeys, and finally by apes, including humans. Only distant lemur relatives are found elsewhere—galagos, or "bushbabies," lorises, and tarsiers. As Jean-Jacques Petter and François Desbordes remark in their beautifully illustrated guide to primates, "It can be imagined that the ancestors of the Malagasy lemurs arrived by sea, borne on rafts of vegetation, and that they subsequently diversified in isolation on Madagascar."[14]

One distinctive difference between Malagasy primates and simians is their wet noses. Prosimians generally have more teeth than apes and monkeys, less expressive faces, reproductive inclinations toward litters rather than single births, and, according to many who study them, lower cognitive abilities. Although most simian species are male dominant, most lemurs are female dominant. (Feminists would agree that this last trait does not argue for lower cognitive abilities among lemurs.) A subfossil extinct lemur the size of a calf has been found, but even including this species, the average size of prosimians is less than the average size of simians. (Madame Berthe's mouse lemur brings the average down: it weighs just over an ounce and could sleep comfortably in a teacup.) Over a hundred lemuroid species, extinct or extant, have been identified, and according to the International Union for the Conservation of

Nature (IUCN), today, 98 percent of them could be extinct within twenty years.[15]

If the baobab radiation is remarkable, the lemur radiation is astounding. Taking an expansive view, lemurs in Madagascar have filled niches which, in Africa and South America, are occupied by apes and monkeys. Focus the lens on a small ecozone—stands of bamboo within the Madagascar rainforest—and you see an even more refined example of lemuriform radiation, all three of them rare: the greater bamboo lemur, the gentle bamboo lemur, and the golden bamboo lemur. Each bamboo lemur eats a different part of the bamboo stalk, or a different species of bamboo. The golden bamboo lemur, in fact, has adapted to consume shoots, narrow stems, and leaf bases full of cyanide, which would kill the other two lemur species sharing the same ecozone. The golden bamboo lemur was almost extinct before it was scientifically described by Patricia Wright in the mid-1980s. During the same period, Gerald, along with Alison Jolly, Roland Albinac, Hanta Rasamimanana, and a number of young Malagasy primatologists were studying lemuroids intensively.[16]

Isolated biological specialists are always more vulnerable than generalists. In a pre-industrialized country, still in recovery from waves of colonization and centuries of swidden (slash and burn) agriculture, where the human population has for a few centuries inflicted enormous pressures on the natural world, specialists do not fare well. All the bamboo lemurs are critically endangered. In 2020, five out of the twenty-five most endangered primates in the world are lemurs of Madagascar: the Bemanasy mouse lemur, Lake Alaotra gentle lemur, James' sportive lemur, Indri, and aye-aye.[17]

Lemurs and their kin have been of special interest to the Durrell team since the late 1970s. The red ruffed is now part of a breeding program at the Jersey Zoo, as are the aye-aye, Alaotran gentle lemur, black and white ruffed lemur, and red fronted brown lemur. The ringtailed lemur is not critically endangered, but since it has proven most adaptable and easiest to breed, it has served as a model for the captive breeding of other lemuroid species. Gerald's approach, which has been adopted worldwide, has been to breed "for practice" the less endangered relatives of the rarest animals. (In the Lemur Conservation Foundation, in Myakka City, Florida, the animal of choice for breeding experiments is the brown lemur.)

Madagascar is an elongated oval, with a point on the northern end. Look at a map of lemuriform distribution on the island: it is a curious

148 THE EVOLUTION OF GERALD DURRELL

thing that these little primates have settled all around the edges of this micro-continent, in dry forest, tropical forest, and spiny forest. That is because now, they avoid the central plateau because the forests are gone. The only lemurs anywhere around the capital city Antananarivo (or Tana, as the locals call it), near the center of Madagascar, are in the Tsimbazaza Zoo. Likewise, there are few roads across the high central plateau except those in and around Tana, and most other roads are poorly maintained.

In the 1980s, traveling around the island was much easier than traveling across it, but getting to the capital required following both coastal and mountain routes. Imagine, then, the difficulty of finding, filming, and capturing lemurs. Some of the larger lemurs are naïve and unconcerned about human interference. The smaller, rarer, more vulnerable, and nocturnal lemurs are just the opposite. The nocturnal aye-aye that Gerald most passionately sought was one of these. Imagine traveling around the island on rough roads and through risky river crossings by bridge or ferry, with truckloads of equipment and supplies, in search of rare animals that just might be saved in the nick of time from a cooking pot, or extermination by an angry farmer. Now imagine that the capture of three or four individuals might make the difference between species survival and extinction. That is what Gerald and his associates were up against.

As he had done in Africa and South America, Gerald made use of colonial political infrastructures, even outdated ones, to find and save creatures pushed toward oblivion by colonial and postcolonial interests. The irony should not be lost. In 1983, the journey began easily enough in Berenty, a private reserve that was home to the ringtailed lemurs and dancing sifakas, whose long leaps and pogo-like gait make them as recognizable as the ringtailed lemurs. On this visit, the primary purpose was filming. Gerald followed Lee, whose lemur Ph.D. research led her down a path walked by Alison Jolly in 1960. In *Lords and Lemurs* (2004), a lemur-centered history of Madagascar, Jolly described Berenty as a paternalistic or kindly colonial enterprise. The reserve was established by the aristocratic de Heaulme family, who settled in Madagascar before the French Revolution and held extensive lands in the south of the island even after formal independence in 1960. The family had cleared large areas of native spiny forest, contributing to the silting up of the river, and employed the local Tandroy people on a vast sisal plantation. These workers remained part of the servant and agricultural worker class. On the other hand, the de Heaulme plantation continued to operate, sometimes at a loss, against a French colonial and postcolonial backdrop of political turmoil and economic extraction, to provide income for the workers.

By 1970, the country was in disarray from ethnic tensions, an anthrax outbreak, political and economic upheaval, famine, and the crumbling tatters of a French legal system, which remained without means of enforcement. In contrast to Madagascar as a whole, Berenty seemed a peaceful island within an island. Fences were whitewashed, the family and members of the Tandroy community were hospitable, and the lemurs were thriving. "I do know a lot about ringtailed lemurs," Jolly's story begins. "As for people, all I can tell you is what they chose to tell me."[18] Nevertheless, she continues, "Any primatologist knows ... that to decipher a dominance hierarchy, you don't watch for aggression in the dominants. You look for signs of fear in the subordinates." The ex-colonial patriarchs were clearly in charge here. Apparently, one purpose of the de Heaulme legacy was to support a population of indigenous sifakas and ringtailed lemurs, as well as a few brown lemurs brought in from the north and east of the island. Just enough forest was left to accommodate them. Jolly comments that, just as many aristocrats have librarians in their libraries, this family seemed to expect primatologists in the reserve.

The Durrell crew arrived in 1981 in a small plane. One purpose was filming a series, *Ark on the Move*, which became a book illustrated with still photography. And like others who describe the Malagasy landscape, both Jolly and Gerald noticed damage from habitat destruction and climate change. Erosion makes the rivers run red; from the air, the land seems to bleed. The Mandrare River feeding Berenty runs merely a fraction of the water it held early in the twentieth century, swidden agriculture has resulted in widespread erosion, the spiny forest has shrunk as commercial interests like the sisal plantation have expanded, and even the "rides" cut through the reserve for convenience have reduced the integrity of the woodland the lemurs occupy.

Still, the rides offer easy interaction with habituated groups. Altogether, this situation has benefited primatologists and wildlife conservationists who study lemurs in efforts to save them from extinction. In the spiny forest near Berenty, the crew managed to capture on film mouse lemurs and lepilemurs, perhaps the most curious lemurs of all. Because they eat leaves almost exclusively, their digestive track is extensive, and they extract the full nutritional value of their food by re-ingesting their waste.

Gerald was charmed by the lepilumurs he encountered in the spiny forest, as he was by all Malagasy fauna, but he particularly enjoyed their official name, Milne-Edwards's sportive lemur. No one seems quite sure why they are "sportive," except that they vault from tree to tree in much the same way as sifakas.

Berenty was unusual in Gerald's experience of Madagascar, though. After they left the area, Professor Roland Albignac would guide the Durrells back to Tana in a roundabout way, along rough roads to Ankarafantsika, a large dry deciduous forest in the northwest of the island. Albignac and his students had divided the reserve into labeled transects which, but for the dangerously spiny trees and lack of rides, resembled Berenty. With this system, the seven species of lemurs inhabiting this corner of the island could be tracked with relative ease, their behaviors noted, and their numbers recorded. Gerald was astonished when a troop of Coquerel's sifaka, creamy colored rather than white, leapt through the thorny tree trunks with unerring speed and grace. When a nocturnal avahi, or wooly lemur, was darted—a new technology at the time—Gerald was once again astonished as he sank his fingers into the soft, thick coat. Fitted with a radio collar, the avahi soon rejoined the group, providing more information for the primatologists studying them than their tracking and recording via marked transects.

Back to the capital the Durrells went before heading toward the final destination for *Ark on the Move*, the northeastern town of Perinet, on the outskirts of Madagascar's most accessible reserve, and one of its oldest. Andasibe-Mantadia consists of two almost contiguous areas, an official reserve and a national park. Of all Madagascar's natural areas, Andasibe-Mantadia is closest to Tana. Here, the goal was filming the indri, large as human toddlers, rare, elusive, and known for their haunting song, which can carry for miles through the rainforest.[19] Day after day, the party heard the indri singing from afar, but never saw them until the crew started to pack for good. Suddenly, as if by magic,

we were all startled . . . by a sudden ear-splitting, ground-vibrating, roaring, howling chorus. . . . The noise was indescribable and made the forest vibrate like a harp. Moving our vantage point we could see, thirty feet above us, taking their ease in the sunlit garden of pink flowers, a troop of five indri, singing their territorial chorus. It had all the rich, sonorous quality of organ music, but—as I later discovered—it sounded more like the weird and beautiful calls of whales.[20]

Again, luck was with Gerald, and the crew.

Filming continued in Nosy Komba, a tropical island off the northwest coast—a veritable lemur paradise, where the age-old fady, or taboo against harming lemurs, persists in the best way possible. According to legend, a local king imported rare black lemurs to this island where no lemurs lived, protected them, and appointed special keepers to insure their wellbeing. That tradition thrives, the lemurs are privileged characters, and Nosy Komba is now a tourist destination. When the Durrell film crew landed for a celebration, they found the lemurs tame and perhaps too curious about the film equipment. Still photographs in *Ark on the Move* show the landing party, the celebration, and the little animals clambering over cine cameras.

These happy moments in Madagascar continued the energy of the market in Tana, the surprisingly luscious Malagasy cuisine served in run-down hotels, the friendly curiosity of the children, and the camaraderie of the adults—from village leaders to local wildlife experts to foreign scholars.

On Gerald's final mission, to Madagascar again in 1990, described in *The Aye-Aye and I*, he would encounter the same warmth, energy, and humor. City life in Antananarivo was as exuberant as ever. The zoma, Tana's large and energetic market, provided a wealth of fruits and vegetables, every colorful spice imaginable, and local goods of every conceivable kind. For blankets, carryalls, and spare garments, Gerald and Lee were able to find piles of lambas, or multi-use lengths of fabric most often employed for clothing. They bought baskets for gifts, storage, and small animal homes. From the upper stories of their hotel, market umbrellas up and down every street in view resembled fields of mushrooms. The Tsimbazaza Zoo cared for some of the creatures headed for Jersey.

Comedy prevails from time to time. Misadventures in the typical Malagasy "hotely" sound like a scene from Michael Frayne's *Noises Off.* The hotel staff managed to survive the shocks of discovering wildlife in and out of their proper cages, climbing curtains and speaking a language that sounded like popping champagne corks. Gerald managed to survive being locked in his room for several hours by a smiling maid. His experiment of introducing a terrified lemur youngster to an old lady of the lemur bunch paid off: "he flung himself onto her.... She was momentarily startled by this sudden invasion but ... clasped him in her arms" until he "tried to feed from her milkless teats and was given a sharp nip for his pains."[21] Fortunately, the baby quickly adapted to getting milk from a syringe, content to get the affection he needed from a foster mother of his own species. All the animals in the Durrells' care on this trip fared well.

But in many ways, this was the most difficult journey of Gerald's life. In the midst of trying to organize transportation back to Jersey, Gerald learned that Lawrence had died, and he was too far away from the rest of the family to offer any comfort. A staff member contracted cerebral malaria. Gerald's health was deteriorating, so travel along "unspeakable" roads and in small planes was sometimes excruciating.[22] The mission was more complicated: it included capturing critically endangered animals as well as filming their natural behaviors in their natural habitat. Although more local and foreign scholars and conservationists were investing time and resources in the Malagasy fauna, the situation had become more dire, as the thin tissue of conservation law was still powerless to stop land clearing for logging and agriculture. Erosion and habitat loss were even more extreme this time.

Capture of endangered local fauna as pets or protein continued, as did persecution of the aye-aye by farmers who blamed them for agricultural losses. Economic and political pressures on the human inhabitants resulted in feeble support for healthcare, education, and poor or nonexistent communication with the Malagasy people about the precious rarity and importance of their own plants and animals. As in every environmental hot spot in the world, pressures on humans translate directly into pressures on wildlife. In *The Aye-Aye and I* (1992), Gerald's last book, along with the usual self-deprecating humor, the anger boils over.

Outside Tana, Gerald and Lee were "depressed" through most of this difficult and complicated journey. Again, the party traveled to the vanishing Lac Alatroa area northeast of the city, where they found the gentle lemurs that created such havoc in the hotel. The lake is vanishing because subsistence rice growers burn more and more of the surrounding woodland or bamboo forest for paddies. Rice is the basis of the Malagasy diet, and the "tavy" agricultural system which produces it is ritually embedded in local cultures throughout much of the island. Growing rice for home consumption in this way is unsustainable, since cleared land wears out after a season or two, and forest takes decades to regrow.[23]

When their homes are burned, the lemurs are easily caught, and, since the disappearance of the taboo against harming them has disappeared, "paper protection" is the only protection they have.[24] A not unjustified fear of the *vazaha*, as Europeans are called, returning to "wrench their land from them" makes the situation all the worse.[25] Newer agricultural methods can be perceived as a threat, and conservation programs as an even greater threat since, even from the beginning, many of these programs set aside land which has been heretofore perceived as open and free. Wildlife conservation, of course, prohibits the consumption of certain animals which historically have been absorbed into protein-poor diets, and the sale of "exotic" pets, which could ease poverty, at least temporarily, could also be interpreted as imperialism, however green and benign the intention.

On this final Durrell mission, Mihanta Rakotoarinosy, a young local helper who later went on to publish scientific papers about Malagasy wildlife, bought a subadult gentle lemur from a cousin, who selected it from several others she sighted at a local market to cook it for dinner. The poor animal was "terrified out of its wits," and the cousin was "astonished" to learn that selling or killing lemurs was illegal.[26] In short order, at other villages, the Durrells managed to buy (for a price that would not encourage further capture) more babies, several subadults, and the unhealthy elderly foster mother (a former pet)—all smuggled successfully into the hotel. The perpetually smiling Mihanta seems to have been a genius at locating villagers with lemurs for sale.

In the middle of their travels to find lemurs, Gerald and Lee traveled north to Boly Bay to monitor the progress of a new captive breeding program for the ynifora, or the ploughshare tortoise, endangered not only because of habitat loss, but because many rural people kept these animals as pets; they believed in the tortoise's protective powers. At the time—and since then to an alarming degree—these large, rare reptiles have also been trafficked by illegal international trade in rare, endangered animals. In 1985, the IUCN Tortoise Specialist Group asked the Durrell Foundation to establish and operate the ploughshare rescue program: it was Lee's first independent project, conducted with wildlife specialists *in situ*.

In the case of the ploughshare tortoise, captive breeding, always difficult, must take into account unusual behavioral patterns. A male ploughshare breeds only after fighting with other males, attempting to topple them onto their backs with the plow-shaped extension under his "chin," the source of the colorful name. Feeding, protecting, and rebuilding habitat is almost never enough for successful captive breeding, and reintroduction is almost never enough to sustain local populations.

After this detour, the Durrells and crew searched in the Kirindy Forest, observing the endangered kapidolo tortoise, giant jumping rat, fosa, mouse lemur, and sifaka. There are also six species of lepilemur in this region. The humans contended with biting flies and other physical discomforts, trapping difficulties, and rare animals blocking traffic—all sources for Gerald's particular brand of humor. But altogether, the successful efforts to film were a calm before the emotional storm of locating aye-ayes at Mananara, back across the island on the east coast,

The Aye-Aye and I begins with Gerald's first face to face meeting with one of these animals. His tiny new acquaintance bit Gerald's walking stick almost in half with its alarming teeth, crawled to his shoulders, combed through his beard and hair, and finally inserted the long, thin middle finger into his ear. This odd "magic finger" adaptation serves more than one purpose. The aye-aye's diet includes insects, echolocated in tree bark by tapping, and, since the introduction of coconuts as a cash crop, green coconuts, which it easily pierces with its huge teeth and scoops out with the strange middle finger. Aye-ayes also feast on sugar cane and cloves. "If you are a villager whose whole livelihood depends on, perhaps, five coconut trees, a tiny patch of sugar cane, and half a dozen clove trees," Gerald wrote, "then the Aye-aye becomes . . . a creature that can ruin your income forever. Therefore, you kill it or starve."[27]

For Gerald the aye-aye was "astonishing and complex," but the encounter also explains to a degree why other humans might consider it threatening. Sometimes, sorcerers add the magic finger to their ritual kits. In fact, though historically most lemurs are protected by "fady," or taboo, the aye-aye is, in contrast, rarely protected and, indeed, usually persecuted by a taboo, from a belief that it is a "harbinger of death."[28] An aye-aye is liable to be killed on sight, its corpse left in the road, fed to dogs, or thrown onto a succession of neighbors' property. Patient with animals, Gerald had to work harder at developing patience with the distinctive cultural patterns he found in Madagascar, no longer sustainable for the humans under economic and political pressure, and more immediately putting the island's distinctive plants and animals at risk.

Mananara was home base in the search for the aye-aye. Almost the first sight at Mananara was a crystal market and factory: a group of young women sat beneath a tree, extracting several kinds of crystal from matrices with small hammers. Team members were delighted with their purchases of the multi-colored stones. How quickly environmental conditions can degenerate! By 2020, such an apparently harmless activity had become a human tragedy. As the world market for crystals has grown and the Malagasy economy has faltered even more, wages have stagnated to the point that an entire family can chip out crystals all day for one cup of rice.[29] At that time, probably no one saw that this burgeoning industry foreshadowed economic exploitation of the worst kind. The scene was simply a bit of local color, much needed in view of the devastation Gerald did see.

For weeks, aye-ayes were impossible for the crew to find and film, much less capture. Some of the investment of time and money was salvaged when Albinac lent them an aye-aye named Verity, the name inspired by *cinema verité*, and perhaps by the mission, to communicate the truth of a dire situation as realistically as possible. Filming Verity up close could fill part of the gap if aye-ayes in their normal habitat, engaging in their usual behavior, refused to reveal themselves. Verity learned to eat from Lee's hand, and his attacks on the sugar cane and coconuts he was given provided plenty of drama for the cinematographers.

The rest of the mission—to help save the species' possible extinction—remained in the balance. A few aye-aye had been moved to Nosy Mangabe, where Eleanor Sterling, a conservationist as devoted as Gerald to rescuing Madagascar's unique faunal community, was studying them.[30] However, successful captive breeding operations usually rely on more than one colony, so rescuing more from mainland Madagascar was still a necessity.

When locating the animals within tangled local relationships and remaining forests began to seem hopeless, the team decided to consult a soothsayer, partly out of belief that he could help, half out of desperation and the need for some kind of stimulation. After channeling an ancestor, the soothsayer felt that they would succeed in their quest because their motives were pure. "If some people want to believe in Jesus, or Mohammed, or Buddha, or their ancestors, who is to say which is right, and which is wrong?" Gerald wrote. "It seems to me that most of the religions in the world are too dogmatic. They preach the 'live and let live' philosophy, but rarely do they practice it."[31]

For all his anger, his delight in stereotypes, and his willingness to make jokes on the basis of gender, sex, race, ethnicity, and nation, at his core, Gerald tried to be open and respectful of the differences among individuals and societies. Everyone in the camp washed and saved tin cans for the village women. The team opened their camp every day so children could visit the animals, and, following Gerald's lifelong custom, they rewarded the children for helping. This approach of respecting the human environment has become, more and more, standard practice for field scientists and environmentalists: it is kind, politically aware, and pragmatic, but not easy.

The days dragged, and the film team had to leave. Now the drama began in earnest. The next day, two farmers showed up at the camp with a mother aye-aye and infant. A few days later, two team members found another female in the forest, but the baby escaped into the forest; if not found, it would need its mother, who would have to be returned to the nest. At the last moment, the infant was found and reunited with its mother in the camp. And soon after, members of Gerald's team captured a large male "of pugilistic mien," almost fulfilling their quota of six.[32] It was as if the Fon of Bafut's juju extended across space and time, this time for the aye-ayes instead of the golden cat.

Then it was time for Gerald's last good-bye to Madagascar. "The morning before we left," he wrote, "Lee and I walked up the road towards the forest and stood listening to the indris, as the sky turned from green to blue. Their haunting, wonderful, mournful song came to us, plaintive, beautiful and sad. It could have been the very voice of the forest, the very voice of Madagascar lamenting."[33] After a terrifying flight back to Tana with the aye-ayes, and complicated arrangements for all their animal charges to get through British customs, Gerald and Lee were back to their own little island. There had been good reason to worry. The return trip would be lengthy. In Gerald's four decades of collecting, he knew animals sometimes died before reaching their destination, and sometimes the draconian British Customs process was to blame.

The healthy collection of Malagasy creatures at the Jersey Zoo and ongoing conservation efforts on the island itself are proof that this last mission was a success. Knowing nothing of that future, Gerald could not refrain from ending with gloomy statistics:

Between 1980 and 1981, over 33,000 wild-caught parrots passed through the Amsterdam airport. Most of these either die on their journey or shortly afterwards because to save costs they are squashed together as slaves used to be. If they survive, they are sold to "bird lovers" in different parts of the world.

Japan and Hong Kong are whittling away at the last of the elephants, turning their tusks (so much more elegant left on the elephants) into artistic carvings. In much the same way, the beautiful furs from leopard, jaguar, snow leopard, clouded leopard and so on, are used to clad the inelegant bodies of thoughtless and, for the most part, ugly women. I wonder how many would buy these furs if they know that on their bodies they wore the skin of an animal that, when captured, was killed by the medieval and agonizing method of having a red-hot rod inserted up its rectum so as not to mark the fur.[34]

The CITES (Convention on International Trade in Endangered Species) treaty is only a start, and only as effective as the expertise of customs agents and the good will of its signatories.

Comedy became increasingly difficult for Gerald to sustain. Failure to capture and film the aye-aye might have meant extinction because, except for the small group on Nosy Komba, there were no other captive colonies in the world at that time. The forced humor, the occasional derogatory remark about his host country, and the hastily constructed conclusion, detailing a quick trip back to Carl Jones' aviary in Madagascar and to Round Island once more, are understandable. Although it is not his best conceived or best written book, Gerald might have known that *The Aye-Aye and I* would be his last book about finding animals, just as the journey to Madagascar would be his last mission. The book had to count, and it had to be published quickly. A review in the *Times Literary Supplement* suggests importance beyond literary qualities: "If only animals could speak they would award Mr. Gerald Durrell one of their first Nobel prizes."[35]

After almost forty years of risking his health, his first marriage, and even his life to search out and find rare and endangered animals, in *The Aye-Aye and I*, Gerald explains why:

> The first [aye-aye] I had ever met had given me a shock, an extraordinary fibrillation of the nerves, a sense of astonishment that no other animal has given me. And yet I have met everything from killer whales to hummingbirds the size of a flake of ash, animals as curious as giraffe to platypus. . . . I thought of all of the animals we had just seen in Mauritius and what we had achieved for them. If only we could do the same for this strange cargo of creatures. . . .[36]

More than the tragic sense Nancy Myers saw in the whole Durrell family, more than the untethered comedy on the other side of Gerald's character, still, at the end of his life, hope and the sense of wonder remained.

Notes

1 G. Durrell, *Golden Bats and Pink Pigeons* (New York: Simon and Schuster, 1977), *42.*

2 Jacques-Henri Bernardin de Saint-Pierre, *Journey to Mauritius* (New York: Interlink Books, 2002).

3 Ibid.,102.

4 David Quammen, *Song of the Dodo: Island Biogeography in an Age of Extinctions* (New York: Simon and Schuster, 1997), 269–73.

5 G. Durrell, *Golden Bats and Pink Pigeons*, 110–11.

6 Ibid., 91.

7 Ibid., 94.

8 Ibid., 124.

9 Frank B. Gill, Christian Jouanin, and Robert W. Storer. "Notes on the Seabirds of Round Island," *The Auk* 87 (3) (July 1970), 518. This article includes photographs illustrating nicely the landscape Gerald describes in *Golden Bats and Pink Pigeons.*

10 G. Durrell, *Golden Bats and Pink Pigeons*, 177.

11 Gerald poses with the aye-aye on the dramatic dust jacket photo of Douglas Botting's official biography.

12 Alison Jolly, *A World Like Our Own* (New Haven, CT: Yale University Press, 1980), xiii.

13 Ibid.

14 Jean-Jacques Petter and François Desbordes, *Primates of the World: An Illustrated Guide* (Princeton, NJ: Princeton University Press, 2013), 10.

15 Lemur Conservation Foundation. https://www.lemurreserve.org/lemurs/#:~:text=Physically%20many%20have%20especially%20pointed,most%20threatened%20groups%20of%20mammals [accessed July 20, 2023].

16 Patricia Wright, *For the Love of Lemurs: My Life in the Wilds of Madagascar* (New York: Lantern Books, 2014).

17 Christoph Schwitzer, Russell A. Mittermeier, Anthony B. Rylands, et al., *Primates in Peril: The World's 25 Most Endangered Primates 2018-20*, (IUCN SSC Primate Specialist Group, 2019), 1. https://www.researchgate.net/publication/338657345_Primates_in_Peril_The_world's_most_endangered_primates_2018-2020

18 Alison Jolly, *Lords and Lemurs: Mad Scientists, Kings with Spears, and the Survival of Diversity in Madagascar* (Boston, MA: Houghton Mifflin, 2004), 2–5.

19 G. Durrell, *Ark on the Move*, 129.

20 Ibid., 136.

21 G. Durrell, *The Aye-Aye and I*, 30.

22 Ibid., 152.

23 Örjan Bodin, Maria Tengö et al., "The Value of Small Size: Loss of Forest Patches and Ecological Thresholds in Southern Madagascar," *ESA: Ecological Applications* 16 (2) (2013), 1–4.

24 Douglas W. Hume, "Malagasy Swidden Agriculture," *Karnataka Journal of Agricultural Sciences*, 2 (1) (2012), 37–54.

25 G. Durrell, *Aye-Aye and I*, 125.

26 Ibid., 17.

27 Ibid., 3.

28 Ibid., 2.

29 Tess McClure, "Dark Crystals: the Brutal Reality behind a Booming Wellness Craze," *Guardian*, September 17, 2019, 26. https://www.theguardian.com/lifeandstyle/2019/sep/17/healing-crystals-wellness-mining-madagascar [accessed July 20, 2019].

30 Eleanor Sterling later went on to work as a conservation biologist with the American Museum of Natural History, where she continued her research on the aye-aye.

31 G. Durrell, *Aye-Aye and I*, 126.

32 Ibid., 146.

33 G. Durrell, *Ark on the Move*, 137.

34 G. Durrell, *Aye-Aye and I*, 154.

35 Ibid., back cover.

36 Ibid., 166–67.

7 THE ZOO

"Porthos." "Poooorthos." A resigned voice drifts across the grove of trees from a hundred yards or so away. I'm standing in a broad gravel path, just at sunset, watching an emperor tamarin, who is watching me from his vantage point on a wooden fence post a few feet high. This is the Tamarin Wood, and I'm guessing this is Porthos. Presumably his fellow "musketeers" have already retired for the night. The zoo is closing, but I'm not in a hurry,

FIGURE 7.1 Emperor tamarin.

and neither is he. After we eye each other for several quiet minutes, I move on, making the circuit to see who else is postponing a good night's sleep. My walk brings me around to the other side of the wood, where a keeper ushers other emperor tamarins, one by one, through a small door above a shelf and into their cabin for the night. Everyone gets a good night snack. I make the connection. What happens to Porthos, I ask, if he doesn't come in for the night. "That's his choice," says the keeper. "Sometimes they decide to stay out for the evening, and sometimes they probably regret it, but there you are." Why, I ask, is the fence so low that Porthos could easily hop down and investigate other parts of the zoo, or even amble down the narrow, wooded road to the Trinity Pub, where congenial human residents of the zoo sometimes assemble at the end of the day? "He won't cross the gravel path. That would expose him to predators."

Not all zoo animals have this kind of freedom. Porthos is guided by his own adaptive behavioral traits and his keepers' understanding of tamarin behaviors. Still, most animals need "freedom" less than average zoo visitors think they do. Catering to this assumption, most zoos are designed for maximum external control of the residents, while at the same time they present the illusion of freedom for the animals. Porthos has some agency here, but not as much freedom as I thought before my conversation with the keeper.

There are many kinds of zoos, and the Jersey Zoo is only one sort, perhaps a unique sort, as it claims to be. In *The Stationary Ark* (1976) and *The Ark's Anniversary* (1990), Gerald outlines the history of the zoo, addresses the constant efforts made by everyone involved to strengthen and improve the organization and the lives of the zoo residents, and reiterates the zoo's unwavering mission of "saving animals from extinction." Everywhere in his nonfiction writing about zoos, Gerald insists on firm principles and best practices. There are many accrediting agencies, and the Jersey Zoo, established in advance of most, could have served as a model for accreditation standards around the world.

Most standards include the need for strong financial and administrative practices. In the early days of the Jersey Zoo, financial health was the most pressing problem, addressed early in the zoo's history by a conservation trust governed by a board of directors. The Trust was reorganized in the 1970s to strengthen its financials: the campus itself, the conservation academy that depends on the zoo for instruction, conservation projects in the zoo and around the planet, and the zoo's function as the primary tourist attraction for the Isle of Jersey—all attest to the financial and administrative health of the organization in the twenty-first century.

Most important, of course, is concern for the animals. Now, all zoo and aquarium accreditation standards emphasize animal health and welfare. However, modern iterations of accreditation criteria insist, as well, on zoos as agents for wildlife conservation and education. It goes without saying that concern for the individual animals and species was the very foundation of Gerald's zoo, and wildlife conservation was always the primary goal. Standards for various accreditation organizations also address the quality of zoo visitor experiences. Zoo design affects both animal welfare and the human visitor experience, and the concern about zoo design is one example of how human and more-than-human needs intersect.

The effects of zoo design and architecture are perhaps underestimated by zoo visitors, in the Jersey Zoo as much as elsewhere: zoo design is not simply a matter of aesthetics. In 1976, after the packing crates and scrap lumber fencing were replaced by carefully designed enclosures, Gerald wrote, "Anyone who has had anything to do with zoos must admit, albeit reluctantly, that there is precious little art in zoo architecture." In his usual hyperbolic language, he continued: "The average architect in a zoo behaves like a child with its first box of bricks and will, if left to himself, produce buildings that are about as much use as they would be if they had been designed by a mentally retarded infant of five".[1]

The London Zoo, founded in 1826 for scientific research, quickly became known as a safe, clean, open space in Regents Park where families could come for a Sunday afternoon outing. Entertainment thus became as important as science, or more so. Cages were designed to frame the large exotic animals, and several buildings fancifully mimicked the most popular animals' countries of origin. For example, the tall doorways of the giraffe house, often represented in cartoons of the time, were shaped a bit like Romanesque cathedral doors, mashed up with Gothic architecture. In one of those cartoons, a giraffe leans over the bars of a small paddock to tug at a visitor's parasol. Three other giraffes seem to look on with benign approval. The London Zoo has been significantly altered and updated, but the pattern of its early architecture appeared in zoos all over the world.

Even though Gerald knew the London Zoo well and cooperated with the staff there, his arch nemesis was Sir Solly Zuckerman, a primatologist who served as secretary and then president (1955–84). Zuckerman held a position against captive breeding, and oversaw a disastrous war among hamadryas baboons on "Monkey Hill" between 1924 and 1931. The females were greatly outnumbered, and most were quickly killed by males. Artificial cliffs resembling the native habitat of the baboons did nothing to quell the artificially imbalanced groups or the overcrowding: free hamadryas live in fission-fusion groups which range over many square miles each day before settling at night into their sleeping cliffs.[2]

As Gerald mentions in *A Bevy of Beasts* and *The Bafut Beagles*, Carl Hagenbeck's enterprise was an inspiration for his first collecting adventure. Half a century after the London Zoo was established, and probably serving superficially as a model, Hagenbeck had radically changed the prevailing zoo aesthetic to display his assemblage of animals as a peaceable kingdom in naturalistic enclosures. His influence lasts until this day and has contributed to a new wave of "immersion experience" zoo architecture, that is, optical effects designed to create for the visitor the illusion of closeness within the animals' habitats.

Some elements in these immersion enclosures—glass barriers and carefully laid out viewing angles—do allow for closeness. Other elements—plants, objects for enrichment such as climbing structures made from or disguised as trees or stones—can resemble objects which might appear in the animal's natural habitat. Jon Coe, a landscape architect responsible for the Woodland Park Zoo gorilla habitat in Seattle, Washington, participated in a trend to design enclosures that unsettle visitors by directing them along passages that are lower than the enclosures, with camouflaged barriers. The excitement of feeling vulnerable to a silverback, lion, or large snake, he has explained, lends respect to the animals as well as entertainment value. In making the enclosure seem more natural, of course, zoo architects often also make it more natural in fact. The "flight distance" designed to give the visitor the illusion of space within such habitats also provides the animal on display some feeling of comfort, safety, and privacy. The exemplary gorilla habitat in Seattle's Woodland Park Zoo, designed in 1977 by Coe and Grant Jones, for example, creates for the visitors a sense of closeness to the animals and presents an illusion of a real gorilla forest.[3] The gorilla habitat in Disney's Animal Kingdom in Orlando, Florida, is similar. Looking natural is not always best, though. One of the keepers there confided that enrichment objects cannot include anything that would look "unnatural" to visitors—no brightly colored toys or cardboard boxes that, in other zoos, are provided because they appeal to primates' hard-wired attraction to color. All of us do, you know, like our colors.

The postage stamp zoo and the naturalistic zoo are not the only models, and Gerald did not follow either one when he established his zoo on the Isle of Jersey. A few professionally operated zoos, generally those with a tight budget, consist of modest structures placed within the landscape as found. As a Floridian, I have come to know the Santa Fe College Teaching Zoo in Gainesville, Florida. (Like the Durrell Zoo, this small collection serves as the public zoo for the city.) Situated within a small, natural Florida hammock, it comprises a gibbon forest with five residents, a meadow for crowned cranes and springbok, and a pond for alligators. Exotic animal species mingle with well-known creatures such as peacocks and Florida natives, many of whom find the zoo a convenient stopping place for a snack or shelter. Its earliest residents were discarded pets. Like Gerald's zoo, this one features the "small uglies," partly because they are interesting and partly because the students who operate the zoo need not work with large or dangerous animals in order to learn their vocation.

One of the few expeditions Gerald and Lee made without collection or conservation as an explicit objective was to the Soviet Union in 1984, where they filmed material for the television series *Durrell in Russia*, which became a lavishly illustrated book in 1986. The journey took months and covered thousands of miles, from Lake Baikal, in the eastern part of the country just north of the border with Mongolia, to Askanaya Nova, almost 28,000 acres on the steppes of (now occupied) Ukraine near the Black Sea. Askanaya Nova was established a hundred years before the Durrells visited, on land granted during the reign of Catherine the Great to the family of the reserve's founder, Friedrich-Jacob Eduardovych Falz-Fein. He brought in animals which had become rare in Russia—swans, bison, Bobac marmots—and imported exotic species such as llamas, eland, and ostrich. Markhor (members of the goat family native to the mountains of central Asia) and Przewalski's horses (Mongolian residents rare almost to the point of extinction), arrived and thrived, as did kulan (wild asses also native to central Asia). Specialists backbred related species such as the horse and the zebra in attempts to revive the extinct quagga. They managed to boost the numbers of endangered equids, the Przewalski's horse and the kula, enough to reintroduce them to their original ranges. Gerald called the area "a zoo within a zoo within a farm."[4] The area is now considered a biosphere reserve.

Such integration of the zoo within the natural features of a landscape is part of the essence of the zoo on the Isle of Jersey. Like Askanaya Nova and the teaching zoo in Gainesville, Florida, the zoo campus in Jersey has enclosures which are adaptations of the landscape itself. The seventeenth-century manor house and outbuildings are built of local granite. The small stream, lake, and water meadow are situated down the hill from the front of the house. On this thirty-acre site are woods, spacious gravel paths, old walls dripping with wallflowers, and historic outbuildings serving newer purposes—offices and a small museum to show the zoo's history and Gerald's memorabilia. One wing of the manor house now houses the aye-ayes. The grounds are managed for conservation of all kinds: most organic materials are recycled on site, and much of the food comes from an organic farm on the campus.

The design of the Tamarin Wood can be extraordinarily and genuinely open because Gerald and the founding staff studied the behaviors of individual animals and species. With due precautions, of course, Chilean flamingoes and Oriental short-clawed otters will stay in or near the stream and water meadow because they prefer water. The Endangered red-breasted geese will stay within confines of the park because they are fed there. The great apes are given places to hide, and they even learn to use the protective bars of their habitats for physical development and entertainment. Porthos can perch on his fence post, taking the evening air and observing humans who seem to be brought in for his entertainment. But the visitor is never encouraged to forget that the lemurs, flamingos, and Endangered island reptiles are expatriates, aboard an ark that may, or may not, ever return them or their descendants to an ancestral home, however desirable that future might be.

We think they are not unhappy where they are. As Gerald pointed out more than once, the residents of any zoo are less concerned about the human concept of freedom than they are with the right "furniture" and dimensions for them to feel safe from predators or prying eyes. Even during his early collecting trips, he constructed traveling cages so that his captive animals had "bedrooms" for escape and privacy. By the time he published *The Stationary Ark* in 1976, Gerald had absorbed an introductory textbook on the subject, *Wild Animals in Captivity* (1950) by Heini Hediger, who introduced the notion of flight distance well before it became part of the vocabulary of zoo architecture in general—and a guiding principle for Coe and Jones in their work for the Woodland Park Zoo.

Flight distance is genuine at the zoo in Jersey. Unless they want to be seen, most of the small monkeys remain invisible to the casual visitor. As

166 THE EVOLUTION OF GERALD DURRELL

Jersey's only zoo, the Durrell zoo maintains popular animals like the emperor tamarins, a species of "Least Concern," for the pleasure of its visitors, and since there are so many of them, it isn't difficult to catch glimpses of these charming little monkeys. However, the most threatened tamarin species—black lions, golden lions, and pied—are now part of rigorously controlled captive breeding programs. They are housed in two other locations in the zoo, in airy cages filled with trees. Otherwise, a virus could wipe out an alarming percentage of the world's tamarin population in a single blow. Sometimes they hide.

The park also provides a convenient hostelry for native species of plants, birds, squirrels, frogs and toads, pipistrelle bats, and insects. In the early days of the Jersey Zoo, a tame chough named Dingle lived there, but choughs were locally extinct on the island due to habitat loss and persecution by farmers. Now they are back—a population restarted from a few pairs of Cornish choughs and bred in a new enclosure furnished with a small replica of their favorite nesting cliffs. Some of the offspring have been released from an aviary on the coast. Once again, these glossy black relatives of the crow, with their brilliant red beaks, nest in the cliffs above the sea.

Although the park looks as if it has always been there, its beginnings in 1959 were tenuous. Before the zoo came the animals, most collected during Gerald's third foray into Africa and residing temporarily in Margo's back garden. Chumley lived in the house, the special charge of Louisa and Margo, who cosseted him. For months, while family and neighbors endured the noisy discomfort of wild animals in their neighborhood, Gerald courted officials, tried to fight his way through red tape, and endured broken promises. Soon, some of the more troublesome or delicate animals had to be boarded at the zoo in Paignton, in Devon.[5] Meanwhile, Gerald kept up a rigorous schedule of writing and television programming. When hope seemed almost gone, his publisher introduced the Durrells to Major Hugh Fraser, who agreed to show them several locations on the Isle of Jersey. None suited.

Then a miracle occurred—when Gerald observed that Fraser's own manor Les Augres would be a perfect location. Apparently without a second thought, the major agreed to lease the property, and after a few months of frantic activity, the zoo opened for visitors on March 26, 1959. But money had been the source of perpetual woes ever since Gerald first mentioned the project to Lawrence in October 1954:

I am now, I think, sufficiently well known to attempt something which I have had in mind for a number of years. To you, no doubt, it will sound completely mad and a lot of rubbish. I want to start a Trust or organization, with land in somewhere like the West Indies, for the breeding of those forms of animal life which are on the borders of extinction, and which without help cannot survive.[6]

But as his friend, the evolutionary biologist Julian Huxley pointed out, however popular such a project would be with zoologists, zoologists have no money. So, Gerald asks his brother, "What I should like to know from you is, who do you know that is stinking rich?" Just as Gerald had used Lawrence's foreign service network to help negotiate his routes into animal collecting in South America, this time, he took advantage of the contacts ("snobs") Lawrence was making as a novelist with a growing and glowing reputation on both sides of the Atlantic. Even in 1954, his correspondence with Lawrence shows that Gerald consulted accountants about structuring the Trust with tax shelters. Les Augres wasn't just a perfect location for its aesthetic and topographical features: Jersey would come to serve Gerald's financial purposes as well.

Gate receipts might have kept afloat an ordinary zoo on a relatively wealthy island, where there had never been one, but this was a zoo with mission, which Gerald outlines in *The Stationary Ark*:

1   To promote interest in wildlife conservation throughout the world.

2   To build up under controlled conditions breeding colonies of various species which were threatened with extinction in the wild state.

3   To organize special expeditions to rescue seriously threatened species.

4   By studying the biology of these species, to mass and correlate data which would help towards protecting these endangered animals in the wild state.[7]

The ramifications of this ambitious agenda proved to be more complex than anyone could have predicted at the outset.

All zoos are more than collections of animals housed in collections of human-made structures. A zoo tells a story, or many stories. Gerald's story was new, and different from the stories told by any other zoo in the world at that time.

The zoo historian Nigel Rothfels has challenged the conservation rhetoric of the contemporary zoo community, not because conservation is unimportant, but because it may often serve as a secondary rationalization for an entertainment industry.[8] The "arks" most zoos claim to be house animals who will never (or very rarely) return to their homes. If they go anywhere, it will be to another zoo. Captive breeding thus has served to replenish zoo stocks, not wild stocks, although, since 1975, international sales and trade of zoo animals have been regulated by the CITES treaty (Convention on International Trade in Endangered Species of Wild Fauna and Flora). Even without CITES, replacing animals by capturing them in the wild would be increasingly difficult or impossible as the animals become more rare. The most responsible (as well as legal) policy toward wild creatures is to leave them alone or increase and protect their endangered habitat. Although breeding animals for zoos is necessary and important as long as there are zoos, it would be a stretch to equate breeding zoo stocks with conservation.

It is also true that some zoos now make significant contributions to conservation. The World Conference on Breeding Endangered Species in Captivity as an Aid to their Survival (WCBESCAS), co-hosted by what is now called the Flora and Fauna International, was initiated at the Jersey Zoo in 1972. A few years later, in 1978, thanks to the captive breeding cooperation fostered by this network, Durrell's zoo received its first pair of golden lion tamarins. In 2020, these beautiful monkeys are merely "Endangered," not Critically Endangered, thanks to the network which includes the Durrell program, the Smithsonian Zoo in Washington D.C., and Zoo Atlanta. In *The Rarest of the Rare* (1997), Diane Ackerman describes the dedication required for relocating these beautiful monkeys to the Atlantic coastal forest in Brazil—some of the earliest releases from a captive breeding project. The challenges are many and include the monkeys' own social structures, which must be managed with established hierarchies and individual temperaments in mind. Some golden lions live at the Jersey Zoo as a potential breeding group for reintroduction into the wild. Unlike the other zoos which have invested in conservation only since the late twentieth century, the Durrell project was different from the beginning. However lovely the setting may be, however interesting the animals, the primary purpose of the Jersey Zoo, even *before* its beginning, was conservation.

At first the zoo had to be supported by gate receipts, so just about any "exotic" animal fit in. Even now, a few species besides the emperor tamarins are maintained at the Jersey Zoo to allow for practice in breeding techniques and to delight visitors. The meercat enclosure is one of the most popular spots in the park, even though the meercat is another species of Least Concern.

However, after 1963, the narrowing focus on conservation and financial restructuring after the establishment of the Trust meant that many of the animals whose upkeep required major expenditures went to other zoos. Claudius, the affectionate tapir Gerald rescued from a Buenos Aires pet shop, was one of the first to go, along with his mate Paula. Juanita the peccary, collected in Jujuy when she was a tiny piglet, and Potsil, a palm civet from West Africa, followed. The chimpanzees were phased out because, for high-maintenance animals, they were not sufficiently endangered for the zoo's mission and resources. A beloved lioness acquired by Deputy Zoological Director Jeremy Mallinson during an expedition to Botswana died as a result of her first pregnancy and was not replaced. Paula the cheetah, who frequently sprinted with Mallinson around the park, and her mate Peter, were the last of their kind at the zoo. With the possible exception of Potsil, who inflicted painful bites on Gerald and his other keepers whenever he could, these animals were much missed.

There were other disasters—deaths of rare white-eared pheasants from an infectious disease hitherto undetected in the ground, deaths of Endangered Mexican volcano rabbits from bureaucratic mishandling. The flamingos uncovered and ingested a cache of lead shot, probably buried by a Jersey local during the Second World War German occupation. Many of the flamingos were poisoned. The most heartbreaking and grotesque loss, perhaps, was the death of a friendly, tame macaw when a zoo visitor sat on him as he paused on a low granite wall, his favorite daytime perch. She neither apologized nor inquired about his injuries later on.

As Douglas Botting has shown in his official biography, Gerald was so overwhelmed with the business of keeping the project afloat that sometimes his only contact with the animals came when he watched them from the windows of his flat in the manor house. Additional stresses resulted from courting celebrities and royalty for financial support, making films and appearing on television, live public appearances (one at the Royal Festival Hall, which seats nearly 3,000 people), and other special fundraising events. Until the Trust was established in 1963, royalties from Gerald's books amounted to the most reliable and largest chunk of the funding, and he had to publish at a frantic pace to repay a large personal loan for everyday operating expenses.

Louisa died in 1964, and soon after, Leslie lost his job in Kenya. Gerald drank and smoked too much, and at one point, contracted mumps. Another time, he committed himself to a rest home for a break from mental stress. Here, he gives Lawrence a progress report on his health:

> the doctors here have decided that my heart is fine, but it's merely general stress and strain that causes something jolly called 'arterial spasm'. They've advised me not to drink spirits at all and to cut down smoking. Whilst there's wine about I am more than willing to follow their advice though cutting the cigarettes down is a bigger problem.[9]

The stress that brought on Gerald's physical illnesses did not diminish. In 1972, tensions developed over administration of the Trust. Eventual reorganization along lines Gerald approved removed some of the administrative responsibility, but writing, traveling, television programming, and zookeeping continued to take a toll. Jacquie left Gerald and the zoo in 1976, their marriage a casualty in Gerald's battle to save all the animals he could from the human onslaught in a world gone haywire.

Despite stressful finances and the hard labor of running a small zoo with an important mission, from the beginning, the staff were exceptionally competent and committed. Of the utmost importance, especially after the early reconstruction of the zoo as a conservation organization, was developing a record system for individual animals—their personalities, body measurements, care, behavior, medical experiences, and breeding. Since boyhood in Corfu, Gerald had obsessively kept records about the animals he collected and other observations about his daily rambles around the island.[10] Mallinson noted in his autobiography that he, too, made detailed flash cards about all the animals he expected to encounter on his own collecting trips—and at the Jersey Zoo.[11]

After the formation of the Trust as a non-profit conservation organization, more detailed records were required. It must have been second nature for Gerald and the staff to invent their unique system of color-coded cards, each the size of standard typing paper, to which photos of each animal were attached. A white card was for the individual's history. Pink was for medical records. Blue was for behavior. Breeding records

THE ZOO **171**

were kept with the same fastidious care on other cards, and keepers wrote daily entries about animal happenings in a large logbook. These cards are still kept, and all the logbooks are safely filed away. The system generated a great deal of necessary redundancy, and within a few years, additional filing systems were added as more kinds of information became obviously important. The cards turned out to be useful in captive breeding of endangered species. Although the staff might not have foreseen this particular importance for the card system at the outset, it would evolve into essential data sets. Now, accredited zoos worldwide use a similar standardized system for the breeding of endangered species.

From the beginning, an additional wish was to collect sound recordings to accompany the information recorded on the cards, but this would not occur until 1978. At that point, Lee McGeorge, whose dissertation research focused on vocalizations of animals in Madagascar, came to the zoo at Gerald's invitation to make these recordings. If the recordings were much desired for the zoo's records, Lee's presence was desired even more. After she and Gerald married the following year, her commitment to the project as a whole and the Madagascar species in particular has remained unflagging.

In his forward to *Breeding Endangered Species in Captivity* (1975), the proceedings of the 1972 collaborative conference held at the Jersey Zoo, Gerald elaborated on the tensions between conservationist organizations and zoos. As usual, he urged readers and participants to greater levels of cooperation. To do otherwise, he suggested, is illogical and irresponsible because conservationists need zoos as sanctuaries for highly endangered species, and zoos need to accept their ethical duty to serve the needs of conservationists and the rare animals they want to save. The Jersey Zoo, he reminded his audience, is only a "small part of the whole complex machinery of conservation." However, he pointed out that this zoo was doing conservation work on a larger scale than other zoos. It was a "practical rescue organization," and the work at Jersey is beginning now, instead of a hazy future, when it might be too late.[12]

Participants in the conference came from Europe, North America, the Commonwealth, India, and the Jersey Zoo itself—and from academic science, government agencies, wildlife conservation organizations, and other zoos. As a result, the quality and approach of the contributions differed considerably, but consistency was hardly the point for this forward-looking conference. The point was to break down prejudice and start sharing useful information. Not merely cautionary, M. A. G.

Warland's foreword to the conference proceedings, "A Cautionary Note on Breeding Endangered Species", includes a list of criteria recently developed by the IUCN as part of its new species survival plans. One of these criteria was the development of an effective studbook for every species an organization such as the Jersey Zoo took on.

Although studbooks for domesticated animals had existed for centuries, and creating studbooks for endangered species began in the late nineteenth century, only in the 1960s did the zookeeping community begin to use these records as a matter of routine.[13] Studbook records depend upon international cooperation among all responsible organizations contributing to breeding groups of endangered animals. The genetic health of these populations—for example, Mauritian kestrels, Malagasy radiated tortoises, or Round Island skinks—depends on sharing information and sharing the animals themselves.

In terms of captive breeding and reintroduction—the applied science of all Gerald's studies on breeding animals—one of the Trust's early successes was the reintroduction of the pink pigeon to Mauritius. David Jeggo, curator of birds, kept the studbook for the pink pigeon. By the mid-1980s, Mark Brayshaw, also on the staff in Jersey, kept the Rodrigues fruit bat studbook. Mammal keeper Tim Wright was responsible for studbooks for the Madagascar jumping rat, the Alaotran gentle lemur, and the aye-aye.[14]

Complete and accurate data already amassed by the Durrell staff from the time the zoo opened in 1959 set a high standard for this newer form of record keeping, which is shared with other organizations around the world. Christopher Clark, a Trust and Grant Fundraiser of the Durrell organization (where he also served as a keeper and educator), believes that in the long view, sharing the science has been the most important contribution made by the zoo.[15] That sharing has been done not only by contributing to studbooks, but in establishing the International Training Center in the late 1970s. Annual reports were written as soon as the Trust was established, and almost immediately afterwards, Gerald began to consider the foundation of a journal, *The Dodo*, which began in 1964 (first entitled "The Annual Report").

All the species for which studbooks were kept by the Durrell staff are island indigenes, of special concern for Gerald not only because of his passion for islands, but because populations of most remote island species are tiny to begin with and highly specialized. In addition, they are small enough to transport and nurture in the Jersey facility. Gerald's understanding of the problems evolved significantly between the 1966 BBC filming excursions described in *Two in the Bush* and the trips to Madagascar and the Mascarenes a decade later. In even more island books published in the 1970s and 1980s, Gerald described the capture of endangered birds and reptiles, and his hopes for reintroduction. In the meantime, tiny residual populations of these rare animals—pigeons, bats, boas, skinks, and geckos, captured in the wild—were residents of the zoo. Finally, in 1984, the organization began to make efforts at reintroduction. *In situ* breeding programs made even more sense as soon as trained staff were available to oversee them.

What is the Jersey Zoo, then? A collection of animals. A group of buildings. A bundle of stories. An heroic attempt for earth justice. The bats at Les Augres show how all these threads, and more, are woven into a fabric which cannot be pulled apart. Worldwide, bat populations are declining: they are victims of prejudice and persecution, pollution and habitat destruction. Wildlife conservationists all over the world have been trying to reverse this trend. One of the most complex and innovative of these attempts is taking place in Jersey.

At the western edge of the zoo, near the organic farm and across a meadow from Les Noyers—The Durrell Conservation Academy—is a long, low shed. Until you realize it is constructed of mud-filled tires, you might mistake this building for farm and garden storage. Once inside, you are face to face with dozens of fruit bats. Light pours through a translucent ceiling and colorful wine bottles set into the walls. Almost all the building materials are recycled. You have access to a walkway at the edge. In the center is a lush, tropical garden. A keeper enters to refill feeding containers along the edges with fruit, and the air explodes with beautiful, puppy-faced flying mammals on their way to lunch—Rodrigues fruit bats and Livingstone's fruit bats, both endemic to small islands in the Indian Ocean.

The golden-furred Rodrigues bats, which weigh a little over half a pound, were brought to the Durrell facility in 1976 and bred in captivity. The other piece of the puzzle is restoration of the animal's habitat on the island of Rodrigues. Doing so has required dialogue with the people of Rodrigues, tree-planting campaigns, and luckily fewer tropical cyclones in recent years. As a result, the bat population on this tiny island has increased to more than 10,000.

The glossy black Livingstone's fruit bats, about twice the size of their roommates and even more endangered, arrived at the zoo in 1992. For the time being, they are not candidates for reintroduction. The human population of their home, the tiny Comoros Islands just off the coast of Mozambique, is growing so quickly that forests have been relentlessly felled to meet human needs. From Jersey, breeding groups of bats have been sent to zoos in Bristol, Chester, the United States, and France, not only to share costs and benefits, but to protect these small, endangered populations from stochastic events or disease.

The Durrell bat habitat tells stories of conservation and recycling, saving animals, sharing information and risk, human need and carelessness, inter-cultural dialogue, natural and human-made beauty, respect, love, and hope.

I came to this project with a different bundle of stories. When I was a child, my family visited the zoo in a large midwestern city. It wasn't my first zoo experience, but it was my last for a very long time. In a bare central paddock about half the size of half an American football field mingled several savannah ungulates, including a camel who spat across the bars at my aunt when she offered a peanut. The big cat cages were classic, smelly "postage stamp" enclosures. A wolf, sequestered at some distance from the other animals, in a cage which couldn't have been more than eight or nine feet long and fewer feet wide, paced frantically back and forth, alone, trapped, and emotionally dead. I could not look away, and I will never forget that stereotyped behavior: caging had driven him literally crazy. Wolves in most zoos have it better these days, with larger, "naturalistic" enclosures. In some zoos, there is room for the wolves to play with their keepers when the visitors have gone home, and, except for indulging their peripatetic inclinations, they behave as they wish, instead of mimicking "wolves in nature"—as they assuredly are not.[16]

But the real measure of an animal's treatment in a zoo, I think, is the extent of its agency. It seems counterintuitive to say that a zoo animal should be allowed to disappear, but that happens at the Jersey Zoo. Apart from the gorillas, orangutans, and Andean bears, there are few large animals. The maned wolf family have dispersed. But on a visit a few years ago, I ambled by their large paddock again and again, hoping to see the one remaining wolf, named Eva. Here are the grassy hillocks, one with a few stones around an opening for her den. Here is a keeper, but Eva stays out of sight.

I know this from looking at photos: although maned wolves aren't really wolves, or dogs, or foxes, they are tall like wolves and red like foxes. The tips of their pointed ears are a bit rounder than a German shepherd's, and their manes resemble a horse's. Among canids, the maned wolf stands out because she is shy and often ranges through the wilds of central South America by herself, instead of with a pack. (Oddly, the favorite food of the zoo's first maned wolf was bananas.)[17] Humans have driven the species to Endangered status by persecution and habitat destruction.

But at the Jersey Zoo, one might say that Eva is happily retired. Her loneliness and privacy are respected, despite frequent complaints by visitors that she and many other animals are hard to see. Eva is well cared for. Reluctantly, the keeper lifts a cover to reveal Eva's evening meal, a little tray of "pinkies," dead mouse pups. In spite of the zoo's perennially tight budget, this rare, elderly, anti-social animal has what she needs for a happy life and a good death.

I look over at the pink granite manor house and across at the tall climbing structures for the orangutans and gorillas. From where I stand, I can just see the highest point of the sociable Sulawesi black crested macaques' paddock, next door to Eva (they are here in the zoo because the humans back home like to eat them for special dinners). I'm listening to evening calls from the lemur lake. There is no pretense that Porthos or the other primates, or the wolf, or almost any other creatures enclosed here—among all of the approximately 1,600 individuals, in 141 species— is at home.[18] They are in a liminal state: exiled, and yet they belong in this special community. Gerald Durrell and his family might have understood this condition more profoundly than almost anyone else in the world.

Notes

1   G. Durrell, *The Stationary Ark*, 27.

2   Shirley C. Strum and Linda Marie Fedigan explain Zuckerman's approach to zookeeping and primatology as an example of poor practices in both enterprises in *Primate Encounters: Models of Science, Gender, and Society* (Chicago, IL: University of Chicago Press, 2002), Chapter 1 and elsewhere.

3   Melissa Greene, "No Rms, Jungle Vu," *Atlantic Monthly*, December 1987, https://www.theatlantic.com/magazine/archive/1987/12/no-rms-jungle-vu/670244/ provides a useful overview of late twentieth-century zoo architecture, and the Woodland Park Zoo in particular. Accessed July 21, 2023.

4   G. Durrell and L. Durrell, *Durrell in Russia* (New York: Simon and Schuster, 1986), 47.

5   Douglas Botting *Gerald Durrell: The Authorized Biography* (New York: Carroll & Graf Publishers, 1999), 252.

6 G. Durrell, unpublished letter, October 20, 1954.

7 G. Durrell, *Stationary Ark*, 23.

8 Felicia R. Lee, "Shaping Nature's Unnatural Homes," *New York Times*, (September 14, 2002), 7. https://www.nytimes.com/2002/09/14/books/shaping-nature-s-unnatural-homes.html [accessed July 21, 2021].

9 G. Durrell, unpublished letter, no date.

10 G. Durrell with Lee Durrell, *The Amateur Naturalist* (New York: Knopf), 1989.

11 Jeremy Mallinson, *The Touch of Durrell: A Passion for Animals.* [Foreword Lee Durrell] (Market Harborough, L eicestershire: Book Guild Publishing, 2009).

12 R. D. Martin, "Introduction," *Breeding Endangered Species in Captivity* (Academic Press: London, 1975), xii.

13 F. P. G. Princée, *Exploring Studbooks for Wildlife Management and Conservation* (New York: Springer, 2016).

14 Angela R. Glatston. "Studbooks the Basis of Breeding Programmes." *Zoo Yearbook*, 25 (1986). https://zslpublications.onlinelibrary.wiley.com/doi/10.1111/j.1748-1090.1985.tb02533.x [accessed July 21, 2023].

15 Interview with Christopher Clark, July 15, 2015.

16 Nigel Rothfels, "Zoos, the Academy, and Captivity," *PMLA*, 124 (2) (March 2009).

17 Botting, *Gerald Durrell*, 274.

18 Interview with Dr. Amy Louise Hall, Animal Registrar, August 29, 2012.

AFTERWORD: HOW TO BE WHOLE

The Durrells were emotionally gifted. By that I mean they experienced and expressed the entire range of human emotions. If they cultivated the "tragic sense," as Nancy Myers Durrell pronounced, Lawrence located tragedy in the failures of human cultures to connect with one another and the failure of individual humans to plumb the depths of the self. Gerald identified tragedy as a human perspective that ignored individual animals' interiority and denied whole species the right to exist unless they served their human neighbors in some material way. In her 1996 preface to a collection of Gerald's best work, Lee Durrell remembers his delight in animals, his wit and humor, and his anger "on seeing the natural world despoiled and its creatures destroyed." On this point, he "was not gentle."[1]

This is environmental grief. At the end of the last century, the concept of "disenfranchised emotion" gained currency in psychology. When grief is a response to something not generally considered worthy of a powerful emotion—a miscarriage or abortion, for example, or the suicide of a loved one, or the death of a pet—that emotion is "disenfranchised." Recently, the concept has been applied to "environmental grief" or "ecological grief," or "climate grief." If scientists, naturalists, and conservationists experience grief (or fear, or rage) that is not shared with either their immediate circle or society at large, those emotions are, to a degree, "disenfranchised." Edward Abbey's famous fictional *Monkey Wrench Gang* were energized by environmental rage. Greta Thunberg offers a powerful example of disenfranchised climate rage. The activists of Greenpeace and Sea Shepherd demonstrate disenfranchised ecological and animal protection rage.

Although his work inspired heartfelt support during his lifetime, Gerald's grief was (and still is) disenfranchised and misunderstood by anyone

FIGURE A.1 Statue of Gerald Durrell with Lemurs, Jersey Zoo.

incapable of seeing beneath the layers of comedy, exaggeration, and ordinary human flaws. Environmental grief is now better understood than it was in Gerald's lifetime—and less "disenfranchised" because it is more widely shared. Still, to the degree that conservation activists are ignored, their emotions are disenfranchised, whether they pour their passion into the fight to eliminate greenhouse gas emissions, clear oceans of the plastic which kills marine life, protect animals from human abuse, or protect wildlife habitat from human encroachment. With every passing year in the twenty-first century, more people experience environmental grief, and most of us do not know how to translate our emotions into meaningful action.

Here are a few instances of what Gerald was up against and the devastation still going on. According to Interpol, in 2020, the international illegal pet trade accounted for the depletion of wild populations to the tune of twenty billion US dollars annually.[2] The IUCN now reports that almost a third of the 150,388 assessed species are threatened with extinction,[3] and the National Wildlife Federation estimated the percentage of declining bird species in the United States at 50 percent.[4] 2023 is at present the hottest year since 1850, when the record begins. Bats are the most easily studied of all animals potentially serving as viral reservoirs.[5] Whether or not they have been the source of the recent zoonotic pandemic, COVID-19 is very likely only a precursor to more diseases, more pandemics, as animals are crowded out of their own habitats. And bats, among other species, will be persecuted because of it.

The enemies of environmental grief are complacency, greed, ignorance, and anthropocentrism. The dangers of environmental grief are depression and stasis. Against the odds, Gerald "tried to rectify the situation in the way he knew best," Lee continues in her preface, "providing a loving sanctuary for threatened animals until they were able to go back to their wild homes."[6] His work has saved several species from extinction and contributed to the rescue of many others.

Gerald was never alone in his quest to save animals from extinction. Within the United Kingdom, for instance, Julian Huxley successfully urged UNESCO to add natural sites to its World Heritage list, and in the early 1960s, Sir Peter Scott followed a series of successful conservation projects focusing on birds by organizing the famous and essential IUCN Red Data Books. David Attenborough, Jane Goodall, Dian Fossey, Gerald's American friend Tom Lovejoy, conservation biologist Leela Hazzah, Jacques Cousteau, and Hardy Jones are a few of the animal heroes, out of thousands well known by the twenty-first century.

But Gerald's journey was unique—an outsider from childhood, he found his own way through travel, interactions with local people in places under threat, intense interest in the animals, and a brilliant literary imagination.[7]

Even within Gerald's lifetime the lovely conservation zoo on the Isle of Jersey was only the most visible expression of his passion and his mission. It all began with Gerald's books, which are still in print and available in electronic form. The Durrell project has included festivals, art events, sports events and organized tours for fund-raising, conferences for zoo workers and administrators, a professional zoo science journal, film and video, and online fora. Now over sixty years old, the Durrell Trust describes itself as a combination of the zoo (sometimes known as the wildlife park, or the animal collection), the Durrell Conservation Academy for wildlife specialists, and field programs all around the world (including a wide range of conservation and breeding activities). Not surprisingly, most of these are island programs.

The influence of the Trust on wildlife conservation would be difficult to overestimate. In 2015, of the sixty-three animal species downlisted to a less alarming status by the IUCN, 67 percent of them were associated with Durrell's conservation projects directly or indirectly, through financial support.[8] The Durrell Index, a hypothetical measure of likely species survival *with*, versus *without* intervention, is based on the IUCN Red List of Endangered Species. The index shows that, by 2021, the conservation impact of the Durrell projects was 135 percent: without

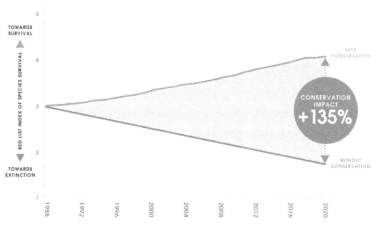

FIGURE A.2 The Durrell Index, 2020.

Durrell's interventions, populations of these Endangered creatures would have plummeted, on average by more than half.

Durrell biologists estimate that some species, such as the Round Island reptiles, would have disappeared entirely decades ago. By 2019, the Trust had overseen the release of over 50,000 individuals of twenty-three species—mammals, birds, reptiles, and amphibians.[9] Although releasing individuals to strengthen local populations occurs with relative frequency, reintroduction of species where they are locally extinct is still relatively rare. Releasing and reintroduction are considered a "success" if sufficient habitat can be restored, and reproduction can be tracked over several generations. Minimal tracking and management are counted full success.

Here are some conservation particulars. Without the Gerald's and the Trust's heartfelt and hard-headed dedication, the tiny bird populations of Mauritius, reptiles of Round Island, Rodrigues and Livingstone's fruit bats, and many of the lemuroids of Madagascar might have vanished. The black lion tamarin of Brazil was thought to be extinct but is now recovering, partly through the efforts of the organization. The Saint Lucia Amazon Parrot is now a beloved mascot for the island, thanks to educational efforts supported by Durrell, and no longer on the brink of extinction. Like most frogs and toads throughout the world, the gargantuan mountain chicken frog was threatened with extinction by the chytridiomycosis disease; until intervention by wildlife conservationists associated with Durrell, 99 percent of the population had disappeared. With Assamese wildlife conservationists, Durrell has contributed to restoration of Himalayan pigmy hog's habitat and helped the population begin to rebound by contributing to captive breeding programs. The pink pigeon population, down to twelve individuals in the 1970s, has increased to almost 500, including both zoo and wild living birds. Durrell also contributes to the protection of the northern bald ibis, Madagascar pochard, Edwards' pheasant, blue-crowned laughing thrush, and Bali starling—some of these animals are in the zoo, some in the wild, some in captivity near their own native, compromised habitat. This list is far from complete—and it will always be, while there are species left for the organization to save in our endangered world.

The third strand of the Durrell mission, woven into the first two—the zoo and the conservation projects—is Gerald's project of educating others to continue this work into the future. The Durrell Conservation Academy has instructed over 6,000 individuals in short or long courses. Some courses, in cooperation with the University of Kent, result in graduate academic credit. The longest and most rigorous Level 3 courses lead to certificates for endangered wildlife species management. The school began simply, in 1979, just months before the first international zookeeping conference hosted at the zoo. The first student, Yousoof Mungroo had to sleep in the reptile house (for warmth), but he learned as the curriculum was being devised and doubtless contributed to it. He rotated through every part of the collection and studied biology, conservation, veterinary care, conservation methods, and zoo administration. Aside from the zoo itself, there were then no facilities for more students, despite Gerald's intuition that training could well be his greatest contribution to wildlife conservation in the future.

Almost as if by magic, Les Noyers, a centuries-old working manor with a rambling white stone house and old granite barns, became available later in 1979—literally next door to the zoo. Les Noyers now adjoins Les Augres' organic farm and a yurt encampment for tourists. The academy was fully established and organized by 1984. The house provides a home for students from all over the world (and tourists, too, when the school is not in session). The barns have been converted into classrooms and laboratories. The back doors of the original house open to an expansive garden and a wide island sky.[10]

Most important is the practical training, of course. When he returned to Mauritius, Yousoof became the first director of Madagascar's first national park. Over the years, students from environmental hotspots all over the world have been supported financially by scholarships and, when they return home, by the Durrell Conservation Learning Network. Since 1985, conservationists from 147 countries have come and gone from Les Noyers. Faculty from institutions all over the world have taught courses, and many instructors are returning graduates from the program.

A Durrell family friend, Edward Whitley, who visited many of the trainees at work back home in the early 1990s, came away with a gloomy picture, which he presented in *Durrell's Army*. However, Gerald reminded him that no one can do it all. "I have to limit myself to what I can achieve. This is why I have kept our projects small and long term."[11] He did not allow himself to be overwhelmed by climate grief. How do you combat climate grief? Here is one answer: do what you can, with work, love, and rapt attention. Successful trainees who have graduated from the school attack their work with the same dedication, the same focus, as Gerald himself.

Marlynn Mendoza, whose early government work In the Philippines included the monitoring of birds, seemed to Whitley to be working in an echo chamber, and he was amazed at her perseverance under the circumstances. Since then, however, she has written and co-authored multiple papers, including one about collaboration between scientists and lay observers in wildlife observation and record-keeping. The data Whitley saw her collecting in her lonely forest hut contributed to the IUCN Red List data, and she has continued for many years to work with conservation programs in her country, including the Philippines' engagement with the International Coral Reef Initiative, of which it was a founding member.[12]

For Kanchana Weerakoon, who founded a conservation program in her native Sri Lanka, training at the Durrell academy in 1999 "changed everything" and inspired her to found ECO-V (Ecofriendly Volunteers) when she returned home. She remains active in the International Conservation community and speaks with something like Gerald's own passion and infectious sense of humor, although she never encountered him in life.[13]

Arturo Muños Saravia, a biologist who founded the Bolivian Amphibian Initiative, remembered the friendships of people all over the world whose desire to save species from extinction resonated with his own and supported his team-building efforts in Latin America. He first trained in Jersey in 2006 and served in a Durrell internship in 2011.[14]

Herizo Andrianandrasana keeps in touch with colleagues around the world, despite patchy internet services in Madagascar, where he served for a time as Durrell's mentoring coordinator for the country. He regards the sharing of conservation information through the Durrell network as critical to his success: "Durrell is small, but it is very efficient and effective."[15]

In 2015, I interviewed Sandra Sarmiento, at that time a zoo director outside Bogota. She had attended courses at Durrell seven times already and was preparing to train an incoming graduate credit class before returning to Colombia, where she teaches at the Universidad de Cundinamarca. Sandra has specialized in development projects and forest animal nutrition. She has worked with accrediting agencies at home and in Europe.

Sandra is only one of the Durrell trainees I met who return again and again—for further training, to teach other students, and to report on their progress in Durrell-supported conservation projects. Some are profiled in the publications of the Trust, and yet there are so many that most of them cannot be acknowledged in this way—an indicator of the breadth and success of the training programs. If these students had no hope, they would not come back. They would not share their experiences—their joy as well as their pain—in the way they do.

Gerald's capacity to suffer on behalf of mistreated animals emerged in childhood and informs the Corfu Trilogy; it underscores all but the earliest of his travel memoirs and reaches almost overwhelming proportions in *The Aye-Aye and I*, his last travel memoir. Such grief could have been a crushing burden, encompassing as it did individual animals, embattled species, endangered plants, and embattled ecosystems. Often, he laughed and loved: the love and laughter almost always infect the persona of the wonderful stories he wrote. But sometimes he isolated himself, against the grain of his own convivial personality, or lashed out in anger. Like others in his family, he ate and drank to cope with stress and pain, and he died too soon.

But Gerald never wavered in his belief that collective action is required to save the planet, or that small projects can help. He never slackened his efforts to remind others that we are connected with all human beings, all animals, and every aspect of every landscape in the world. While his legacy survives, his life and work can remind anyone who loves animals and fears for the future of the planet that we are not alone.

In an address delivered in 2009, David Attenborough weighed the significance of the Durrell project:

What you are doing now in Durrell is more important than it ever was because Gerry could not know the extremes to which we have been driven right now. This institution, Durrell, has never been more important. There have never been more endangered species in the world than there are right now, and neither has there been such an accomplished, admirable, and wonderful institution as Durrell before in this world. Nobody else, *nobody else*, has accumulated the sort of expertise in how to breed endangered species and how, not only to do it here, but how to export that expertise to the countries where the endangered animal is indigenous, where it should be, so that Durrell has become far more important perhaps than even Gerry realized it would be. The worldwide importance of this institution, I assure you, is tremendous so on this, its fiftieth birthday, I wish it every success. And may it go on for another fifty years—and more—because I do assure you that the world needs you.[16]

186 THE EVOLUTION OF GERALD DURRELL

Gerald believed that animals understood natural boundaries—rivers and mountains, islands and oceans, air currents and magnetic fields—and were threatened with the artificial boundaries imposed by human interference. His life and work suggest that wholeness for all beings on earth depends on crossing those artificial divisions to care for others, human and more-than-human.

When Gerald's career as a conservationist began in the 1950s, few people were even aware that the biosphere would be doomed if the industrialized world continues to hurtle toward the future with unchecked assumptions about "progress" and consumption. But he teaches us that if ecology, biophilia, and a cosmopolitan world view merge in a deep and profound bond, there is hope.

Notes

1 Lee Durrell, "Introduction," *The Best of Gerald Durrell* (New York: HarperCollins, 1996), 3.

2 Interpol, "Wildlife Crime: Closing Ranks on Serious Crime in the Illegal Animal Trade, December 21, 2020. https://www.interpol.int/en/News-and-Events/News/2020/Wildlife-crime-closing-ranks-on-serious-crime-in-the-illegal-animal-trade [accessed 21 July, 2023].

3 "IUCN Red List of Threatened Species." https://www.iucn.org/resources/conservation-tool/iucn-red-list-threatened-species

4 "State of the Birds Report Highlights How Dedicated Funding Can Recover Species." https://www.nwf.org/Latest-News/Press-Releases/2022/10-12-22-State-of-the-Birds-Report

5 "'Bat Man of Mexico' Says Bats Deserve Thanks, Not A Bad Rap (April 8, 2021). https://www2.stetson.edu/today/2021/04/bat-man-of-mexico-says-bats-deserve-thanks-not-a-b [accessed May 1, 2021].

6 Lee Durrell, "Introduction," 3.

7 In *Beloved Beasts* (New York: Norton, 2021), Michelle Nijhuis offers a history of early days in the international wildlife conservation movement through a series of short biographies of early and mid-twentieth-century activists. Durrell's absence from these pages reflects his outsider status, perhaps, and his unique combination of approaches to wildlife conservation.

8 "The Durrell Index," *On the Edge* (Durrell Wildlife Conservation Trust, 2015), 18–19, supplemented by private correspondence with Lee Durrell and Mike Hudson.

9 BIAZA (British Irish Association of Zoos and Aquaria), "Sixty Years of Saving Species." https://biaza.org.uk/news/detail/sixty-years-of-saving-

species#:~:text=Durrell%20is%20proud%20of%20its,choughs%20and%20 21%20Madagascar%20pochards. In addition, the Trust has trained 5,500 conservationists from 142 countries around the world, protected 435,445 hectares of habitat, and generated 382 scientific publications.

10 The history of the zoo and the academy are part of the local lore, but among the best sources are Gerald's books about the zoo, *The Stationary Ark* (London: Collins, 1976) and *The Ark's Anniversary* (New York: Little, Brown and Company, 1990), and Jeremy Mallinson's *The Touch of Durrell*, with "Foreword" by Lee Durrell (Brighton: Book Guild, 2009).

11 Edward Whitley, *Gerald Durrell's Army* (London: John Murray, 1992), 236.

12 Many of Mendoza's prolific publications are listed in ResearchGate and LinkedIn.

13 Durrell Wildlife Conservation Trust, "Conservation Training Prospectus 2012," 26. Weerakoon's internet presence is impressive. See, for example, her address to the Indian Green Building Council, posted on YouTube (December 7, 2017).

14 https://www.amphibianark.org/arturo-munoz-saravia/. In "Amphibian Ark," Muñoz credits Durrell: the experience "changed my life." He is profiled in *On the Edge* (Autumn 2011), 20. See also Durrell Wildlife Conservation Trust, "Conservation Training Prospectus 2021," 31.

15 *News from Durrell* (2011), 11. Andrianandrasana and other graduates of the academy are profiled in this publication, one of several in-house Durrell periodicals.

16 David Attenborough, "Speech about Durrell," YouTube, September 24, 2009. Accessed July 21, 2023.

SELECT BIBLIOGRAPHY

A Note on Sources

For biographical facts about the Durrell family, see Douglas Botting's biography of Gerald, Ian MacNiven's biography of Lawrence, and *The Durrells of Corfu* by Michael Haag. The richest vein of information is, of course, found in books and ephemera by the Durrells themselves—Gerald, Lawrence, Margo, and Jacquie. These sources are listed below.

Information about the species Gerald encountered is available from multiple sources online, which are omitted from this bibliography, but available in the end notes. Gerald worked with a series of talented illustrators, who probably represented individual animals as he himself saw them.

I have also listed some important sources for information about trends in environmental science, extinction, postcolonial studies, animal studies, zoo studies, and travel literature. All such listings have influenced the general structure of the argument in this book, even if they do not appear in notes.

Gerald worked with publishers in Great Britain, the Commonwealth, and the United States. In the interest of the paper trail for my research, I have listed the editions which I consulted in the end notes and the first (UK) editions here.

Ackerman, Diane. *The Moon by Whale Light and Other Adventures among Bats, Penguins, Crocodilians, and Whales.* New York: Vintage, 1992.

Ackerman, Diane. *The Rarest of the Rare: Vanishing Animals, Timeless Worlds.* New York: Vintage, 1997.

Botting, Douglas. *Gerald Durrell: The Authorized Biography.* New York: Carroll & Graf Publishers, 1999.

Crosby, Alfred. *Ecological Imperialism: The Biological Expansion of Europe, 900–1900.* New Edition. New York: Cambridge University Press, 2004.

Durrell, Gerald. *The Ark's Anniversary.* New York: Arcade Publishing, 1990.

Durrell, Gerald. *Ark on the Move.* New York: Coward-McCann, 1983.

Durrell, Gerald. *The Aye-Aye and I: A Rescue Mission in Madagascar.* New York: Arcade Publishing, 1992.

Durrell, Gerald. *The Bafut Beagles.* London: Rupert Hart Davis, 1953.

Durrell, Gerald. *Beasts in My Belfry.* Glasgow: Fontana Collins, 1976. [Published in the United States as *A Bevy of Beasts.*]

Durrell, Gerald. *Birds, Beasts, and Relatives.* New York: Viking, 1971.

Durrell, Gerald. *Catch Me a Colobus.* New York: Penguin, 1972.

Durrell, Gerald. *The Drunken Forest*. New York: Berkley Publishing Corporation, 1956.

Durrell, Gerald. *Fillets of Plaice*. New York: Viking, 1971.

Durrell, Gerald. "Foreword." *Breeding Endangered Species in Captivity*. Ed. R. D. Martin. Academic Press: London, 1975. vii–xii.

Durrell, Gerald. *The Garden of the Gods*. Glasgow: Fontana Collins, 1980.

Durrell, Gerald. *Golden Bats and Pink Pigeons: A Journey to the Flora and Fauna of a Unique Island*. New York: Simon and Schuster, 1984.

Durrell, Gerald. "Introduction." *Okavango*, June Kay. London: The Adventurers Club, 1963. 13.

Durrell, Gerald. "Introduction." *On the Track of Unknown Animals*, Bernard Heuvelmans. Trans. Richard Garnett. London: Rupert Hart-Davis, 1958.

Durrell, Gerald. *Marrying Off Mother and Other Stories*. New York: Arcade Publishing, 1991.

Durrell, Gerald. *Menagerie Manor*. Hammersmith: Penguin, 1964.

Durrell, Gerald. *The Mockery Bird*. Glasgow: Fontana Collins, 1981.

Durrell, Gerald. *My Family and Other Animals*. London: Penguin, 1956.

Durrell, Gerald. *The New Noah*. Hammersmith: Collins, 1955.

Durrell, Gerald. *The Picnic and Suchlike Pandemonium*. Glasgow: Fontana Collins, 1981.

Durrell, Gerald. *The Overloaded Ark*. London: Faber and Faber, 1953.

Durrell, Gerald. *Rosie Is My Relative*. Glasgow: Fontana Collins, 1969.

Durrell, Gerald. *The Stationary Ark*. London; Collins, 1976.

Durrell, Gerald. *Two in the Bush*. New York: Viking, 1966.

Durrell, Gerald. *The Whispering Land*. New York: Viking Penguin, 1964.

Durrell, Gerald. *Three Singles to Adventure* London: Rupert Hart-Davis, 1954. [Published in the United States as *Three Tickets to Adventure*.]

Durrell, Gerald. *A Zoo in My Luggage*. New York: Viking [Penguin], 1960.

Durrell, Gerald with Lee Durrell. *The Amateur Naturalist*. New York: Knopf, 1989.

Durrell, Gerald with Lee Durrell. *Durrell in Russia*. New York: Simon and Schuster, 1986.

Durrell, Lawrence. *Bitter Lemons of Cyprus*. London: Faber, 2021.

Durrell, Lawrence. *Prospero's Cell. A Guide to the Landscape and Manners of Corfu* (NP: Open Road. Kindle Edition).

Durrell, Lawrence and Henry Miller. *Lawrence Durrell and Henry Miller: A Private Correspondence*. Ed. George Wickes. New York: E. P. Dutton, 1963.

Durrell, Jacquie. *Beasts in My Bed*. London: Fontana Collins, 1968.

Durrell, Margaret. *Whatever Happened to Margo?* London: Time Warner Books, 1996.

Durrell Wildlife Conservation Trust. *The Durrell Guidebook: Saving Species from Extinction*. Trinity, Jersey. Guidebook to the Durrell Zoo, n. p., n. d., 2015.

Euxküll, Jacob von. *A Foray into the Worlds of Animals and Humans with A Theory of Meaning*. Trans. Joseph D. O'Neil. Minneapolis: University of Minnesota Press, 2010.

Heise, Ursula. *Imagining Extinction: The Cultural Meanings of Extinction*. Chicago: University of Chicago Press, 2016.

Huggan, Graham. *Celebrity Conservationists in the Television Age*. London. New York: Routledge, 2013.

Huggan, Graham and Helen Tiffin. *Postcolonial Ecocriticism: Literature, Animals, Environment*. New York: Routledge, 2010.

Grazian, David. *American Zoo: A Sociological Safari*. Princeton: Princeton University Press, 2015.

Jolly, Alison. *Lords and Lemurs: Mad Scientists, Kings with Spears, and the Survival of Diversity in Madagascar*. Boston: Houghton Mifflin, 2004.

Jolly, Alison. *A World Like Our Own: Man and Nature in Madagascar*. New Haven: Yale University Press, 1980.

Kolbert, Elizabeth. *The Sixth Extinction: An Unnatural History*. New York: Henry Holt, 2014.

Louv, Richard. *Last Child in the Woods: Saving Our Children from Nature-Deficit Disorder*. Chapel Hill: Algonquin, 2006.

Louv, Richard. *Our Wild Calling: How Connecting with Animals Can Transform Our Lives—and Save Theirs*. Chapel Hill: Algonquin, 2020.

MacNiven, Ian. *Lawrence Durrell: A Biography*. London: Faber and Faber, 1998.

Nyman, *Jopi. The Postcolonial Animal Tale*. Delhi: Nice Printing Press, 2003.

Pettinger, Alasdair and Tim Youngs. *The Routledge Research Companion to Travel Writing*. New York: Routledge, 2020.

Pratt, Mary Louise. *Imperial Eyes: Travel Writing and Transculturation*. New York: Routledge, 1992.

Quammen, David. *The Song of the Dodo: Island Biogeography in an Age of Extinctions*. New York: Simon and Schuster Touchstone, 1997.

Rothfels, Nigel. *Savages and Beasts Savages and Beasts: The Birth of the Modern Zoo*. Baltimore: Johns Hopkins University Press, 2008.

Wilson, E. O. *Biophilia, the Diversity of Life, Naturalist*. Ed. David Quammen. New York: Library of America, 2021.

Wilson, E. O. and Robert MacArthur. *The Theory of Island Biogeography*. Princeton: Princeton University Press, 1967.

Whitley, Edward. *Gerald Durrell's Army*. London: John Murray, 1992.

INDEX

Abbey, Edward 179
Achirimbi II; *See* Fon of Bafut
Ackerman, Diane 169, 189n
Adichi, Chimamanda Ngozi 88n
Agamben, Giorgio 52, 59n
Albinac, Roland 148, 151, 156
Andrianandrasana, Herizo 185, 188n
Animal Kingdom (Disney) 164
Attenborough, David, Sir 69, 181, 186, 188n
AZA (American Zoo and Aquarium Association) 174

BBC 1, 14n, 80–3, 87, 88n, 121, 122, 127, 130
Beale, Captain 51, 52, 61
Borges, Jorge Luis 99
Botting, Douglas 14n, 23, 26, 38n, 39n, 40n, 78, 89, 113n, 137n, 159n, 170, 176n, 177n, 189n
Brayshaw, Mark 173
Breeze, Jack 42
British Council 98, 113n
British East India Company 131
Brown, Jack 11n
Buffon, Georges-Louis Leclerc, Compte de 95

Chalikiopoulos, Spiro 3, 16, 28, 30, 37
Chaillu, Paul du 69
Channel Television (Jersey) 11n, 14n, 145
Chatwin, Bruce 14n, 99, 113n
CITES (Convention on International Trade in Endangered Species) 158, 169

Clark, Christopher 173, 177n
climate grief 18, 179. 181, 184, 186
Coco 10, 109–112n, 117
Coe, John 164, 166
conservation biology 3, 13n
Cousteau, Jacques 181
CSIRO (Commonwealth Scientific and Industrial Research Organization) 127

Darwin, Charles 22, 44, 100, 104, 105, 112n, 114n–118, 127
Duke University 39n, 88n
Durrell Conservation Academy 174, 177n, 182, 183, 184, 188n
Durell Wildlife Park 7, 8, 120, 121, 132, 145, 148, 157, 162, 163, 167, 169, 170–175, 182
Durrel Wildlife Trust 7, 83, 132, 145, 162, 168, 170, 171, 173, 182, 183, 185, 187n, 188n
Durrell, Eve 98, 99
Durrell, Gerald
   A Bevy of Beasts (Beasts in my Belfry) 51, 59n, 61, 88n, 164, 189n
   A Zoo in My Luggage 63, 66, 75, 78, 79, 88n, 102, 190n
   adolescence in London and Bournemouth 2, 4, 13n, 16, 17, 18, 20, 24, 29, 39n, 44–46, 50, 51, 58n, 72, 78, 80, 81, 88n, 90n, 101, 113n, 114n, 163, 164, 177n, 188n–191n
   Ark on the Move 150, 151, 152, 159n, 160n, 189n

Birds, Beasts, and Relatives 20, 21, 37, 38n, 39n, 40n, 189n
Catch Me a Colobus 13n, 66, 81, 82, 90n, 189n
childhood in Corfu 1, 2, 3, 6, 9, 13n, 15–31, 33–38n, 41–44, 46–50, 58n, 61, 115, 116, 117, 122, 136n, 171, 186
Durrell in Russia, with Lee Durrell 11n, 14n, 165, 176n, 190n
Fillets of Plaice 58n, 77, 90n, 190n
Golden Bats and Pink Pigeons: A Journey to the Flora and Fauna of a Unique Island 142, 144, 159n, 190n
Marrying Off Mother and Other Stories 38n, 40n, 190n
Menagerie Manor 8, 48, 190n
My Family and Other Animals 1, 13n, 16, 20, 21, 22, 25, 26, 28, 33, 39n, 40n, 49, 58n, 113n, 190n
Rosie is My Relative 6, 190n
The Amateur Naturalist, with Lee Durrell 24, 26, 29, 39n, 115, 117, 136n, 177n, 190n
The Ark's Anniversary 162, 188n, 189n
The Aye-Aye and I: A Rescue Mission in Madagascar 147, 152, 153, 155, 158, 160n, 186, 189n
The Bafut Beagles 66, 73, 75, 96, 164, 189n
The Drunken Forest 98, 101, 113n, 114n, 190n
The Garden of the Gods 17, 20, 32, 35, 36, 38n, 39n, 40n, 190n
The Mockery Bird 6, 9, 10, 120, 190n
The New Noah 67, 89n, 190n
The Overloaded Ark 66, 68, 69, 73, 89n, 96, 190n
The Picnic and Suchlike Pandemonium 59n, 190n
The Stationary Ark 162, 166, 168, 176n, 188n, 190n
The Whispering Land 10, 14n, 38n, 93, 99, 103, 106, 108, 110, 112n, 113n, 114n, 190n
Three Singles to Adventure (Three Tickets to Adventure) 23, 93, 96, 97, 112n, 190n
travels in Africa 3–5, 61–69, 78, 80, 82–84, 88n, 91–93, 116, 121, 148, 149, 167
travels in Australia 5, 10, 61, 116, 120–122, 124, 125, 127–131, 135, 136n, 146
travels in Madagascar 4, 5, 8, 12, 70, 141, 145–152, 155–160n, 172–174, 183, 185, 189n
travels in Mascarenes 4, 12, 115, 118, 120, 140–145, 158, 159n, 173, 174, 183, 184
travels in Maylasia 7, 116, 120, 122, 130, 131, 133–138n, 143
travels in New Zealand 5, 10, 116, 120–125, 127, 131, 135, 137n, 144, 145
travels in South America 4, 5, 62, 68, 92, 98, 100, 112n–114n, 116, 120, 121, 148, 149, 168, 176n
Two in the Bush 10, 23, 116, 122, 124, 125, 126, 127, 131, 132, 134, 136n, 137n, 138n, 174, 190n
Durrell, Jacquie Wolfenden 4, 5, 78, 79, 80, 81, 88n, 98, 100, 101, 102, 104, 108, 123, 171, 189n, 190n
Beasts in My Bed 78, 88n, 90n, 101, 114n, 190n
Durrell, Lawrence 2, 3, 4, 6, 9, 11n, 14n, 16, 17, 18, 19, 21, 22, 24, 28, 29, 31, 32, 34–43, 49, 51, 58n, 98, 99, 100, 115, 136n, 153, 167, 168, 171, 179, 189n, 190n, 191n
Bitter Lemons of Cyprus 6, 14n, 35, 190n
Prospero's Cell 6, 15, 19, 34, 37, 38n, 40n, 41, 58n, 115, 136n, 190n
Durrell, Lawrence Samuel 2, 17

Durrell, Lee McGeorge 172
Amateur Naturalist, The, with
Gerald Durrell 24, 26, 29, 39n,
115, 117, 136n, 177n, 190n
Durrell in Russia, with Gerald
Durrell 11n, 165
Durrell, Leslie 3, 17, 30, 32, 42, 48, 50
Durrell, Margo 3, 4, 6, 16, 17, 20, 22,
41, 42, 47, 48, 58, 72, 81, 167,
189n
Whatever Happened to Margo?
58n, 190n
Durrell, Nancy Myers 16, 158, 179
Durrell, Roger 3, 16, 18, 20, 25, 32–34,
40n, 49
de Heaulme family 149, 150

Elias 69, 72
Euxküll, Jacob von 1, 13n, 190n
Evans, Pat (Peter) 26, 27

Ferrerya, Bebita 99, 101–103
Ferrerta, Monono 99, 103, 113n
Fon of Bafut 9, 76, 157
Fossey, Dian 181
Fraser, Hugh, Major 5, 167

Grazian, David 59n, 191n
Greenpeace 179

Hagenbeck, Karl 45, 54, 61, 74, 164
Hare, Bryan 33, 40n
Hartley, John 7, 48, 82, 87, 139, 144
Hazzah, Leela 181
Hearn, Vicki 40n
Hediger, Heini 166
Heise, Ursula 8, 14n
Huichi, Señor 104–109, 112n
Humboldt, Alexander von 92, 93, 117
Hutchinson, C. Evelyn 23, 117, 120,
136n
Huxley, Julian 168, 181

island biogeography 3, 9, 36, 100, 116,
117, 119, 120, 136n, 145, 159n,
191n; *See* conservation biology

IUCN (International Union for the
Conservation of Nature) 55,
148, 154, 159n, 173, 181, 182,
185, 187n
IUCN Red Data Book 54, 181

Jacob 13n, 74, 165, 190n
Jeggo, David 173
Jersey Zoo; *See* Durrell Wildlife Park
Jolly, Alison 136n, 146, 148, 149, 150,
159n, 191n
Jones, Carl 164, 166

Krajewsky (Kralefsky) 27–9, 46
Kummer, Hans 68, 89n

Latour, Bruno 62, 88n
Lofting, Hugh 112n, 114n
London Zoo 44–46, 51, 58n, 72, 80,
88n, 101, 163, 164
Louv, Richard 2, 13n, 38n, 191n
Lovejoy, Thomas 12, 117, 119, 120,
136n, 137n, 181
Luna 110, 112n

MacArthur, Robert 118, 119, 136n,
191n
Mallinson, Jeremy 113n, 170, 171, 177n
Mavrodaki, Countess 28, 35, 49
McKelvey, Dave 139, 140
megadiversity 130
Mendoz, Marlynn 185, 188n
Miller, Henry 21, 22, 28, 29, 39n, 42,
43, 51, 58n, 190n
Mungroo, Yousoof 184
Muñoz Saravia, Arturo 185, 188n
Mussolini, Benito 41

Nyman, Jopi 74, 89n, 191n
Gonzalo Fernández de Oviedo 95

Perlès, Alfred 22
Person, Juan 109
Peters, Ann 142
Pious 73, 77
Pratt, Mary Louise 34, 40n, 191n

Quammen, David 116, 118, 120, 121, 123, 136n, 137n, 159n, 191n

Rabelais, Francois 22
Rakotoarinosy, Mihanta 148
Raleigh, Walter, Sir 91–94, 97
Rasamimanana, Hanta 148
Revol, Enrique 99
Rosaldo, Renato 66, 89n
Rothfels, Nigel 58n, 89n, 169, 177n, 191n

Santa Fe College Teaching Zoo 11n, 165
Schomburgk, Robert 92–94, 96, 113n
Scott, Peter, Sir 67, 69, 181
Sea Shepherd 179
Shakespeare, William 37
Smithsonian Zoo 169
Spiro Americano; *See* Spiro Chalikiopoulos
Spivak, Gayatri; *Can the Subaltern Speak?* 74
Stephanides, Theodore (Theo) 3, 21, 26, 28, 29, 30–32, 35, 37–39n, 42, 52, 99, 117
Sterling, Eleanor 156, 160n

Terrall, Mary 39n, 62, 88n
Thunberg, Greta 179
Tsimbazaza Zoo 149, 152

Umwelt 1
Uncle Ambrose 83, 87
United Africa Company 67

Valdes Peninsula World Heritage Site
Vinson, Jean 144

Wallace, Alfred Russel 130
Walton, William 99
Weerakoon, Kanchana 185
Whipsnade Zoo 4, 44, 45, 51, 53–57, 61, 94, 125
Whitley, Edward 184, 185, 188n, 191n
Wilkinson, George 18, 24, 29
Wilkinson, Pam 24,
Wilson, E.O. 2, 13n, 14n, 136n, 191n
Woburn Park 55, 56
Wood, Vanessa 33, 161, 166
World Wildlife Fund 56, 134, 142
Wright, Tim 173

Yerkes, Robert and Ada 134, 138n

Zoo Atlanta 169
Zuckerman, Solly, Sir 163, 176n

www.ingramcontent.com/pod-product-compliance
Ingram Content Group UK Ltd.
Pitfield, Milton Keynes, MK11 3LW, UK
UKHW020917060225
454753UK00003B/5